Philosophical and Sociological Foundation of Education

Philosophical and Sociological Foundation of Education

Shiv Shanker Tiwary

KUNAL BOOKS

New Delhi-110002, India

KUNAL BOOKS
4596/1A, First Floor, Daryaganj,
New Delhi-110002
Phones: 9868071411, 011-30125412
E-mail--*Kunalbooks@gmail.com*

Philosophical and Sociological Foundation of Education

First Published 2009
Reprint 2016
ISBN - 978-81-907129-5-8

Published in India by P.S. Bisht for Kunal Books, and printed at Deepak Offset Press, Delhi.

Contents

Preface

Education in its broadest sense is any act or experience that has a formative effect on the mind, character, or physical ability of an individual (e.g., the consciousness of an infant is educated by its environment through its interaction with its environment); and in its technical sense education is the process by which society deliberately transmits its accumulated knowledge, values, and skills from one generation to another through institutions.

Philosophy of education is the philosophical study of the purpose, process, nature and ideals of education. Philosophy of education can naturally be considered a branch of both philosophy and education. Philosophy of education is commonly housed in colleges and departments of education, yet it is applied philosophy, drawing from the traditional fields of philosophy (ontology, ethics, epistemology, etc.) and approaches (speculative, prescriptive, and/or analytic) to address questions regarding education policy, human development, education research methodology, and curriculum theory, to name a few.

Philosophy of education is a field of applied philosophy, drawing from the traditional fields of philosophy (ontology, ethics, epistemology, etc.) and its approaches (speculative, prescriptive, and/or analytic) to address questions regarding education policy, human development, and curriculum theory, to name a few. Put another way, philosophy of education is the philosophical study of the purpose, process, nature and ideals of education. For example, it might study what constitutes upbringing and education, the values and norms revealed through upbringing and educational practices, the limits and legitimization of education as an academic discipline, and the relation between educational theory and practice.

Philosophy of education can be considered a branch of both philosophy and education. The multiple ways of conceiving education coupled with the multiple fields and approaches of philosophy make philosophy of education not only a very diverse field but also one that is not easily defined. Although there is overlap, philosophy of education should not be conflated with educational theory, which is not defined specifically by the application of philosophy to questions in education.

The social foundations of education course are an exploration and analysis of the underlying issues within contemporary educational policies, practices, and theories. It is an attempt to ground the day-to-day realities of the classroom within a larger philosophical, historical, anthropological, political, and sociological context. Such an interdisciplinary perspective will allow students to begin to reflect upon the structures and practices of American education and provide a foundation from which to continue becoming reflective and critical educational practitioners and leaders. It is also an opportunity to investigate the role of schooling and education within a democracy.

1

Introduction

Education can be seen as a product or a process and considered in a broad sense or a technical sense. In its broad sense, education refers to any act or experience that has a formative effect on the mind, character, or physical ability of an individual...In its technical sense education is the process by which society, through schools, colleges, universities, and other institutions, deliberately transmits its cultural heritage—its accumulated knowledge, values, and skills—from one generation to another. In popular discourse, use of the term education usually connotes the technical sense and is generally limited to the context of teachers instructing students.

Teachers may draw on many subjects, including reading, writing, mathematics, science and history. Teachers in specialized professions such as astrophysics, law, or zoology may teach only a certain subject, usually as professors at institutions of higher learning. There is also instruction in fields for those who want specific vocational skills, such as those required to be a pilot. In addition to such formal and technical education there is an array of education, in the technical and broad sense, possible at the informal level, e.g., at museums and libraries, with the Internet, and in life experience. A philosophy is a comprehensive system of ideas about human nature and the nature of the reality we live in. It is a guide for living, because the issues it addresses are basic and pervasive, determining the course we take in life and how we treat other people.

The topics that philosophy addresses fall into several distinct fields. Among those of fundamental concern are:

- Metaphysics (the theory of reality).
- Epistemology (the theory of knowledge)
- Ethics (the theory of moral values)
- Politics (the theory of legal rights and government)
- Aesthetics (the theory of the nature of art)

The most widespread systems of ideas that offer philosophical guidance are religions such as Buddhism, Christianity, Judaism, and Islam. Religions differ from philosophies not in the subjects they address, but in the method they use to address them. Religions have their basis in mythic stories that pre-date the discovery of explicitly rational methods of inquiry. Many religions nowadays appeal to mystical faith and revelation—modes of belief that claim validity independent of logic and the scientific method, at least for the biggest questions. But most religions are in their origins pre-rational rather than anti-rational, a story-teller's account of philosophic issues rather than a scientist's.

In Greek, "philosophy" means "love of wisdom." Philosophy is based on rational argument and appeal to facts. The history of the modern sciences begins with philosophical inquiries, and the scientific method of experimentation and proof remains an instance of the general approach that a philosopher tries to bring to a question: one that is logical and rigorous. However, while today the sciences focus on specialized inquiries in restricted domains, the questions addressed by philosophy remain the most general and most basic, the issues that underlie the sciences and stand at the base of a world-view.

Philosophy raises some of the deepest and widest questions there are. Addressing the issues in each branch of philosophy requires integrating everything one knows about reality (metaphysics) or humanity (epistemology, ethics, politics, and aesthetics). Proposing reasonable positions in philosophy is therefore a difficult task. Honest philosophers have often disagreed about key issues, and dishonest ones have been able to slip their own positions into the mix as well. For this reason, there is not one philosophy worldwide, as there is one physics. Instead, there are many philosophies. Over the course of history, philosophers have offered entire systems that pulled together positions in each of the branches of philosophy.

Aristotle, the father of logic, authored such a system in ancient times, teaching that we could know reality and achieve happiness. In more modern times, philosophers such as John Locke and Immanuel Kant have written systematic accounts of their thought. Most modern philosophers, however, have specialized in one area or another within philosophy, although some schools of philosophy have emerged that are marked by the general positions of their members on a variety of issues and the members' shared admiration for a chain of historical figures.

These schools have included Pragmatism, Logical Positivism, and Existentialism, but are little-known outside of university classes in modern philosophy. Today philosophic issues often enter public life through political or social movements, some religious in inspiration, such as Christian conservatism, and others secular, such as left-wing environmentalism and socialism. The ideas of such movements are often called ideologies. That term, "ideology," is another name for the systems of ideas we have been talking about. Though the focus of ideological movements is political, their political beliefs tend to be rooted in shared conceptions of reality, human nature, and values.

Sociology enables us to understand the structure and dynamics of society, and their intricate connections to patterns of human behaviour and individual life changes. It examines the ways in which the forms of social structure

— groups, organizations, communities, social categories (such as class, sex, age, or race), and various social institutions (such as kinship, economic, political, or religious) affect human attitudes, actions, and opportunities. The discipline also explores how both individuals and collectivities construct, maintain, and alter social organization in various ways.

Sociology asks about the sources and consequences of change in social arrangements and institutions, and about the satisfactions and difficulties of planning, accomplishing, and adapting to such change. Areas studied in examining social dynamics include: culture, values, socialization, cooperation, conflict, power, exchange, inequality, deviance, social control, violence, order and social change.

Social and Philosophical Foundations of Education

Foundations of education courses aim to develop in teachers and other school professionals such as administrators, counselors, and psychologists the ability to interpret knowledge within its historical, philosophical, cultural, and social contexts. The aim of interpretation is to produce clear normative and critical perspectives on education both within, and outside of, schools. The Council of Learned Societies in Education (CLSE) has provided definitions and standards regarding Foundations of Education on behalf of its twenty member societies. Representatives of CLSE and its member societies serve actively on the advisory boards of NCATE, and provide ongoing input into NCATE standards.

The CLSE member organizations are:

- American Educational Studies Association
- Association for Philosophy of Education
- Comparative and International Education Society
- Florida Foundations of Education and Policy Studies Society
- History of Education Society

- International Society of Educational Biography
- The John Dewey Society
- Middle Atlantic States Philosophy of Education Society
- Midwest History of Education Society
- Midwest Philosophy of Education Society
- New York State Foundations of Education Association
- Ohio Valley Philosophy of Education Society
- Pennsylvania Educational Studies Association
- Philosophy of Education Society
- The Society for Educational Reconstruction
- Society for the Philosophy and History of Education
- Society of Professors of Education
- South Atlantic Philosophy of Education Society
- Southeast Philosophy of Education Society
- Texas Educational Foundations Society

The study of Social Foundations of Education relies heavily on the disciplines and methodologies of the humanities, particularly history and philosophy, and the social sciences, such as sociology and political science. The purpose of foundations study is to bring these disciplinary resources to bear in developing interpretive, normative, and critical perspectives on education, both inside and outside of schools. The general objectives of these foundational studies are to introduce students to interpretive uses of knowledge germane to education and to establish a basis for life-long learning through normative and critical reflection on education within its historical, philosophical, cultural, and social contexts. The interpretive perspectives use concepts and theories developed within the humanities and the social sciences to assist students in examining, understanding, and explaining education within different contexts.

Foundational studies promote analysis of the intent, meaning, and effects of educational institutions, including schools. Such studies attend particularly to the diverse contexts within which educational phenomena occur, and how interpretation can vary with different historical, philosophical, and cultural perspectives. The normative perspectives assist students in examining and explaining education in light of value orientations. Foundational studies promote understanding of normative and ethical behaviour in educational development and recognition of the inevitable presence of normative influences in educational thought and practice. Foundational studies probe the nature of assumptions about education and schooling. They examine the relation of policy analysis to values and the extent to which educational policymaking reflects values.

Finally, they encourage students to develop their own value positions regarding education on the basis of critical study and their own reflections. The critical perspectives employ normative interpretations to assist students to develop inquiry skills, to question educational assumptions and arrangements, and to identify contradictions and inconsistencies among social and educational values, policies, and practices. In particular, the critical perspectives engage students in employing democratic values to assess educational beliefs, policies, and practices in light of their origins, influences, and consequences. Study in Foundations of Education shall NOT be equated with "Introduction to Education" coursework unless such study clearly addresses the three perspectives indicated in this Standard and is taught by individuals specifically trained in Foundations of Education.

The Philosophy of Education Society was founded to:

- promote the fundamental philosophic treatment of the problems of education.
- promote the clarification of agreements and differences among the several philosophies of education through the opportunities for discussion afforded by annual meetings.
- advance and improve teaching in the philosophy of education both in schools for the education of teachers and in other educational institutions.

- cultivate fruitful relationships between workers in general philosophy and workers in philosophy of education.
- cultivate fruitful relationships between scholars in philosophy of education and those in other areas of education, and
- encourage promising students in the field of philosophy of education.

Philosophy of Education

Philosophy of education is the philosophical study of the purpose, process, nature and ideals of education. Philosophy of education can naturally be considered a branch of both philosophy and education. Philosophy of education is commonly housed in colleges and departments of education, yet it is applied philosophy, drawing from the traditional fields of philosophy (ontology, ethics, epistemology, etc.) and approaches (speculative, prescriptive, and/ or analytic) to address questions regarding education policy, human development, education research metho-dology, and curriculum theory, to name a few.

The multiple ways of conceiving education coupled with the multiple fields and approaches of philosophy make philosophy of education not only a very diverse field but also one that is not easily defined. Although there is overlap, philosophy of education should not be conflated with educational theory, which is not defined specifically by the application of philosophy to questions in education. A chronological summary of the work of some of the most important and influential educational philosophers in Western culture follows:

Plato

Plato is the earliest important educational thinker. He saw education as the key to creating and sustaining his Republic. He advocated extreme methods: removing children from their mothers' care and raising them as wards of the state, with great care being taken to differentiate children suitable to the various castes, the highest receiving the most education, so that they could act as guardians of the city and care for the less able. Education would be holistic, including facts, skills, physical discipline, and music and art, which he considered the highest form of endeavour.

For Plato the individual was best served by being subordinated to a just society. Plato's belief that talent was distributed non-genetically and thus must be found in children born in any social class. His belief moves us away from aristocracy as a political system. He builds on this by insisting that those suitably gifted are to be trained by the state so that they may be qualified to assume the role of a ruling class. What this establishes is essentially a system of selective public education premised on the assumption that an educated minority of the population are, by virtue of their education (and inborn educability), sufficient for healthy governance. Today's tracking systems could be justified with Plato's ideas.

Plato should be considered foundational for democratic philosophies of education both because later key thinkers treat him as such, and because, while Plato's methods are autocratic and his motives leaned toward a meritocracy, he nonetheless prefigures much later democratic philosophy of education. This is different in degree rather than kind from most versions of, say, the American experiment with democratic education, which has usually assumed that only some students should be educated to the fullest, while others may, acceptably, fall by the wayside.

Plato's writings contain some of the following ideas: Elementary education would be confined to the guardian class till the age of 18, followed by two years of compulsory military training and then by higher education for those who qualified. While elementary education made the soul responsive to the environment, higher education helped the soul to search for truth which illuminated it. Both boys and girls got the same kind of education. Elementary education consisted of music and gymnastics, designed to train and blend gentle and fierce qualities in the individual and create a harmonious person.

At the age of 20, a selection was made. The best one would take an advanced course in mathematics, geometry, astronomy and harmonics. The first course in the scheme of higher education would last for ten years. It would be for those who had a flair for science. At the age of 30 there would be another selection; those who qualified would study dialectics and metaphysics, logic and philosophy for the next five years. They would study the idea of good and first principles of being. After accepting junior positions in the army for 15 years, a man would have completed his theoretical and practical education by the age of 50.

Aristotle

Only fragments of Aristotle's treatise On Education are still in existence. We thus know of his philosophy of education primarily through brief passages in other works. Aristotle considered human nature, habit and reason to be equally important forces to be cultivated in education. Thus, for example, he considered repetition to be a key tool to develop good habits.

The teacher was to lead the student systematically; this differs, for example, from Socrates' emphasis on questioning his listeners to bring out their own ideas (though the comparison is perhaps incongruous since Socrates was dealing with adults). Aristotle placed great emphasis on balancing the theoretical and practical aspects of subjects taught. Subjects he explicitly mentions as being important included reading, writing and mathematics; music; physical education; literature and history; and a wide range of sciences. He also mentioned the importance of play.

Avicenna

In the medieval Islamic world, an elementary school

was known as a maktab, which dates back to at least the 10th century. Like madrasahs (which referred to higher education), a maktab was often attached to a mosque. In the 11th century, Ibn Sina (known as Avicenna in the West), wrote a chapter dealing with the maktab entitled "The Role of the Teacher in the Training and Upbringing of Children", as a guide to teachers working at maktab schools. He wrote that children can learn better if taught in classes instead of individual tuition from private tutors, and he gave a number of reasons for why this is the case, citing the value of competition and emulation among pupils as well as the usefulness of group discussions and debates.

Ibn Sina described the curriculum of a maktab school in some detail, describing the curricula for two stages of education in a maktab school. Ibn Sina wrote that children should be sent to a maktab school from the age of 6 and be taught primary education until they reach the age of 14. During which time, he wrote that they should be taught the Qur'an, Islamic metaphysics, language, literature, Islamic ethics, and manual skills (which could refer to a variety of practical skills). Ibn Sina refers to the secondary education stage of maktab schooling as the period of specialization, when pupils should begin to acquire manual skills, regardless of their social status.

He writes that children after the age of 14 should be given a choice to choose and specialize in subjects they have an interest in, whether it was reading, manual skills, literature, preaching, medicine, geometry, trade and commerce, craftsmanship, or any other subject or profession they would be interested in pursuing for a future career. He wrote that this was a transitional stage and that there needs to be flexibility regarding the age in which pupils graduage, as the student's emotional development and chosen subjects need to be taken into account.

Jean-Jacques Rousseau

Rousseau, though he paid his respects to Plato's

philosophy, rejected it as impractical due to the decayed state of society. Rousseau also had a different theory of human development; where Plato held that people are born with skills appropriate to different castes (though he did not regard these skills as being inherited), Rousseau held that there was one developmental process common to all humans.

This was an intrinsic, natural process, of which the primary behavioural manifestation was curiosity. This differed from Locke's 'tabula rasa' in that it was an active process deriving from the child's nature, which drove the child to learn and adapt to its surroundings. Rousseau wrote in his book Emile that all children are perfectly designed organisms, ready to learn from their surroundings so as to grow into virtuous adults, but due to the malign influence of corrupt society, they often fail to do so. Rousseau advocated an educational method which consisted of removing the child from society—for example, to a country home—and alternately conditioning him through changes to environment and setting traps and puzzles for him to solve or overcome. All human societies, past and present, have had a vested interest in education; and some wits have claimed that teaching (at its best an educational activity) is the second oldest profession.

While not all societies channel sufficient resources into support for educational activities and institutions, all at the very least acknowledge their centrality—and for good reasons. For one thing, it is obvious that children are born illiterate and innumerate, and ignorant of the norms and cultural achievements of the community or society into which they have been thrust; but with the help of professional teachers and the dedicated amateurs in their families and immediate environs (and with the aid, too, of educational resources made available through the media and nowadays the internet), within a few years they can read, write, calculate, and act (at least often) in culturally-appropriate ways.

Some learn these skills with more facility than others,

and so education also serves as a social-sorting mechanism and undoubtedly has enormous impact on the economic fate of the individual. Put more abstractly, at its best education equips individuals with the skills and substantive knowledge that allows them to define and to pursue their own goals, and also allows them to participate in the life of their community as full-fledged, autonomous citizens. But this is to cast matters in very individualistic terms, and it is fruitful also to take a societal perspective, where the picture changes somewhat. It emerges that in pluralistic societies such as the Western democracies there are some groups that do not wholeheartedly support the development of autonomous individuals, for such folk can weaken a group from within by thinking for themselves and challenging communal norms and beliefs; from the point of view of groups whose survival is thus threatened, formal, state-provided education is not necessarily a good thing.

But in other ways even these groups depend for their continuing survival on educational processes, as do the larger societies and nation-states of which they are part; for as John Dewey put it in the opening chapter of his classic work *Democracy and Education* (1916), in its broadest sense education is the means of the "social continuity of life". Dewey pointed out that the "primary ineluctable facts of the birth and death of each one of the constituent members in a social group" make education a necessity, for despite this biological inevitability "the life of the group goes on". The great social importance of education is underscored, too, by the fact that when a society is shaken by a crisis, this often is taken as a sign of educational breakdown; education, and educators, become scapegoats. It is not surprising that such an important social domain has attracted the attention of philosophers for thousands of years, especially as there are complex issues aplenty that have great philosophical interest.

Even a cursory reading of these opening paragraphs

reveals that they touch on, in nascent form, some but by no means all of the issues that have spawned vigorous debate down the ages; restated more explicitly in terms familiar to philosophers of education, the issues the discussion above flitted over were: education as transmission of knowledge versus education as the fostering of inquiry and reasoning skills that are conducive to the development of autonomy (which, roughly, is the tension between education as conservative and education as progressive, and also is closely related to differing views about human "perfectibility"—issues that historically have been raised in the debate over the aims of education); the question of what this knowledge, and what these skills, ought to be—part of the domain of philosophy of the curriculum; the questions of how learning is possible, and what is it to have learned something—two sets of issues that relate to the question of the capacities and potentialities that are present at birth, and also to the process (and stages) of human development and to what degree this process is flexible and hence can be influenced or manipulated; the tension between liberal education and vocational education, and the overlapping issue of which should be given priority—education for personal development or education for citizenship (and the issue of whether or not this is a false dichotomy); the differences (if any) between education and enculturation; the distinction between educating versus teaching versus training versus indoctrination; the relation between education and maintenance of the class structure of society, and the issue of whether different classes or cultural groups can—justly—be given educational programs that differ in content or in aims; the issue of whether the rights of children, parents, and socio-cultural or ethnic groups, conflict—and if they do, the question of whose rights should be dominant; the question as to whether or not all children have a right to state-provided education, and if so, should this education respect the beliefs and customs of all groups and how on earth would this be accomplished; and a set of complex issues about the relation between education and social reform, centering upon whether education is essentially conservative, or whether it can be an (or, *the*) agent of social change.

It is impressive that most of the philosophically-interesting issues touched upon above, plus additional ones not alluded to here, were addressed in one of the early masterpieces of the Western intellectual tradition—Plato's *Republic*. A.N. Whitehead somewhere remarked that the history of Western philosophy is nothing but a series of footnotes to Plato, and if the *Meno* and the *Laws* are added to the *Republic,* the same is true of the history of educational thought and of philosophy of education in particular. At various points throughout this essay the discussion shall return to Plato, and at the end there shall be a brief discussion of the two other great figures in the field—Rousseau and Dewey. But the account of the field needs to start with some features of it that are apt to cause puzzlement, or that make describing its topography difficult. These include, but are not limited to, the interactions between philosophy of education and its parent discipline.

Problems in delineating the field

There is a large—and ever expanding—number of works designed to give guidance to the novice setting out to explore the domain of philosophy of education; most if not all of the academic publishing houses have at least one representative of this genre on their list, and the titles are mostly variants of the following archetypes: *The History and Philosophy of Education, The Philosophical Foundations of Education, Philosophers on Education, Three Thousand Years of Educational Wisdom, A Guide to the Philosophy of Education,* and *Readings in Philosophy of Education.* The overall picture that emerges from even a sampling of this collective is not pretty; the field lacks intellectual cohesion, and (from the perspective taken in this essay) there is a widespread problem concerning the rigor of the work and the depth of scholarship—although undoubtedly there are islands, but not continents, of competent philosophical discussion of difficult and socially-important issues of the kind listed earlier. On the positive side—the obverse of the lack of cohesion—there is, in the field as a whole, a degree of adventurousness in the form of openness to ideas and radical approaches, a trait that is sometimes lacking in other academic fields. This is not to claim, of course, that taken individually philosophers of education are more open-minded than their philosophical cousins!

Part of the explanation for this diffuse state-of-affairs is that, quite reasonably, most philosophers of education have the goal (reinforced by their institutional affiliation with Schools of Education and their involvement in the initial training of teachers) of contributing not to philosophy but to educational policy and practice. This shapes not only their selection of topics, but also the manner in which the discussion is pursued; and this orientation also explains why philosophers of education—to a far greater degree, it is to be suspected, than their "pure" cousins—publish not in philosophy journals but in a wide range of professionally-oriented journals (such as *Educational Researcher, Harvard Educational Review, Teachers College Record, Cambridge Journal of Education, Journal of Curriculum Studies*, and the like).

Some individuals work directly on issues of classroom practice, others identify as much with fields such as educational policy analysis, curriculum theory, teacher education, or some particular subject-matter domain such as math or science education, as they do with philosophy of education. It is still fashionable in some quarters to decry having one's intellectual agenda shaped so strongly as this by concerns emanating from a field of practice; but as Stokes (1997) has made clear, many of the great, theoretically-fruitful research programs in natural science had their beginnings in such practical concerns—as Pasteur's groundbreaking work illustrates.

It is dangerous to take the theory versus practice

dichotomy too seriously. However, there is another consequence of this institutional housing of the vast majority of philosophers of education that is worth noting—one that is not found in a comparable way in philosophers of science, for example, who almost always are located in departments of philosophy—namely, that experience as a teacher, or in some other education-related role, is a qualification to become a philosopher of education that in many cases is valued at least as much as depth of philosophical training. (The issue is not that educational experience is irrelevant—clearly it can be highly pertinent—but it is that in the tradeoff with philosophical training, philosophy often loses.) But there are still other factors at work that contribute to the field's diffuseness, that all relate in some way to the nature of the discipline of philosophy itself.

The open nature of philosophy

In describing the field of philosophy, and in particular the sub-field that has come to be identified as philosophy of education, one quickly runs into a difficulty not found to anything like the same degree in other disciplines. For example, although there are some internal differences in opinion, nevertheless there seems to be quite a high degree of consensus within the domain of quantum physics about which researchers are competent members of the field and which ones are not, and what work is a strong contribution (or potential contribution). The very nature of philosophy, on the other hand, is "essentially contested"; what counts as a sound philosophical work within one school of thought, or socio-cultural or academic setting, may not be so-regarded (and may even be the focus of derision) in a different one.

Coupled with this is the fact that the borders of the field are not policed, so that the philosophically-untrained can cross into it freely—indeed, over the past century or more a great many individuals from across the spectrum of real and pseudo disciplines have for whatever reason exercised their right to self-identify as members of this broad and loosely defined category of "philosophers" (as a few minutes spent browsing in the relevant section of a bookstore will verify). In essence, then, there are two senses of the term "philosopher" and its cognates: a loose but common sense in which any individual who cogitates in any manner about such issues as the meaning of life, the nature of social justice, the essence of sportsmanship, the aims of education, the foundations of the school curriculum, or relationship with the Divine, is thereby a philosopher; and there is a more technical sense referring to those who have been formally trained or have acquired competence in one or more areas such as epistemology, metaphysics, moral philosophy, logic, philosophy of science, and the like.

If this bifurcation presents a problem for adequately delineating the field of philosophy, the difficulties grow tenfold or more with respect to philosophy of education. This essay offers a description and assessment of the field as seen by a scholar rooted firmly in the formal branch of "philosophy of education", and moreover this branch as it has developed in the English-speaking world (some of which, of course, has been inspired by Continental philosophy); but first it is necessary to say a little more about the difficulties that confront the individual who sets out, without presuppositions, to understand the topography of "philosophy of education".

The different bodies of work traditionally included in the field

It will not take long for a person who consults several of the introductory texts alluded to earlier to encounter a number of different bodies of work (loosely bounded to be sure) that have by one source or another been regarded as part of the domain of philosophy of education; the inclusion of some of these as part of the field is largely responsible for the diffuse topography described earlier. What follows is an informal and incomplete accounting. First, there are works of advocacy produced by those non-technical, self-identified "philosophers" described above, who often have an axe to grind; they may wish to destroy (or to save) common schooling, support or attack some innovation or reform, shore-up or destroy the capitalist mode of production, see their own religion (or none at all) gain a foothold in the public schools, strengthen the place of "the basics" in the school curriculum, and so forth.

While these topics certainly can be, and have been, discussed with due care, often they have been pursued in loose but impressive language where exhortation substitutes for argumentation—and hence sometimes they are mistaken for works of philosophy of education! In the following discussion this genre shall be passed over in silence. Second, there is a corpus of work somewhat resembling the first, but where the arguments are tighter, and where the authors usually are individuals of some distinction whose insights are thought-provoking—possibly because they have a degree of familiarity with some branch of educational activity, having been teachers (or former teachers), school principals, religious leaders, politicians, journalists, and the like. While these works frequently touch on philosophical issues, they are not pursued to any philosophical depth and can hardly be considered as contributions to the scholarship of the discipline. However, some works in this genre are among the classics of "educational thought"—a more felicitous label than "philosophy of education"; cases in point would be the essays, pamphlets and letters of Thomas Arnold (headmaster of Rugby school), John Wesley (the founder of Methodism), J.H. (Cardinal) Newman, T.H. Huxley, and the writings on progressive schooling by A.S. Neill (of Summerhill school).

Some textbooks even include extracts from the writings or recorded sayings of such figures as Thomas Jefferson, Ben Franklin, and Jesus of Nazareth (for the latter three, in works spanning more than half a century). Books and extracts in this genre—which elsewhere I have called "cultured reflection on education"—are often used in teacher-training courses that march under the banner of "educational foundations", "introduction to educational thought", or "introduction to philosophy of education". Third, there are a number of educational theorists and researchers, whose field of activity is not philosophy but—for example—might be human development or learning theory, who in their technical work and sometimes in their non-technical books and reflective essays explicitly raise philosophical issues or adopt philosophical modes of argumentation—and do so in ways worthy of careful study.

If philosophy (including philosophy of education) is defined so as to include analysis and reflection at an abstract or "meta-level", which undoubtedly is a domain where many philosophers labor, then these individuals should have a place in the annals of philosophy or philosophy of education; but too often, although not always, accounts of the field ignore them. Their work might be subjected to scrutiny for being educationally important, but their conceptual or philosophical contributions are rarely focused upon. (Philosophers of the physical and biological sciences are far less prone to make this mistake about the meta-level work of reflective scientists in these domains.)

Te educational theorists and researchers I have in mind as exemplars here are the behaviourist psychologist B.F. Skinner (who among other things wrote about the fate of the notions of human freedom and dignity in the light of the development of a "science of behaviour", and who developed a model of human action and also of learning that eschewed the influence of mental entities such as motives, interests, and ideas and placed the emphasis instead upon "schedules of reinforcement"); the foundational figure in modern developmental psychology with its near-fixation on stage theories, Jean Piaget (who developed in an abstract and detailed manner a "genetic epistemology" that was related to his developmental research); and the social psychologist Lev Vygotsky (who argued that the development of the human youngster was indelibly shaped by social forces, so much so that approaches which focused on the lone individual and that were biologically-oriented—he had Piaget in mind here—were quite inadequate).

Fourth, and in contrast to the group above, there is a type of work that is traditionally but undeservedly given a prominent place in the annals of philosophy of education, and which thereby generates a great deal of confusion and misunderstanding about the field. These are the books and reflective essays on educational topics that were written by mainstream philosophers, a number of whom are counted among the greatest in the history of the discipline. The catch is this: Even great philosophers do not always write philosophy! The reflections being referred-to contain little if any philosophical argumentation, and usually they were not intended to be contributions to the literature on any of the great philosophical questions. Rather, they expressed the author's views (or even prejudices) on educational rather than philosophical problems, and sometimes—as in the case of Bertrand Russell's rollicking pieces defending progressive educational practices—they explicitly were "potboilers" written to make money. (In Russell's case the royalties were used to support a progressive school he was running with his current wife.) Locke, Kant, and Hegel also are among those who produced work of this genre.

John Locke is an interesting case in point. He had been requested by a cousin and her husband—possibly in part because of his medical training—to give advice on the upbringing of their son and heir; the youngster seems to have troubled his parents, most likely because he had learning difficulties. Locke, then in exile in Europe, wrote the parents a series of letters in which alongside sensible advice about such matters as the priorities in the education of a landed gentleman, and about making learning fun for the boy, there were a few strange items such as the advice that the boy should wear leaky shoes in winter so that he would be toughenedup! The letters eventually were printed in book form under the title *Some Thoughts Concerning Education* (1693), and seem to have had enormous influence down the ages upon educational practice; after two centuries the book had run through some 35 English editions and well over thirty foreign editions, and it is still in print and is frequently excerpted in books of readings in philosophy of education.

In stark contrast, several of Locke's major philosophical writings—the *Essay Concerning Human Understanding* and the *Letter on Toleration*—have been overlooked by most educational theorists over the centuries, even though they have enormous relevance for educational philosophy, theory, policy, and practice. It is especially noteworthy that the former of these books was the foundation for an approach to psychology—associationism—that thrived during the nineteenth century. In addition it stimulated interest in the processes of child development and human learning; Locke's model of the way in which the "blank tablet" of the human mind became "furnished" with simple ideas that were eventually combined or abstracted in various ways to form complex ideas, suggested to some that it might be fruitful to study this process in the course of development of a young child.

Fifth, and finally, there is a large body of work that clearly falls within the more technically-defined domain of philosophy of education. Three historical giants of the field are Plato, Rousseau, and Dewey, and there are a dozen or more who would be in competition for inclusion along with them; the short-list of leading authors from the second-half of the 20th century would include Richard Peters, Paul Hirst, and Israel Scheffler, with many jostling for the next places—but the choices become cloudy as we approach the present-day, for schisms between philosophical schools have to be negotiated.

The diversity and clashes between philosophical approaches

As sketched earlier, the domain of education is vast,

the issues it raises are almost overwhelmingly numerous and are of great complexity, and the social significance of the field is second to none. These features make the phenomena and problems of education of great interest to a wide range of socially-concerned intellectuals, who bring with them their own favored conceptual frameworks—concepts, theories and ideologies, methods of analysis and argumentation, metaphysical and other assumptions, criteria for selecting evidence that has relevance for the problems that they consider central, and the like. No wonder educational discourse has occasionally been likened to Babel, for the differences in backgrounds and assumptions means that there is much mutual incomprehension. In the midst of the melee sit the philosophers of education.

It is no surprise, then, to find that the significant intellectual and social trends of the past few centuries, together with the significant developments in philosophy, all have had an impact on the content and methods of argument in philosophy of education—Marxism, psycho-analysis, existentialism, phenomenology, positivism, post-modernism, pragmatism, neo-liberalism, the several waves of feminism, analytic philosophy in both its ordinary language and more formal guises, are merely the tip of the iceberg. It is revealing to note some of the names that were heavily-cited in a pair of recent authoritative handbooks in the field (according to the indices of the two volumes, and in alphabetical order): Adorno, Aristotle, Derrida, Descartes, Dewey, Habermas, Hegel, Horkheimer, Kant, Locke, Lyotard, Marx, Mill, Nietzsche, Plato, Rawls, Richard Rorty, Rousseau, and Wittgenstein. Although this list conveys something of the diversity of the field, it fails to do it complete justice, for the influence of feminist philosophers is not adequately represented.

No one individual can have mastered work done by such a range of figures, representing as they do a number of quite different frameworks or approaches; and relatedly no one person stands as emblematic of the entire field of philosophy of education, and no one type of philosophical writing serves as the norm, either. At professional meetings, peace often reigns because the adherents of the different schools go their separate ways; but occasionally there are (intellectually) violent clashes, rivaling the tumult that greeted Derrida's nomination for an honorary degree at Cambridge in 1992.

It is sobering to reflect that only a few decades have passed since practitioners of analytic philosophy of education had to meet in individual hotel rooms, late at night, at annual meetings of the *Philosophy of Education Society* in the USA, because phenomenologist and others barred their access to the conference programs; their path to liberation was marked by discord until, eventually, the compromise of "live and let live" was worked out. Of course, the situation has hardly been better in the home discipline; an essay in *Time* magazine in 1966 on the state of the discipline of philosophy reported that adherents of the major philosophical schools "don't even understand one another", and added that as a result "philosophy today is bitterly segregated. Most of the major philosophy departments and scholarly journals are the exclusive property of one sect or another". Traditionally there has been a time-lag for developments in philosophy to migrate over into philosophy of education, but in this respect at least the two fields have been on a par.

Inevitably, however, traces of discord remain, and some groups still feel disenfranchised, but they are not quite the same groups as a few decades ago—for new intellectual paradigms have come into existence, and their adherents are struggling to have their voices heard; and clearly it is the case that—reflecting the situation in 1966—many analytically-trained philosophers of education find postmodern writings incomprehensible while scholars in the latter tradition are frequently dismissive if not contemptuous of work done by the former group. In effect, then, the passage of time has made the field more—and not less—diffuses. All this is evident in a volume published in 1995 in which the editor attempted to break-down borders by initiating dialogue between scholars with different approaches to philosophy of education; her introductory remarks are revealing:

Philosophers of education reflecting on the parameters of our field are faced not only with such perplexing and disruptive questions as: What counts as Philosophy of Education and why?; but also *Who* counts as a philosopher of education and why?; and What need is there for Philosophy of Education in a post-modern context? Embed-ded in these queries we find no less provocative ones: What knowledge, if any, can or should be privileged and why?; and Who is in a position to privilege particular discursive practices over others and why? Although such questions are disruptive, they offer the opportunity to take a fresh look at the nature and purposes of our work and, as we do, to expand the number and kinds of voices participating in the conversation.

There is an inward-looking tone to the questions posed here: Philosophy of education should focus upon itself, upon its own contents, methods, and practitioners. And of course there is nothing new about this; for one thing, almost forty years ago a collection of readings—with several score of entries—was published under the title *What is Philosophy of Education?* .It is worth noting, too, that the same attitude is not unknown in philosophy; Simmel is reputed to have said a century or so ago that philosophy is its own first problem. Having described the general topography of the field of philosophy of education, the focus can change to pockets of activity where from the perspective of this author interesting philosophical work is being, or has been, done—and sometimes this work has been influential in the worlds of educational policy or practice. It is appropriate to start with a discussion of the rise and partial decline—but lasting influence of—analytic philosophy of education This approach (often called "APE" by both admirers and detractors) dominated the field in the English-speaking world for several decades after the second world war, and its eventual fate throws light on the current intellectual climate.

Analytic philosophy of education, and its influence

Conceptual analysis, careful assessment of arguments, the rooting out of ambiguity, the drawing of clarifying distinctions—which make up part at least of the philosophical analysis package—have been respected activities within philosophy from the dawn of the field. But traditionally they stood alongside other philosophical activities; in the *Republic*, for example, Plato was sometimes analytic, at other times normative, and on occasion speculative/metaphysical. No doubt it somewhat over-simplifies the complex path of intellectual history to suggest that what happened in the twentieth century—early on, in the home discipline itself, and with a lag of a decade or more in philosophy of education is that philosophical analysis came to be viewed by some scholars as being the major philosophical activity (or set of activities), or even as being the *only* viable or reputable activity (for metaphysics was judged to be literally vacuous, and normative philosophy was viewed as being unable to provide compelling warrants for whatever moral and ethical positions were being advocated).

Contemporary social, political and moral philosophy

By the 1980s, the rather simple if not simplistic ordinary language analysis practiced in philosophy of education, was reeling under the attack from the combination of forces sketched above, but the analytic spirit lived on in the form of rigorous work done in other specialist areas of philosophy—work that trickled out and took philosophy of education in rich new directions. Technically-oriented epistemology, philosophy of science, and even metaphysics, flourished as did the interrelated fields of social, political and moral philosophy. John Rawls published *A Theory of Justice* in 1971; a decade later MacIntyre's *After Virtue* appeared; and in another decade or so there was a flood of work on individualism, communitarianism, democratic citizenship, inclusion, exclusion, rights of children versus rights of parents, rights of groups (such as the Amish) versus rights of the larger polity.

From the early 1990s philosophers of education have contributed significantly to the debates on these and related topics—indeed, this corpus of work illustrates that good philosophy of education flows seamlessly into work being done in mainstream areas of philosophy. Illustrative examples are *Creating Citizens: Political Education and Liberal Democracy*, Callan (1997); *The Demands of Liberal Education*, Levinson (1999); *Social Justice and School Choice*, Brighouse (2000); and *Bridging Liberalism and Multiculturalism in American Education*, Reich (2002). These works stand shoulder-to-shoulder with semi-classics on the same range of topics by Gutmann, Kymlicka, Macedo, and others.

An excerpt from the book by Callan nicely illustrates that the analytic spirit lives on in this body of work; the broader topic being pursued is the status of the aims of education in a pluralistic society where there can be deep fundamental disagreements:

> The distinction must be underlined between the ends that properly inform political education and the extent to which we should tolerate deviations from those ends in a world where reasonable and unreasonable pluralism are entangled and the moral costs of coercion against the unreasonable variety are often prohibitive. Our theoretical as well as our commonsense discourse do not always respect the distinction.... If some of the teachings of the Roman Catholic Church conflict with our best theory of the ends of civic education, it does not follow that we have any reason to revise our theory; but neither does it mean we have any reason to impose these ends on Catholic schools and the families that they serve.

The debate between liberals and communitarians is far more than a theoretical diversion for philosophers and political scientists. At stake are rival understandings of what makes human lives and the societies in which they unfold both good and just, and derivatively, competing conceptions of the education needed for individual and social betterment. It should be appended here that it is not only "external" world events that have stimulated this body of work; events internal to a number of democratic societies also have been significant.

To cite one example that is prominent in the literature in North America at least, the US Supreme Court issued a ruling in which members of the Amish sect were allowed to withdraw their children from public schools before they had reached the age of sixteen—for, it had been argued, any deeper education would endanger the existence of the group and its culture. In assessing this decision—as of course philosophers have frequently done—a balance has to be achieved between (i) the interest of civic society in having an informed, well-educated, participatory citizenry; (ii) the interest of the Amish as a group in preserving their own culture; and (iii) the interests of the Amish children, who have a right to develop into autonomous individuals who can make reflective decisions for themselves about the nature of the life they wish to lead.

These are issues that fall squarely in the domain covered by the works mentioned above. So much work is being produced on the complex and interrelated issues just outlined, that in a different context it seemed fair for me to remark (descriptively, and not judgmentally) that a veritable cottage industry had sprung up in post-Rawlsian philosophy of education. There are, of course, other areas of activity, where interesting contributions are being made, and the discussion will next turn to a sampling of these.

Other areas of contemporary activity

As was stressed at the outset, and illustrated with a cursory listing of examples, the field of education is huge and contains within it a virtually inexhaustible number of issues that are of philosophical interest. To attempt comprehensive coverage of how philosophers of education have been working within this thicket would be a quixotic task for a large single volume, and is out of the question for a solitary encyclopedia entry. Nevertheless, a valiant attempt to give an overview was made in the recent *A Companion to the Philosophy of Education,* which contained more than six-hundred pages divided into forty-five chapters each of which surveyed a subfield of work.

The following random selection of chapter topics gives a sense of the enormous scope of the field: Sex education, special education, science education, aesthetic education, theories of teaching and learning, religious education, knowledge and truth in learning, cultivating reason, the measurement of learning, multicultural education, education and the politics of identity, education and standards of living, motivation and classroom management, feminism, critical theory, postmodernism, romanticism, purposes of universities in a fluid age, affirmative action in higher education, and professional education.

There is no non-arbitrary way to select a small number of topics for further discussion, nor can the topics that are chosen be pursued in great depth. The choice of those below has been made with an eye to filling out—and deepening—the topographical account of the field that was presented in the preceding sections. The discussion will open with a topic that was not included in the *Companion,* despite it being one that is of great concern across the academic educational community, and despite it being one where adherents of some of the rival schools of philosophy (and philosophy of education) have had lively exchanges.

Philosophical disputes concerning empirical education research

The educational research enterprise has been criticized for a century or more by politicians, policymakers, administrators, curriculum developers, teachers, philosophers of education, and by researchers themselves—but the criticisms have been contradictory. Charges of being "too ivory tower and theory-oriented" are found alongside "too focused on practice and too a theoretical"; but particularly since publication of the book by Stokes mentioned earlier, and also in light of the views of John Dewey and William James that the function of theory is to guide intelligent practice and problem-solving, it is becoming more fashionable to hold that the "theory v. practice" dichotomy is a false one.

A similar trend can be discerned with respect to the long warfare between two rival groups of research methods—on one hand quantitative/statistical approaches to research, and on the other hand the qualitative/ethnographic family. (The choice of labels here is its not entirely risk-free, for they have been contested; furthermore the first approach is quite often associated with "experimental" studies, and the latter with "case studies", but this is an over-simplification.) For several decades these two rival methodological camps were treated by researchers and a few philosophers of education as being rival paradigms (Kuhn's ideas, albeit in a very loose form, have been influential in the field of educational research), and the dispute between them was commonly referred-to as "the paradigm wars".

In essence the issue at stake was epistemological: members of the quantitative/experimental camp believed that only their methods could lead to well-warranted knowledge claims, especially about the causal factors at play in educational phenomena, and on the whole they regarded qualitative methods as lacking in rigor; on the other hand the adherents of qualitative/ethnographic approaches held that the other camp was too "positivistic" and was operating with an inadequate view of causation in human affairs—one that ignored the role of motives and reasons, possession of relevant background knowledge, awareness of cultural norms, and the like.

Few if any commentators in the "paradigm wars" suggested that there was anything prohibiting the use of both approaches in the one research program—provided that if both were used, they only were used sequentially or in parallel, for they were underwritten by different epistemologies and hence could not be blended together. But recently the trend has been towards rapprochement, towards the view that the two methodological families are, in fact, compatible and are not at all like paradigms in the Kuhnian sense(s) of the term; the melding of the two approaches is often called "mixed methods research", and it is growing in popularity. The most lively contemporary debates about education research, however, were set in motion around the turn of the millennium when the US Federal Government moved in the direction of funding only rigorously scientific educational research—the kind that could establish causal factors which could then guide the development of practically effective policies. (It was held that such a causal knowledge base was available for medical decision making.)

The definition of "rigorously scientific", however, was decided by politicans and not by the research community, and it was given in terms of the use of a specific research method—the net effect being that the only research projects to receive Federal funding were those that carried out randomized controlled experiments or field trials (RFTs). It has become common over the last decade to refer to the RFT as the "gold standard" methodology.

The National Research Council (NRC)—an arm of the U.S. National Academies of Science—issued a report, influenced by post-positivistic philosophy of science (NRC, 2002), that argued this criterion was far too narrow. Numerous essays have appeared subsequently that point out how the "gold standard" account of scientific rigor distorts the history of science, how the complex nature of the relation between evidence and policy-making has been distorted and made to appear overly simple (for instance the role of value-judgments in linking empirical findings to policy directives is often overlooked), and qualitative researchers have insisted upon the scientific nature of their work.

2

Philosophy of Education

The philosophy of education may be either the philosophy of the process of education or the philosophy of the discipline of education. That is, it may be part of the discipline in the sense of being concerned with the aims, forms, methods, or results of the process of educating or being educated; or it may be metadisciplinary in the sense of being concerned with the concepts, aims, and methods of the discipline. However, even in the latter case it may be thought of as part of the discipline, just as metaphilosophy is thought of as a part of philosophy, although the philosophy of science is not regarded as a part of science.

Historically, philosophies of education have usually taken the first form, but under the influence of analytical philosophy, they have sometimes taken the second. In the first form, philosophy of education was traditionally developed by philosophers - for example, Aristotle, Augustine, and John Locke - as part of their philosophical systems, in the context of their ethical theories. However, in the twentieth century philosophy of education tended to be developed in schools of education in the context of what is called foundations of education, thus linking it with other parts of the discipline of education - educational history, psychology, and sociology - rather than with other parts of philosophy. It was also developed by writers such as Paul Goodman and Robert M. Hutchins who were neither professional philosophers nor members of schools of education.

Types

As there are many kinds of philosophy, many philosophies, and many ways of philosophizing, so there are many kinds of educational philosophy and ways of doing it. In a sense there is no such thing as the philosophy of education; there are only philosophies of education that can be classified in many different ways. Philosophy of education as such does not describe, compare, or explain any enterprises to systems of education, past or present; except insofar as it is concerned with the tracing of its own history, it leaves such inquiries to the history and sociology of education. Analytical philosophy of education is meta to the discipline of education - to all the inquiries and thinking about education - in the sense that it does not seek to propound substantive propositions, either factual or normative, about education.

It conceives of its task as that of analysis: the definition or elucidation of educational concepts like teaching, indoctrination, ability, and trait, including the concept of education itself; the clarification and criticism of educational slogans like "Teach children, not subjects"; the exploration of models used in thinking about education (e.g., growth); and the analysis and evaluation of arguments and methods used in reaching conclusions about education, whether by teachers, administrators, philosophers, scientists, or laymen. To accomplish this task, analytical philosophy uses the tools of logic and linguistics as well as techniques of analysis that vary from philosopher to philosopher. Its results may be valued for their own sake, but they may also be helpful to those who seek more substantive empirical of normative conclusions about education and who try to be careful about how they reach them.

This entry is itself an exercise in analytical philosophy of education. Normative philosophies or theories of education may make use of the results of such analytical work and of factual inquiries about human beings and the psychology of learning, but in any case they propound views about what education should be, what dispositions it should cultivate, why it ought to cultivate them, how and in whom it should do so, and what forms it should take. Some such normative theory of education is implied in every instance of educational endeavor, for whatever education is purposely engaged in, it explicitly or implicitly assumed that certain dispositions are desirable and that certain methods are to be used in acquiring or fostering them, and any view on such matters is a normative theory of philosophy of education. But not all such theories may be regarded as properly philosophical. They may, in fact, be of several sorts. Some simply seek to foster the dispositions regarded as desirable by a society using methods laid down by its culture.

Here both the ends and the means of education are defined by the cultural tradition. Others also look to the prevailing culture for the dispositions to be fostered but appeal as well to experience, possibly even to science, for the methods to be used. In a more pluralistic society, an educational theory of a sort may arise as a compromise between conflicting views about the aids, if not the methods, of education, especially in the case of public schools. Then, individuals or groups within the society may have conflicting full-fledged philosophies of education, but the public philosophy of education is a working accommodation between them. More comprehensive theories of education rest their views about the aims and methods of education neither on the prevailing culture nor on compromise but on basic factual premises about humans and their world and on basic normative premises about what are good or right for individuals to seek or do.

Proponents of such theories may reach their premises either by reason (including science) and philosophy or by faith and divine authority. Both types of theories are called philosophies of education, but only those based on reason and philosophy are properly philosophical in character; the others might better be called theologies of education. Even those that are purely philosophical may vary in complexity and sophistication. In such a full-fledged philosophical normative theory of education, besides analysis of the sorts described, there will normally be propositions of the following kinds:

1. Basic normative premises about what is good or right;
2. Basic factual premises about humanity and the world;
3. Conclusions, based on these two kinds of premises, about the dispositions education should foster;
4. Further factual premises about such things as the psychology of learning and methods of teaching; and
5. Further conclusions about such things as the methods that education should use.

For example, Aristotle argued that the Good equals happiness equals excellent activity; that for a individual there are two kinds of excellent activity, one intellectual (e.g., doing geometry) and one moral (e.g., doing just actions); that therefore everyone who is capable of these types of excellent activity should acquire a knowledge of geometry and a disposition to be just; that a knowledge of geometry can be acquired by instruction and a disposition to be just by practice, by doing just actions; and that the young should be given instruction in geometry and practice in doing just actions. In general, the more properly philosophical part of such a full normative theory of education will be the proposition it asserts in (1), (2), and (3); for the propositions in (4) and hence (5) it will, given those in (3), most appropriately appeal to experience and science. Different philosophers will hold different views about the propositions they use in (1) and (2) and the ways in which these propositions may be established.

Although some normative premises are required in (1) as a basis for any line of reasoning leading to conclusions in (3) or (5) about what education should foster or how it should do this, the premises appearing in (2) may be of various sorts - empirical, scientific, historical, metaphysical, theological, or epistemological. No one kind of premise is always necessary in (2) in every educational context. Different philosophers of education will, in any case, have different views about what sorts of premises it is permissible to appeal to in (2). All must agree, however, that normative premises of the kind indicated in (1) must be appealed to. Thus, what is central and crucial in any normative philosophy of education is not epistemology, metaphysics, or theology, as is sometimes thought, but ethics, value theory, and social philosophy.

Role

Let us assume, as we have been doing, that philosophy may be analytical, speculative, or narrative and remember that it is normally going on in a society in which there already is an educational system. Then, in the first place, philosophy may turn its attention to education, thus generating philosophy of education proper and becoming part of the discipline of education. Second, general philosophy may be one of the subjects in the curriculum of higher education and philosophy of education may be, and presumably should be, part of the curriculum of teacher education, if teachers are to think clearly and carefully about what they are doing.

Third, in a society in which there is a single system of education governed by a single prevailing theory of education, a philosopher may do any of four things with respect to education: he may analyze the concepts and reasoning used in connection with education in order to make people's thinking about it as clear, explicit, and logical as possible; he may seek to support the prevailing system by providing more philosophical arguments for the dispositions aimed at and the methods used; he may criticize the system and seek to reform it in the light of some more philosophical theory of education he has arrived at; or he may simply teach logic and philosophy to future educators and parents in the hope that they will apply them to educational matters.

Fourth, in a pluralistic society like the United States, in which the existing educational enterprise or a large segment of it is based on a working compromise between conflicting views, a philosopher may again do several sorts of things. He may do any of the things just mentioned. In the United States in the first half of the twentieth century professional philosophers tended to do only the last, but at the end of the twentieth century they began to try to do more. Indeed, there will be more occasions for all of these activities in a pluralistic society, for debate about education will always be going on or threatening to be resumed. A philosopher may even take the lead in formulating and improving a compromise theory of education. He might then be a mere eclectic, but he need not be, since he might defend his compromise plan on the basis of a whole social philosophy.

In particular, he might propound a whole public philosophy for public school education, making clear which dispositions it can and should seek to promote, how it should promote them, and which ones should be left for the home, the church, and other private means of education to cultivate. In any case, he might advocate appealing to scientific inquiry and experiment whenever possible. A philosopher may also work out a fully developed educational philosophy of his own and start an experimental school in which to put it into practice, as John Dewey did; like Dewey, too, he may even try to persuade his entire society to adopt it. Then he would argue for the desirability of fostering certain dispositions by certain methods, partly on the basis of experience and science and partly on the basis of premises taken from other parts of his philosophy - from his ethics and value theory, from his political and social philosophy, or from his epistemology, metaphysics, or philosophy of mind.

It seems plausible to maintain that in a pluralistic society philosophers should do all of these things, some one and some another. In such a society a philosopher may at least seek to help educators concerned about moral, scientific, historical, aesthetic, or religious education by presenting them, respectively, with a philosophy of morality, science, history, art, or religion from which they may draw conclusions about their aims and methods. He may also philosophize about the discipline of education, asking whether it is a discipline, what its subject matter is, and what its methods, including the methods of the philosophy of education, should be. Insofar as the discipline of education is a science (and one question here would be whether it is a science) this would be a job for the philosopher of science in addition to one just mentioned. Logicians, linguistic philosophers, and philosophers of science may also be able to contribute to the technology of education, as it has come to be called, for example, to the theory of testing or of language instruction.

Finally, in a society that has been broken down by some kind of revolution or has newly emerged from colonialism, a philosopher may even supply a new full-fledged normative philosophy for its educational system, as Karl Marx did for Russia and China. In fact, as in the case of Marx, he may provide the ideology that guided the revolution in the first place. Plato tried to do this for Syracuse, and the philosophers did it for France in the eighteenth century. Something like this may be done wherever the schools "dare to build a new society," as many ask schools to do. Dewey once said that since education is the process of forming fundamental dispositions toward nature and our fellow human beings, philosophy may even be defined as the most general theory of education.

Here Dewey was thinking that philosophy is the most general normative theory of education, and what he said is true if it means that philosophy, understood in its widest sense as including theology and poetry as well as philosophy proper, is what tells us what to believe and how to feel about humanity and the universe. It is, however, not necessarily true if it refers to philosophy in the narrower sense or means that all philosophy is philosophy of education in the sense of having the guidance of education as its end.

This is not the whole end of classical philosophy or even of philosophy as reconstructed by Dewey; the former aimed at the truth rather than at the guidance of practice, and the latter has other practical ends besides that of guiding the educational enterprise. Certainly, analytical philosophy has other ends. However, although Dewey did not have analytical philosophy in mind, there is nevertheless a sense in which analytical philosophy can also be said to be the most general theory of education. Although it does not seek to tell us what dispositions we should form, it does analyze and criticize the concepts, arguments, and methods employed in any study of or reflection upon education. Again it does not follow that this is all analytical philosophy is concerned with doing. Even if the other things it does - for example, the philosophy of mind or of science - are useful to educators and normative theorists of education, as, it is hoped, is the case, they are not all developed with this use in mind.

Current Trends

Philosophy of education is a field characterized not only by broad theoretical eclecticism but also by a perennial dispute, which started in the mid-twentieth century, over what the scope and purposes of the discipline even ought to be. In the "Philosophy of Education" article that was included in the previous edition of this encyclopedia, William Frankena wrote, "In a sense there is no such thing as the philosophy of education". During certain periods of the history of the philosophy of education, there have been dominant perspectives, to be sure: At one time, the field was defined around canonical works on education by great philosophers (Plato of ancient Greece, the eighteenth-century Swiss-born Frenchman Jean-Jacques Rousseau, and others); at other times, the field was dominated, in the

United States at least, by the figure of John Dewey (1859 - 1952) and educational Progressivism; at other times, the field was characterized by an austere analytical approach that explicitly rejected much of what had come before in the field as not even being proper "philosophy" at all.

But even during these periods of dominance there were sharp internal disputes within the field (such as feminist criticisms of the "Great Man" approach to philosophy of education and vigorous critiques of the analytical method). Such disputes can be read off the history of the professional societies, journals, and graduate programs that institutionalize the field, and they can be documented through a succession of previous encyclopedia articles, which by definition attempt to define and delimit their subject matter. These sorts of struggles over the maintenance of the disciplinary boundary, and the attempt to define and enforce certain methods as paramount are hardly unique to philosophy of education. But such concerns have so preoccupied its practitioners that at times these very questions seem to become the substance of the discipline, nearly to the exclusion of thinking about actual educational problems.

And so it is not very surprising to find, for example, a book such as Philosophers on Education. Consisting of a series of essays written by professional philosophers entirely outside the discipline of philosophy of education, the collection cites almost none of the work published within the discipline; because the philosophers have no doubts about the status of the discipline of philosophy of education, they have few qualms about speaking authoritatively about what philosophy has to say to educators. On the other hand, a fruitful topic for reflection is whether a more self-critical approach to philosophy of education, even if at times it seems to be pulling up its own roots for examination, might prove more productive for thinking about education, because this very tendency toward self-criticism keeps fundamental questions alive and open to reexamination.

Implications of the Impulses for Philosophy of Education

Given the existence of these three impulses, how can they help in providing an overview of the field of philosophy of education that does not fall into arguments about disciplinary boundary maintenance? First, these very broad orientations are in many respects easier to generalize within the field than would be any specific set of disciplinary criteria; many different kinds of philosophy of education can manifest these sorts of inclinations. Indeed, it makes for strange bedfellows when people consider that despite their vigorous paradigmatic differences they are actually motivated by very similar underlying philosophical commitments. Perhaps this recognition might create a stronger incentive for them to engage one another respectfully across those differences.

Second, it is beneficial for philosophers to consider that the validity they attribute to certain kinds of arguments may not be driven simply by the objective force of those arguments, but also by a particular appeal those kinds of arguments have for them. This sort of reflectiveness might be fruitful for various reasons, but a significant benefit could be in raising a person's appreciation for why others may not be moved by the arguments that seem so patently obvious to that person; and why the force of argument alone may not be sufficient to generate philosophical agreement or reconcile disagreement. Given the pervasively eclectic and interdisciplinary nature of the field of philosophy of education, such a spirit of tolerance and inclusiveness, while not needing to be unbounded entirely, would be a valuable corrective to the historical tendency to establish the methods or the philosophical school that will separate proper philosophy of education from the imposters.

Advocates of more prescriptive approaches typically buttress their case for dominance by reference to canonical Great Works (Plato, ancient Greek philosopher Aristotle, Locke, Rousseau, Dewey). This sort of system-building across epistemological, ethical, and social/political issues is what the great philosophers do, and it is revealing that for them philosophy of education was rarely seen as a distinct area of inquiry but merely the working out in practice of implications for teaching and learning that were derived from their larger positions about truth, value, justice, and so on. Advocates of more analytical approaches, as noted, tend to put more reliance upon the tools of philosophical investigation, and less on particular authors or sources.

In the twentieth century, versions of these approaches tended to dominate philosophy of education, especially in the English-speaking world, as they have many departments of philosophy itself. Indeed, when one surveys accounts of the field of philosophy of education from the 1990s forward, they nearly all chart the history as one of the rise to dominance of an analytical approach and then a succession of critiques and attacks upon it. Advocates of more critical approaches suffer from a particular difficulty - carrying out their philosophical work in a way that is consistent with their broader commitments.

Naturally, any philosophical approach aspires to consistency of some sort; but to the extent that critically oriented philosophers are concerned with challenging power structures, hegemonic belief systems, and universalisms that obscure, not to say squelch, the particular beliefs, values, and experiences of those whom they seem to empower, such philosophers must also endeavor to avoid these potentially oppressive tendencies in their own writing and teaching. This tension is perhaps felt most acutely by contemporary post-modern philosophers of education, but it can be seen in much of the work of neo-Marxists, critical theorists, feminists, and Foucauldians as well: how to argue for and promote an emancipatory approach to education that does not itself fall into the habits of exclusionary language, authoritative (if not authoritarian) postures, and universalizing generalizations that are excoriated when detected in the work of others.

An encyclopedia entry for a topic such as "philosophy of education" might be expected to begin with a simple definition of the subject, followed by a delineation of its major branches of thought. Several writers have undertaken such a project in recent years. In reading these accounts, one finds that a central theme is the essentially contested status of what philosophy of education is (a point illustrated, much earlier on, in the collection "What is Philosophy of Education" Indeed, proposing and arguing for competing conceptions of the field has been one of the reliable cottage industries for its scholars and an arena of debate over criteria for participation in the professional organizations, academic departments, and journals that take on the label. The most striking characteristic of "philosophy of education," then, has been that from the very first uses of the term the negotiation of what the field itself is has been one of its primary objects of preoccupation. Such debates have had a principled philosophical dimension, but have also had specific consequences for the inclusion and exclusion of potential participants.

For this reason, any new attempt to stipulate a definition of "philosophy of education" – even one that attempts to be even-handed and comprehensive – is itself implicated within such contests of boundary maintenance. Encyclopedia entries tend to encourage such disputes, as in the competing entries on "Phenomenology" written by Husserl, and then Heidegger, for successive editions of the Encyclopedia Britannica, through which they expressed their struggle over the meaning of that philosophy. Thus a very different way of sketching the meaning and scope of a field might be to recount its contests of boundary maintenance, highlighting them as such and not merely as philosophical disputes. Such debates in philosophy of education, which are ongoing to this day, have become a perennial feature of professional meetings, hiring decisions, and so forth – the institutionalized conditions of practice that give shape to a discipline, and an important reference point for speculations about where philosophy of education might be headed in the future.

An ironically inclined reader will be amused, I suspect, that only a philosopher would be so chronically self-questioning and obstinate as to resist even the simple question of what his field of study is. Yet, perhaps, at the level of enactment this is an explanation – or demonstration – of what the field is and of what philosophers of education try to do. Rather than taking the task of offering a definition for granted, one might question the possibility of defining the discipline and explore the implications of offering a definition when the consequence of doing so is to rule in or out work that different groups may believe is philosophically worthwhile. For a reader wanting a more literal definition, and not a performative one, I would recommend any of the excellent overviews of the field cited above.

The first difficulty in tracing the development of the term "philosophy of education" is that throughout most of Western thought what might be regarded broadly as philosophical reflections on education were never regarded as constituting a distinct discipline or branch of philosophy. On the one hand, for most of the great writers in the philosophy of education pantheon (such as Plato, Aristotle, or Rousseau) such reflections were continuous with their accounts of epistemology, ethics, politics, or human nature. It would never have occurred to them that a philosophy of education could be developed that was not, at heart, an elaboration of such "purely" philosophical themes. (Though in some cases the ruminations of philosophers on education has had little or nothing to do with their actual philosophical positions and has merely expressed their own predilections.)

At the same time, and from what might be termed the opposite direction of the theory-practice dialectic, what today is called "philosophy of education" has also long been regarded as continuous with the serious reflections of practicing educators, curriculum theorists, and educational policymakers. Having a "philosophy of education," in this sense of the term, is simply a phrase for the process in which educational practitioners or reformers develop thoughtful, and to varying degrees systematic or coherent, justifications for their educational practices and commitments (something with which, not surprisingly, few academic philosophers have had very much experience or direct concern). Hence, while in the contemporary context a central tension within philosophy of education has been between its philosophical, disciplinary aspirations and its relevance to educational policy and practice, at earlier points in its development this dichotomy would not have been recognized, either from the perspective of the philosopher or from the perspective of the educationist.

These continuities are particularly striking when viewed in an international context, where philosophy of education has been a less professionalized and institutionalized endeavor and where, as a consequence, it has been less isolated from other educational concerns. In European thought, for example, education has consistently been considered in a broader context apart from schooling, and so a "philosophy of education" has usually been regarded as continuous with concerns about childrearing generally. In many non-European traditions, issues of intellectual development are frequently not regarded as separate from matters of spiritual, moral, or cultural development. Here, something that could be termed a "philosophy of education" would need to be also a philosophy of faith or duty to some larger source of identity and identification.

The repeated use of quotation marks here is therefore necessary because in fact the phrase "philosophy of education" rarely comes up in such contexts: in many European contexts, for example, the phrase "pedagogical science" or "theory" encompasses many of the same activities that philosophers of education take as their domain. This is revealing, first, in helping to introduce the question of what the very name "philosophy of education" assumes about the nature of philosophy and its relation to educational concerns and, second, in leading us to ask where the phrase does come from, and why it has gained the meanings, particularly in English-speaking contexts, that it has.

This becomes a particularly delicate, even intractable, problem when attempting to offer an institutionalized perspective on a field, as in this chapter. In both contexts across nations and contexts across disciplines of practice, many people are involved in teaching and writing about issues that could be called, in the broadest sense, "philosophies of education" (rather like "philosophies of life," one might say). Yet only a portion of these are identified with the organizations, graduate programs, and journals that use this particular label and hence authorize what counts as official knowledge in this field. Should a proposed account of philosophy of education be drawn broadly enough to encompass all activities that might be identified as such, or narrowly in terms of a label that has professional and institutional authorization? I have settled for the narrower, institutionalized account, largely because it is a story that deserves to be considered for its own sake, but also because documentation is more easily available to substantiate it. As a result, I am dealing with philosophy of education within the context of a particular history of concepts and debates, which is a subset of all the possible activities that might be classified as part of it. Others would certainly offer a different criterion of demarcation.

The Formation of Philosophy of Education

The origins of philosophy of education as a distinct discipline arrived with the 19th century in English-speaking countries, most notably the United States. First of all, they accompanied the spread of an Enlightenment faith in the reasoned formulation of public policy, the attempt to ground policy on a systematic, consistent foundation of purposes and justifications. At the same time, they accompanied a growing institutionalization and professionalisation of the teaching endeavor itself, especially as it was expressed in the ideals of public education and the common school. In this context, a philosophy of education was intimately linked with the argument for a conception of personal betterment and social perfectibility that would serve to initiate, guide, and inspire practitioners, and to justify this set of aims to a broader public that was being asked to support and fund educational programs on an unprecedented scale.

While still not described by the name "philosophy of education," such formulations of purpose and justification can be seen as the first explicit attempts to develop a reasoned, general account of the meaning and aims of education. And what is most significant about this development is the assumption, difficult for us to recognize today as it has become so widely accepted, that it is either possible or desirable to provide such a general account. Soon, having a philosophy of education was seen as an indispensable dimension of competent, responsible practice in education. Such a belief was centrally established on the educational agenda by the life's work of John Dewey. No one before him had so persistently argued for the need for educational practice to be grounded in sound philosophical principles (and, of equal importance to him, but often neglected by commentators, the corresponding need for philosophical reflection to be informed by educational practice).

Certainly no philosopher writing about education has ever, before or since, been so prolific. Dewey, through his voluminous publications and his many talks and articles as a public intellectual, had a singular effect on the theory and practice of education. His approach, broadly termed "Progressive education," but often conflated with the wider movement of Progressivism in the U.S. after the turn of the century, emphasized the independent motivations of the learner, the need for schools to be small-scale laboratories for experiments in democratic social reform, and the basis of authentic learning in inquiry and experience. Yet the lasting legacy of Dewey must be traced, not only in terms of the shifting fortunes of Progressivism as an educational philosophy (about which even Dewey voiced skepticism as it took various shapes in U.S. schools), but in the establishment of the idea that practitioners must have an educational philosophy, and the relentless promotion of a particular one as the potential basis of all educational thought and practice.

It is during this period that we see the first codified account of the phrase "philosophy of education" in Paul Monroe's Cyclopedia of Education in 1911-13. We see the beginnings of the argument for requiring courses in the preparation of educators that seek to promote the systematic, grounded formulation and justification of educational aims. And we see, significantly, the first professional organization dedicated to philosophical reflection on education, the John Dewey Society (JDS), in 1935. The emergence of professional organizations is crucial for a variety of reasons. As these took shape across a range of academic disciplines in the U.S. just after the turn of the century, they were not simply the institutionalized embodiment of fields of intellectual practice, nor simply convocations of like-minded scholars seeking an opportunity to share their ideas. They had consistent effects in reshaping the fields they represented. As we will see, this is strikingly true in the case of philosophy of education. For this reason, it is not an exaggeration to consider "the possibility that the origins of educational philosophy were better attached to the organizations of its embodiment than to their annotated bibliographies".

This claim becomes even more plausible when one considers the shifting fortunes of the publications sponsored by these organizations – the publications that, by accepting and rejecting certain articles, determine what can be included on "annotated bibliographies". In the case of the John Dewey Society, as with other professional organizations in the social sciences and humanities, debates often centered around the degree and forms of social activism and advocacy that were appropriate to a professional organization, as such. Inspired by Dewey's own role as a public intellectual and his involvement across a range of political issues throughout his career, the members of JDS saw a close connection between their teaching, writing, and social commitments.

Yet within this shared understanding, there were strong disagreements over the substance of political issues and over the kinds of activism that were appropriate. Many of these debates revolved around the journal The Social Frontier, which, under the editorship of George S. Counts, expressed positions that rested uneasily with many members of JDS and, indeed, with Dewey himself. Over time, these concerns were manifested in the formation of a new, separate organization, the Philosophy of Education Society (PES), in 1941. In many respects, this event marks a crucial turn in the development of philosophy of education as a discipline (indeed, of its aspiration to regard itself as a distinct discipline). R. Bruce Raup and the other founders of PES were quite explicit about defining their organization, in contrast with JDS, as a professional society and not an advocacy group.

This insistence took the form of, first, beginning with a self-selected charter membership of 34 persons who explicitly distanced themselves from the policies and views of JDS; second, establishing strict criteria of membership, and levels of membership, that would insure that "professional" philosophers of education would always constitute a voting majority of the organization; and, third, proclaiming that philosophical method was the disciplinary core that provided the field with its substance and credibility. It is important to see the fundamental interdependence of these three choices: of excluding activism and partisanship, of establishing strict "professional" criteria of membership, and of proclaiming a disciplinary method as the principle uniting PES's members. Choices about intellectual method or the scope of a discipline need to be seen, in this context, as implicated in decisions about the inclusion and exclusion of people and their points of view. Soon after this, in 1954, a select PES committee sought to formalize philosophy of education as a discrete discipline, based on suitable philosophical methods.

The formation of PES was followed, in Great Britain, by the formation of a similar society, the Philosophy of Education Society of Great Britain (1966), which was seen as heralding a "revolution in philosophy of education," involving a "greater consciousness of and involvement with the methods and results of philosophy as an academic discipline". Partly because of the dominance of the influence of R.S. Peters and P.H. Hirst, and their analytic conception of philosophy of education, Kaminsky calls PESGB during this period a "profoundly conservative" organization, characterized by a narrow preoccupation with that analytic approach to philosophical method. The force of this hegemony was so strong that a commentator such as Dearden could say, with no sense of self-contradiction, that "I do not myself think that philosophy of education stands in need of a single paradigm," then follow this by saying that whatever it is, philosophy of education must be concerned with "general concepts, principles, positions and practices"; that it should make "necessary distinctions to clarify meaning," should "explore conceptual possibilities," "identify what is necessary and what is contingent," "expose question-begging...and inconsistency," "draw implications," "reveal absurd consequences," "test assumptions," "probe the validity of justifications," and so forth – all activities which, whatever their merit, clearly express the orientations of a particular conception of philosophical method.

The prominence of R.S. Peters in Britain, his influence on contemporaries such as Hirst and Dearden, and his many students who carried forth his reputation and commitment to analytic philosophy make him a pivotal figure in the philosophy of education. His argument that the term "education" itself required analysis, and the results of his investigations – that the term refers to a process of "initiation" into a form of life, and that to call something "educational" is to valorize the means and ends of that process (as opposed to socialization into norms that may be instrumentally beneficial but not of intrinsic value) – defined an agenda of questions, and a method of inquiry, that helped shape the approach of a generation of philosophers of education throughout the English-speaking world.

At the same time, during the 1960s and 70s, the analytic approach gained predominance in the U.S. as well, especially through the influence of Israel Scheffler (although he was never active in PES). Scheffler, even more than Peters, focused on the justifiability of the means and ends of education from an epistemological point of view: Do the activities of teaching support the development of reason, both as a process of learning and as an educational aim it? Where do relativism and activism in education threaten this ideal of rationality? How can the analysis of educational language detect the effects of slogans and ideologies of belief? In many respects, the faith in analytic methods in philosophy of education was stronger and more absolute in the U.S. than in Britain.

Hence, although it is often assumed that the influence of the analytic school ran from the British side of the Atlantic toward the U.S., a good argument can be made that the main influences actually ran in the other direction. Either way, in both contexts analytic work in philosophy came to dominate the articles found in the respective journals sponsored by PES and PESGB. Educational Theory, originally established by JDS in 1951 but soon co-sponsored by PES as well, came to represent what Kaminsky calls a "thoroughly professional version" of philosophy of education. The Proceedings of the PES meetings during these years show a similar convergence around specific issues and styles of philosophical argumentation. At the height of this analytic period, as Kaminsky tells it, "At the 1971 meeting of the Philosophy of Education Society, [Jonas] Soltis declared that 'we are all analytical philosophers,' and no one laughed."

In yet another English-speaking context, Australia and New Zealand, the Philosophy of Education Society of Australasia (PESA) was formed in 1970. Educational Philosophy and Theory, which was to become its sponsored journal, actually preceded the formation of PESA by one year. While the influence of analytic work was felt strongly in these countries as well (and one might argue – that the influential work of C.D. Hardie brought analytic method to philosophy of education there long before its influence was much realized in either the U.S. or Great Britain), in both Australia and New Zealand there was from the very beginning a more skeptical attitude toward the dominance of analytic philosophy and, during the 70s, a much wider acceptance of Left scholarship as legitimate terrain for philosophers of education, although this perspective was also seen increasingly in work presented at PES (which came to see itself increasingly as an international organization, comprising not only scholars from the United States and Canada, but from around the world) and at PESGB.

The Methods of Philosophy of Education

This account reveals a particular consequence of the professionalisation of philosophy of education, as it was expressed in the aspiration to ground itself on philosophical method. It meant, during the period being described here, a desire to establish standards of rigor and tough-mindedness that could help this emergent field attain academic credibility. The methods of philosophical analysis were ideally suited to a stance of clear-eyed skepticism in the face of educational claptrap; of reasoned, balanced objectivity in the face of highly contested educational disputes; and of providing a helpful, elucidative service that colleagues in education – whether in pedagogy, policy,, or research – could find amenable to their concerns. Without neglecting the philosophical arguments that were posed in favor of analytic method, to which I will turn in a moment, there can be little doubt that these stances also suited the professional self-interest of a discipline seeking academic credibility as philosophically rigorous, in part through stronger affiliations with professional associations in philosophy. They also reinforced a position of nonpartisanship in the constantly shifting arena of competing educational fads and trends.

Analytic philosophy of education made substantial contributions in elucidating such concepts as "authority," "indoctrination," and even the terms "teaching" and "education" themselves. This method specialized in offering fine-grained distinctions and typologies; diagnosing hidden equivocations or blurriness in the ordinary concepts found within educational slogans or clichés; and criticizing faulty logic or misleading uses of statistics or other evidence. In many cases, educators found such analyses salutary and helpful: this was philosophy in the service of plain speaking and no nonsense. This analytic movement within philosophy of education followed (though lagging by several years) developments within Anglo-American philosophy: notably the movement of logical positivism and various forms of linguistic philosophy. But the arguments raised in favor of analytic methods had the widespread appeal that they did within philosophy of education, in large part, because of their congruence with other imperatives within the field as an increasingly professionalized discipline.

First, as Maloney points out, there is a certain ambivalence that has often accompanied philosophy of education: on the one hand seeking credibility in relation to the traditions of philosophy; on the other seeking legitimacy within the often-utilitarian climate of schools of education. This tension tends to pull philosophy of education in competing, incompatible directions and helps to account for what she calls the relentless need to explain and justify the discipline – hence the perennial business of negotiating and renegotiating just what philosophy of education is. Analytic method seemed to hold promise as the indisputably philosophical core that would uncontroversial link the discourses of philosophy of education with mainstream philosophy. At the same time, its appeal to clarity and logic meant that philosophers of education would not have to endure the accusations of abstraction, obscurantism, and irrelevance they often heard within schools of education – here, finally, was something useful that philosophers could offer policymakers and practitioners.

Second, the rise of analytic method clearly severed the chains joining philosophy of education, especially in the U.S., to the ghost of Dewey. While the polymorphous Dewey continued, and continues, to be read and reread in light of shifting philosophical trends (so that topics such as "Dewey and Marxism," "Dewey and Karl Popper," "Dewey and Feminism," "Dewey and Foucault," and so on, remain a hardy staple of scholarship in the field), the analytic period established the independence of philosophy of education (and, in the U.S. and Canada, the Philosophy of Education Society) from Progressivism (and the John Dewey Society). Once again, there were both professional and philosophical reasons for this split.

Third, the analytic movement in philosophy of education took a particular shape in opposition to the movement that had preceded it, the so-called "isms" approach: the recounting of traditional philosophical positions – with varying degrees of philosophical depth and accuracy – then tracing their "implications" for education. One of the central tenets of the analytic school, repeated often, was that there were no direct implications of substantive philosophical positions for education: that a person may believe in Realism, for instance, but still favor any of a variety of educational aims and practices. The attempt to provide encapsulated summaries of complex, difficult philosophical positions, and then to read off from them neat implications for practice, was regarded as being philosophically sloppy, first of all, and as over promising what philosophy could provide to education. This debate and transition away from the "isms" approach can be traced across a series of NSSE Yearbooks devoted to philosophy of education, published in 1942, 1955, 1972, and 1981.

Yet, not incidentally, this rejection of the "isms" approach and the attendant view that philosophies had implications for education also put at one more remove the concerns of professional philosophy of education from those of practitioners. No longer would a required course for teachers, for example, promise to help students acquire or formulate their own "philosophy of education" – instead, these courses promised to help them "think philosophically" about their educational aims and practices, whatever they were. This transition to a philosophically grounded discipline reached its apotheosis in the subtitle of the 1981 NSSE Yearbook: "Philosophy and Education" (emphasis added). Similarly, the journal Studies in Philosophy and Education, which ran from 1960-1976, then lay dormant until 1989, was acquired by a commercial publisher and resuscitated as a journal with an emphasis on "clarity and excellence in philosophical argumentation" as its chief editorial criteria.

New Perspectives in Philosophy of Education

Yet this evolution had other, less intended, consequences. Over time, the desire to seek a grounding for philosophy of education in philosophy meant that more and more scholars, including students studying for graduate degrees in the field, went into philosophy departments or the relevant aisles in libraries and bookstores and started reading (or, in some cases, returning again to) work in existentialism, phenomenology, and other "Continental" philosophies. It meant that many philosophers of education read or re-read primary sources in philosophy (from the pre-Socratics to Nietzsche, Heidegger, de Beauvoir, or Wittgenstein) and looked increasingly outside Anglo-American philosophy to more international sources. They also turned to texts on the margins of what had been counted as "philosophy" before: critical theory, feminism, and those (such as Foucault) who would later be termed "postmodern" writers.

Their scholarship made substantial contributions to understanding such topics as power and inequality in education, and the critique of cultural intolerance in both the tacit and the "hidden" curricula. In many ways returning to the older vision of philosophy of education as necessarily implicated in issues of politics, critique, and reform, these philosophers eschewed the methods of analysis but, even more profoundly, rejected its vision of philosophy of education as an exercise in rational or objective reconnaissance. Hence, no sooner did it happen that Jonas Soltis offered his widely accepted characterization of philosophy of education in 1971 than, within a year, essays were already appearing with titles like "Analytic philosophy of education at the crossroads".

Criticisms of analytic philosophy, some though not all from critical theory or feminist points of view, gained wider credibility during this decade. These criticisms included, chiefly, the question of whose concepts were being taken for granted; the criticism that the methods of analysis, ostensibly neutral and objective, in fact imported substantive value commitments; the argument that the view of language under girding this method was culturally bounded and a historical; and the complaint that its focus on "merely verbal" concerns often made its results trivial and irrelevant. Even such sympathetic commentators as Barrow, Ericson, and Phillips give some weight to these criticisms, though they differ in their assessments of analytic philosophy of education today. For Barrow (1994, 4444), these criticisms are mostly "irrelevant" and the "objections can be met."

For Phillips (1994, 4454), on the other hand, "antisepsis triumphed" as "analytic philosophy became more technical and more inward looking, directed at issues of interest to other philosophers of education to the neglect of issues of relevance to a broad range of educationists." For Ericson (1994), the criticisms held weight, but a "second generation" of analytic philosophy of education still survived. This second generation of analytic philosophers, including many of these selfsame authors (as well as Robert Ennis and Harvey Siegel) made substantial contributions to understanding issues of critical thinking, the forms of knowledge, and philosophical problems in educational research, for example. What is unmistakable, however, is that by the end of the decade of the 70s, no one could say any longer "we are all analytical philosophers of education." The philosophical work in education from critical theory or neo-Marxist, feminist, and postmodern perspectives, beginning during this period and expanding to the present day, brought not only a shift in philosophical perspectives and methods, but a more explicitly political commitment.

The tone of speakers and writers changed. Issues of class, gender, race, and other dimensions of disadvantagement and exclusion became explicit topics of investigation and focal points of advocacy. As we will see in a moment, these issues were raised, reflexively, as points of critique against the field of philosophy of education itself. These shifts in philosophical outlook, in turn, shaped and were shaped by the articles published in the professional journals of the field, and in the papers presented at conferences. Such manifestations have a dual relation to the scope and content of a field: representing the work with which people are actually engaged, yet also reflecting back to the field what literatures, topics, and perspectives are of current interest or importance. To the extent that scholars, especially younger scholars, are influenced by what they read and by what they find is publishable, such shifting trends play an active part in encouraging and giving legitimacy to new styles of work.

This is a role about which journal editors and conference organizers are usually quite aware, and lends a responsibility to them, and to their reviewers, that goes beyond simply filtering and selecting "the best" from the work that is submitted to them. For at the same time, they are helping to define, either narrowly or broadly, the field that they are representing. The circular process by which a field becomes what it is thought to be, in the minds of its members – and this can either be a highly conservative and static or a highly experimental and fluid intellectual process – is exemplified practically in these activities of peer review and selection (just as they are also exemplified in the courses and degree requirements of graduate programs that prepare students with the imprimatur of the field upon their degrees).

For philosophy of education in the post-analytic period, the contents of leading journals and conference publications (such as those sponsored by PES, PESGB, and PESA) became increasingly eclectic, interdisciplinary, and iconoclastic toward traditional conceptions of "the field." That this partly was an indication of a changing state of affairs, and partly a cause of it, was quite apparent to those involved in making such selections. Something else momentous was happening to philosophy of education during this period, I believe, represented by two related sets of changes. The first concerned the demographics of the field, especially during the 70s and into the 80s, as more and more women entered what had been virtually all-male organizations or, among those women who were already participants, as more shifted their interests away from analytic philosophy or other traditional topics toward women's status within education.

The second was the rise of feminism as a perspective on philosophical and professional issues within philosophy of education. Feminists pointed out that the questions of who was part of certain philosophical debates, and what philosophical language those debates privileged, were interdependent issues. They argued that the forms of philosophical argumentation, in which rigorous, aggressive debate was assumed to be the best way of testing new propositions, had the effect of narrowing the range of perspectives available for discussion and actively intimidating or silencing those who did not debate their points in that manner. They argued that the methods of analytic philosophy, such as the tendency to isolate conceptual issues from actual contexts, gave artificiality to philosophical discussions, notably in cases of ethics where, they believed, situated, interpersonal factors needed to be topics of philosophical consideration from the very start.

In these and other ways they argued the interdependence of issues of content and issues of representation. Which philosophical issues were being discussed, how they were discussed, and which issues were never discussed directly influenced and were influenced by the fact of who was part of those conversations, and who was not. Initially, this concern spoke directly to the under representation of women in the professional organizations and journals of the field; eventually, such concerns began to be extended to other underrepresented groups as well – including, once again, the question of the relevance of philosophy of education to the concerns, needs, and interests of teachers (most of whom, of course, are female). One concrete manifestation of this shift has been a resurgence of interest in moral education, literature, and more relational views of personhood.

These changes – the increased eclecticism of philosophical sources seen as relevant to philosophy of education, and the increased awareness of the interdependence of issues of content and of representation – are fundamentally transforming the field today. Chambliss summarizes the contemporary scene in this way: "In the last decade of the twentieth century, philosophy of education scarcely resembles a discipline with a distinct purpose and a clearly established agenda. It is more accurately characterized as a field of study defined by the variety of its research and interpretive projects" (1996, 472). What is most interesting about this characterization is the implication that philosophy of education ever was a "discipline with a distinct purpose and a clearly established agenda."

As noted, the very idea of "philosophy of education" as a distinct discipline is an artifact of a particular set of philosophical and institutional conditions, ones more typical of certain English-speaking contexts. Beyond this, the idea that this discipline ever had a unified purpose and agenda fits only certain brief periods of its development (notably, during the period of Progressivism and the period of analytic dominance) – yet even these periods were characterized by a good deal of internal friction and resistance to such unifying trends, and were followed by periods of reaction that explicitly challenged the boundaries established to define what truly counted as philosophy of education and what did not.

The Futures of Philosophy of Education

Today, this reflexive awareness of how such philosophical boundaries also have institutional effects, and how these boundaries of inclusion and exclusion, in turn, feed back on which philosophical issues and perspectives are or are not represented within what officially counts as "philosophy of education," has ushered in a new period for the field. What Chambliss characterizes as a diffuse focus, or lack of focus, can be characterized just as accurately as a period of experimentation and expansion in philosophy of education. Consider, for example, Phillips' alternative characterization: "The situation in the 1990s is complex and relatively healthy – philosophers are working with a variety of approaches, in a variety of fields, and the discipline is marked by eclecticism perhaps unrivaled in previous periods".

There are paired centripetal and centrifugal forces at work in the field today, matching philosophers of education who prefer to draw the boundaries of the field more narrowly, around a strict disciplinary view of philosophical method (and within this view of philosophy a primary focus on matters of logic, epistemology, philosophy of science, and philosophy of mind), and those drawing the boundaries more broadly, blurring distinctions of philosophy and theory, and emphasizing the interdisciplinary cross-fertilization of philosophy with literary interpretation, political theory, women's studies, and other fields. These debates, it should be emphasized, arise as much from different views about who is a philosopher of education, who belongs at professional meetings, or who should be published in sponsored journals, as they do from the relative merits of disciplinary and interdisciplinary perspectives on the field.

Yet, as Chambliss' assessment also reveals, if there is no disciplinary core whatsoever, is there anything that does characterize and unify philosophy of education as a field today? I will return to this question in a moment. A related issue about such boundary-drawing is the effect of the professionalisation of philosophy of education upon the involvement of philosophically minded practitioners and their concerns. As noted, from the very beginnings of the Philosophy of Education Society, for example, structures were put in place that would limit the involvement and influence of those without academic credentials in philosophy. While one can say that philosophers of education should continue to focus on issues of educational practice, this position stands in tension with actual policies that discourage the participation of those who hold these concerns closest to heart.

In the case of PES, for example, this tension is expressed in the uncomfortable, and occasionally alienated, relation between the national organization, which is the most philosophically sophisticated and professionally oriented, and which has the strongest representation in the major sponsored publications of the field, and the ten or so "regional" branches of the Society, many of which have a much higher rate of participation by colleagues in other fields of educational scholarship and practice – many of whom rarely attend, or would even consider attending, the national meeting. Similar interactions undoubtedly arise in other national contexts as well. As a result of these dynamics, philosophy of education is once again in a period of self-examination about its scope and mission.

The lead article in a recent collection of essays chosen to survey the field, written by Maxine Greene, is entitled "What counts as philosophy of education?" The responses by Feinberg and Phillips show how far from a consensual answer the field remains today. Yet the title of that collection, Critical Conversations in Philosophy of Education, and its design as a series of constructive engagements around a set of educational concerns, gives a different and, I think, more hopeful characterization of the field. For if disciplinary boundary-drawing is regarded with more suspicion today, and if any prospective philosophical criteria for what counts as "philosophy of education" have come to be scrutinized partly in terms of which voices and perspectives they privilege and which they disadvantage or exclude, then the only alternative demarcations of the field must be more procedural and "boot-strapped."

In this sense, philosophy of education today represents those engaged in ongoing conversations, in person or in print, about certain issues, in full awareness of their diversity and eclecticism of method, while retaining a degree of openness about who else might need to be drawn into those conversations. What counts as philosophy of education is simply what these collective processes of deliberation, paper reviewing, and public discourse acknowledge and accept as pertinent to a set of shared concerns. At the same time, these processes tacitly invite or exclude different participants, and even set the standards of what it means to be involved. Hence adopting or changing these processes is a decision with immediate consequences for who is to be involved; and the converse is also the case. The identification of those concerns, the boundaries of the discipline, and the representation of participants in professional societies, graduate programs, and publications, are shifting, interdependent strands of what is the field, each changing in response to the others.

Such a perspective itself raises a new challenge to the field, however, which is how this dynamic of self-examination and redefinition can maintain a sense of continuity; how a discipline that is continually remaking itself can respect the cumulative gains of sustained lines of inquiry, without discarding substantial bodies of scholarship as simply the outmoded musings of philosophical paradigms that have been transcended or surpassed. Will contemporary philosophers of education read earlier academic work with respect and interest, for example? Or will each new generation of philosophers of education become amnesiac about their predecessors? Will the suspicion toward "canonical texts" mean that reading lists and syllabi are continually discarded with each passing fashion? Or will traditions of inquiry in such areas as ethics, democratic theory, what counts as "knowledge," and so forth, continue as sustained conversations among diverse texts and perspectives, to which each is regarded as making a distinct contribution?

Finally, within this decentered characterization of philosophy of education, what trends stand out for the future? Without stipulating what the changing boundaries of the field will look like (a process I have obviously, painstakingly resisted throughout this essay), are there good guesses that can be offered about the future of philosophy of education? One avenue, I have suggested, is to recognize how current topics of interest such as identity, difference, power, a suspicion toward "metanarratives," and so on, have become not only issues for philosophical investigation, but leverage points for reflection and critique within the field of philosophy of education itself. How difficult and sensitive this process has become can be seen in the dynamics surrounding the reception of Harvey Siegel's Presidential Address to a joint meeting of the Philosophy of Education Society and the Philosophy of Education Society of Australasia in 1995 – an interchange that perfectly crystallized some of the key issues at debate today, and an event that might come to be regarded, with hindsight, as a kind of watershed for the field.

At heart an appeal to and argument for "inclusion," Siegel's account was sharply criticized for assuming as criteria for whom should be included, factors that are in fact exclusionary (some of these comments came from the responses of Bailin 1995 and Morgan 1995; others came from the floor). Yet, of course, all criteria are exclusionary – or else they would not be criteria. For certain philosophers, such as Siegel, the question of standards of philosophical merit, and the matter of their social effects, are entirely separate issues – and a perspective excluded as being non philosophical, if it "is" non philosophical, need not be of concern to an organization devoted to establishing and maintaining standards of integrity and excellence within the discipline. If prospective participants lack these criteria, the goal should be to find ways to help people acquire them, not to question the criteria. In criticism of this view, it was argued that the persistent effects of such standards, in terms of the exclusion of people, groups, and their perspectives, must be taken into account if a field is not to become increasingly hermetic and self-rationalizing – to say nothing of the possible effects of personal or professional harm upon those persons and groups by excluding them.

Where there are important cultural or historical reasons why prospective participants have not acquired the characteristics defined by particular institutions as criteria of participation, one must consider the nature of those criteria as one potential factor. Hence, as the boundaries of philosophy of education are being stretched and blurred, considerations of their role in including and excluding participation are becoming a topic of explicit, reflexive concern. If all criteria exclude someone, then the question of which exclusions will be found livable, and which ones not, is an element in weighing their relevance and merit. In my view, this is not a matter of abandoning all philosophical criteria, or of focusing solely on the question of inclusion and exclusion, but of becoming more sensitive to the complex interaction between them, and judging each in terms of the other. To the extent that professional organizations, graduate programs, and journals and other publications are the institutional embodiment of the field, their decisions along these lines have profound implications for the intellectual and moral qualities of what the field turns out to be.

This is particularly true in assessing the consequences of particular philosophical methods and content for attracting the interest and participation of educators from the arenas of policy, research, or practice. The time has passed when the demographics of a field can be regarded as irrelevant to its diversity and vitality. Just as women, once and for all, made the question of who was, and who was not, part of disciplinary conversations a matter of professional and philosophical concern, the field of philosophy of education must stand today in awareness of its roots in a particular conception of "philosophy of education" that emerged from predominantly English-speaking countries; and recognize that in certain contexts its participants are still predominantly male, and, where more equally male and female, almost entirely White.

The increased globalization of academic work, brought about by relative ease and speed of travel; the growth of international organizations and conferences (such as INPE, the International Network of Philosophers of Education, formed in 1990); the increase in contact among a multicultural group of colleagues; and the widespread use of the Internet as a means of global communication and electronic publication of scholarship, all portend a time when diversity and difference will move centrally onto the agenda of issues of concern to educational philosophers – including, naturally, the question of who is being respected as such. As new partners enter the conversation, further questions of how, where, and under what terms that conversation is occurring will inevitably become objects of philosophical reflection. This shift is already taking place, and provides, I suggest, the best indicator of where the field called "philosophy of education" is headed. What this label will be taken to delimit, and by what criteria, will be the determination of that shifting population, as it has been for many previous generations of participants in the field. The one lasting change may be that the question, "What is philosophy of education?" will never again be asked in the expectation that a single, unified definition is either possible or desirable.

Buddhist relations with Brahmanism and Hinduism

In December 1999, scholars of Indology from different parts of the world (China, Indian, Belgium and the United States) met in New Delhi: at issue lay their different approaches to the Buddhist relations with Brahmanism and Hinduism. One might assume that the differences may be explained by either Buddhism was an anti-ritualistic tendency of Vedic origin or an independent religion of different tradition: the reality is more complex, for some of them, especially, Indians have expressed with a strong mind of faith of religion, whereas other scholars would demonstrate only from the theoretical and historical point of view, and still others face major problem in their misinterpretations of the prehistoric study. The existence alone of those world scholars argues for the complexity of the issue.

For over four decades, these differences in approaches have caused many problems in the issue of academic study of religion and subsequently much literature written in different languages (English, Chinese, Hindi, Japanese, French and German) has been produced on these particular issues. In the foreword of the work of 2500 Years of Buddhism (New Delhi, 1956), the most prominent Indian scholar, Dr. S. Radhakrishnan has described Buddhism as: an offshoot of the more ancient faith of the Hindus, perhaps a schism or a heresy. Since the Brahmanical standpoint has possessed India's scholastic field for about a millennium, it is no doubt and quiet certain that Indian scholars, such as Dr. S. Radhakrishnan, have sought to sum up the history of Buddhism in India largely from this particular standpoint.

The conflict between Buddhism and Brahmanism, the transformation of the Buddhist heritage in India and the disappearance of Buddhism as a living faith from Indian soil during the early medieval centuries, were largely responsible for the growth of misconception on ancient Indian civilization and for the propagation of the Brahmanical standpoint during the medieval through modern times. Nevertheless, Buddhism should be studied from the Buddhist standpoint and its relations with Brahmanism and Hinduism should be studied from the historical standpoint and the scientific line. In this chapter, I will focus on my disagreement with those current theories of the origin of Buddhism, of its early relation with Brahmanism and of its position with regard to Hinduism.

The origin of Buddhism

It has been told that in India it is a fashion to speak and to write: Buddhism is a sect of Hinduism, Buddha was a Hindu, and Hinduism is so catholic as to tolerate and worship a heretical and anti-Vedic teacher like the Buddha. This comfortable theory has been so thoroughly propagated in the Indian soil that it will take a long years for scholars and historians to sweep away its illusions and clear the way for the growth of Buddhist study from historical standpoint and on scientific senses. These current theories, presented India's prevailing standpoints towards the origin of Buddhism, refer mainly to the Indian general faith, their attitude towards Buddhism, and the scholastic interpretations of Buddhism.

The Indian general faith means that almost from all circles of life of Indian people has a strong faith of belief in Hinduism rather than Buddhism at the present stage of the Indian society even though Buddhism has given deeply an influence to Hinduism either theoretically or practically. It's a common sense of Indian that Hinduism (actually a newly born religion in the Indian soil), having converted most of Indians to its own faith, monopolizes not only the India's ideology, but also the India's way of life and thinking either in the political or economic or scientific fields. However, this kind of tendency - the fundamentalist way of thinking - set the Indians apart from the people of the world even today in the 21st century.

The Indian attitude towards Buddhism means that in the mind of the ordinary Indian people, they do concede that Buddhism merged into Hinduism, that the Buddha was a great Hindu reformer and that the Buddha was a great Hindu master. This last is important because it leads us, from beginning to end, to examine carefully and to think differently that Buddhism, as a separate and independent world religion cannot be studied beyond the historical and scientific perspectives. We may see that the people of India today are so sensitive and admired of their most beloved religion, their Vedic culture, and their mythological doctrines when we happened to meet them and have a further discussion with them.

The scholastic interpretation means that some Vedic and Brahmanical minded Indian scholars (modern Indian historians, national leaders and ideologists) have described: Buddhism as an off-shoot of the more ancient faith of Hindus, perhaps a schism or heresy. A few educated Hindus - have specialized in Buddhist studies or studied something of Buddhism or some book on Buddhism - do concede that Buddhism was deeply influenced by the Vedic thought in its origin and it was a heresy of Brahmanism. Archaeologically, at least, we cannot treat Buddhism merely as a heresy against a prevailing Brahmanical orthodoxy, but, on the contrary, Buddhism should be considered as a historical and independent practice- the way of life - and that has nothing to do with the so called the more ancient faith of Hindus.

As we see from the above, the current theory on the origin of Buddhism tells us that the Vedic and Brahmanical standpoint of tendency has possessed and monopolized not only the field of Indian ideology, but also the field of social and historical studies of Buddhist relation with Brahmanism. The story of the origin of Buddhism, told in one sentence, is a matter of street-talk for every grown-up Hindu irrespective of his or her knowledge of ancient Indian religious history and archaeology. In order to reveal and clarify the true features of Buddhism, we may figure most notable question of how Buddhism related itself with the more ancient faith - the orthodox - Brahmanism of its time.

Buddhist relation with Brahmanism

We shall refer to the view of the most eminent Indian scholar, Dr. S. Radhakrishan, whose viewpoint might be considered as a prevailing Indian standpoint towards Buddhist relation with Brahmanism. Dr. S. Radhakrishan's most mature opinion on this point is summarized: the Buddha did not feel that he was announcing a new religion; he was born, grew up, and died a Hindu; he was restating with a new emphasis the ancient ideals of the Indo-Aryan civilization. The ideological tendency of the Indian scholar towards Buddhism refers mainly to the traditional interpretation, the materialistic interpretation, and the fundamentalist interpretation of Buddhism related with Brahmanism.

The traditional interpretation means that Buddhism arose out of anti-ritualistic tendency within the religion of the brahmanas, held by those the Brahmanical standpoint possessed scholars. The fact is that the history of ancient India is a record of the two opposite ideologies, that of world-affirmation represented by the priestly brahmanas of the Vedic tradition (Brahmanism) and that of world-denial and world-transcendence represented by the ascetic sramanas of non-Vedic tradition (Buddhism). It is no doubt, historically, Buddhism and Brahmanism represent two separate traditions, the Vedic tradition and the Sramanic tradition respectively, and therefore, it is irrelevant to establish the theory of Vedic origin of Buddhism.

The materialist interpretation means that some scholars, under influence of the materialist interpretation of history of popularized by Karl Marx have sought to correlate the rise of ascetic and intellectual thought-currents of the age of Buddha (624-544 B.C.) to the rise of capitalism and mercantile middle class economy. This, however, is entirely speculative, for there is no clear evidence to prove the existence of capitalism neither in the Marxian sense nor of a money-economy controlled entirely by an organized middle class of society in the seventh and sixth centuries B.C. Moreover, it is impossible to demonstrate that the spiritual ideas of Bodhisattva (potential Buddha) are determined by that social consciousness being consequent on material progress; indeed, the materialist interpretation of Buddhism is an evidence only of the philosophical crudity of theories of theirs.

The fundamentalist interpretation means that in some Hindu's minds, the Buddha was the destroyer of Brahmanical idolatry because the most fundamental elements of pre-Buddhist Brahmanism, the doctrine of sacrifice and the doctrine of four castes were criticized and rejected totally by the Buddha. In spite of its preaching of mercy to animals, in spite of the sublime ethical religion, and in spite of the hair-splitting discussion about existence or non-existence of a permanent soul, the whole building of Buddhism, ultimately, had tumbled down and was ruined at last. The criticism and condemnation made to the Buddha and his religion is not merely due to the study of philosophy and history of the religion but the fundamentalist tendency towards other religions as well.

As we see from the above, Buddhist relation with Brahmanism, elaborated by some Indian scholars represent the traditional standpoint of monopoly of India's scholastic field extended in the aspect of dialogue among different religions, ideological tendency of the Indian society and the academic study of religion. Some modern Indian scholars, with a strong Vedic and Brahmanical mind have attempted to make an assimilation of the doctrine of Buddhism with that of Brahmanism. Boldly stated, they wanted to show that Buddhism, as deeply influenced by Vedic thought, arose out of anti-ritualistic tendency within the religion of brahmanas; in other words, it is a heresy or a heretic of Brahmanism.

Buddhist relation with Hinduism

Either in the eyes of the ordinary Indian or in the eyes of the scholastic Indian people, both Buddhism and Hinduism are considered as one, because there are some similarities within each of their doctrines and practices, even though Buddhism and Hinduism are absolutely two different systems or religious traditions. Dr. P. V. Kane, a famous Indologist has observed: Buddha was only a great reformer of the Hindu religion as practiced in his time; he did not feel or claim that he was not forming a new religion, nor did he renounce the Hindu religion and all its practices and beliefs. However, when we talk about Buddhist relation with Hinduism, we should observe and examine carefully the term of "Hindu" from the historical perspective, the linguistic perspective and the archaeological perspective respectively.

The historical perspective means that Buddhist relation with Hinduism should be studied from historical standpoint and on scientific line; the study of Buddhism from the Hindu View would be a study of Hinduism but not Buddhism. It has been wrongly employed to support the modern Hindu view that Buddha himself claimed to teach the path of the ancient "Hindu" sages and to show that Buddha did not feel that he was announcing a new religion. The word "Hindu" does not occur in the statement of Buddha; nor does he refer to Vedic sages or Indo-Aryan seers or brahmanas (priests) as the teachers of that ancient path which he followed and practised.

The linguistic perspective means that the term "Hindu" is foreign coinage, of Persian and Arabic origins and stands for the medieval forms of Indian and Brahmanical religions. The word Hinduism began to be used for Indian religious traditions usually with a view to distinguish them from Christian and Islamic traditions in India. We cannot use the word Hinduism for pre-Puranic Brahmanism of the Vedic and Upanisadic age, though medieval Hinduism is based to some extent on the Vedic religion, just as Judaism before the birth of Jesus Christ cannot be properly called Christianity though Christianity is founded on pre-Christian Judaism.

The archaeological perspective means that the occurrence of the word "Hindu" in any ancient Indian archaeological or literary source has yet been discovered since the time of Alberuni (cir. 1030 A. D.), perhaps, he first referred to Indians of non-Islamic faiths as the "Hindus" meant "infidels". The term "Hindu", a form of "Sindhu", used first by the Persians, occurs along with the word "Gadara", a form of "Gandhara", in an inscription of King Darius of Iran; and here is used in a geographical sense denoting people or country on the river Sindhu conquered by that monarch. In old Persian "Sa" is pronounced as "Ha"; "Sindhu" is called "Hindu" from which the Greeks further corrupted it into "Sintos" or "Indos" from which are derived the Arbic and Persian words Hindu and Hindustan and the English words Indian and India.

As we see from the above, Buddhism and Hinduism are differed completely either from the historical point of view or from the linguistic and archaeological point of view, although there is a partial similarities between later Buddhism and the teachings of some of Hinduism. There is a strong evidence of Buddhist influence in the language as well as in the doctrines of the Hinduism; therefore, it must be admitted that we cannot imagine Buddhism was an assimilation of Hinduism (actually the latter had smuggled some of important terms and teachings from the former). We can say it is wrong to treat the Buddha as a "Hindu", or a great reformer of the Hindu religion, since there was no Hinduism in his time.

From the above discussion, we may conclude here that the current theories of the origin of Buddhism and its relations with Brahmanism and Hinduism elaborated by those- the Vedic and Brahmanical standpoint strongly possessed - the modern Indian scholars are, however, entirely speculative. Furthermore, it is understood that historically Buddhism - the most constituent of the anti-Vedic and Brahmanical movement (the Sramanic tradition) - arose out as an independent and separate religion in the India of the sixth century B. C. cannot be deeply influenced by Vedic thought in its origin or an assimilation of Hinduism. Contrary to both Brahmanism and Hinduism, the doctrine of four castes and sacrifice was denounced and rejected totally by the Buddha while it has been practiced even today in the communities of the former.

We can't study religion from this or that particular ideological standpoint merely because of our faith or merely because of our special favor to this or that religion; otherwise our eyes will be blurred even if we are taking an important task of a comparative study of religion. It has been wrongly employed to support the modern Hindu view that Buddha himself claimed to teach the path of the ancient "Hindu" sages and to show that Buddha did not feel that he was announcing a new religion. Furthermore, there is no correspondence or agreement between the basic view of early Brahmanism and early Buddhism; the two religious traditions had different backgrounds in the prehistoric Vedic epoch, and in the age of the Buddha.

As we just mentioned in the above, linguistically and archaeologically, the word of "Hindu" has something to do with Persians and Arabs in the medieval age of India. We are, therefore, not justified in using the words Hindu and Hinduism in the history context of the age of the Buddha; the phrase of "Hindu religion" in connection with pre-Muslim India is altogether meaningless and misleading. The Buddha was neither a Hindu nor a great reformer of Hinduism, since there was no "Hindu religion" in his time but only primitive Brahmanism and Vedicism; the teachings of the Buddha, no doubt, reformed many of the debased practices of Vedic religion, but he did not claim to be a reformer, neither Hindu scriptures nor Brahmanical texts recognize him as a reformer.

The Islamic Philosophy of Education

The educational philosophy is an important screen for selecting and eliminating educational objectives. In this, three important elements that are necessary ingredients in the formulation of a philosophy of Islamic education - namely, learner, knowledge, and means of instruction - will be discussed briefly. The learner, being human, is made up of a dual nature of spirit and body. The spiritual faculty is known as the ruh (soul), 'aql (mind or intellect), qalb (emotion), or nafs (self) according to the function that is ascribed to it. 'Aql (the faculty of reason), unique to human beings, elevates them above the rest of creation. The soul could be elevated to the noblest of positions but it could also be debased to the lowest of the low. The body consists of several faculties corresponding to the physical senses. The nature of the learner with regards to learning has been the subject of study in psychology. It is common knowledge that the learner is inquisitive and flexible and can be molded especially at a tender age. The learner has physical needs for food, activity, and sex; social needs for affection, belonging, and status within a social group; and spiritual needs relating to something larger and beyond one's self, that is, the need to reach for God.

Islam believes in the possibility of obtaining knowledge of Truth and Reality. In Islam there has not been much debate on this matter, unlike in the Western philosophical tradition where there has been constant debate since Greek philosophy, as demonstrated by Plato's Theatetus. We know that man is equipped with a soul and physical senses and prepared by Allah to acquire knowledge. According to Al-Attas, 'ilm (knowledge) is the arrival of the ma'na (meaning) of an object in the soul or the arrival of the soul at the meaning of an object of knowledge. Thus the soul is not merely passive but active too.

Wahy (revelation) and intuition are received by the soul. The five physical senses are the windows of the mind, particularly for obtaining empirical and the rational knowledge. In the Islamic worldview, there exists a hierarchical structure to knowledge, and, just as there exist a dual nature in mankind, there exists two categories of knowledge, the 'ilm alnaqliyah (revealed)—some of which is fard 'ayn, individual duty—and the 'ilm alnaqliyah—which is fard kifayah, which is a communal duty. These correspond to the different degrees of certainty of knowledge and the means of procuring it. Fard 'ayn knowledge is finite, certain, and obligatory for every individual Muslim to acquire. It includes the knowledge about the pillars of the religion, the articles of faith, and the Shari'ah. On the other hand, fard kifayah knowledge is obligatory upon the community. Each community should ensure that there are some people who are knowledgeable in the acquired or intellectual knowledges essential for the survival of the society, such as medicine, mathematics, natural and applied sciences, and social sciences.

In this manner, Islam ensures that every individual is

anchored to his faith while exploring new horizons. The analogy of flying a kite can be used to describe the relationship between faith and reason, where faith is the string and reason is the kite itself. There is always tension between faith and reason just as there is between the kite and the string; if for some reason the string is broken, the kite will fly off in any direction. Similarly, if reason is not grounded in faith, then it will wander in all directions without knowing its limit. Knowledge is integral or holistic as suggested by the "tawhidic" worldview. There is no compartmentalization of knowledge into religious and secular spheres. Both fard 'ayn and fard kifayah knowledge have the purpose of strengthening faith, the former through careful study of the words of Allah in the Holy Qur'an and the latter through a meticulous, systematic study of the world of man and nature.

Knowledge is integral to action, spirituality, and ethics. The nature of the knowledge that provides the content of education is the major concern of the curriculum, and these views of man and knowledge have a great bearing upon Islamic education. Education (ta'dib, disciplining; some still prefer tarbiyah, upbringing) is adab (proper way or virtue), progressively instilled in man. Adab refers to the discipline of body, mind, and spirit. It endows the possessor with the knowledge of the proper places of things or objects (hikmah) in the scheme of Creation and subsequently to act in a just manner ('adl).

Al Attas defines "education" as the progressive instilling of "the recognition and acknowledgment of the proper place of things in the order of creation, such that it leads to the recognition and acknowledgment of the proper place of God in the order of being and existence" of mankind. Therefore the primary goal of education is to lead man to recognize and acknowledge his Creator. This acknowledgment is manifested in obedience and adherence to His commandments. In other words, the primary goal of Islamic education is to produce the good being, who, by developing all his/her potentials accordingly, ensures him or her to be the servant (`abd) and the vicegerent (khalifah) of Allah who has undertaken the amanah (trust) of maintaining prosperity on earth. To this effect education is designed to produce the God-fearing (taqwa) servant of Allah who is aware of his individual vertical relations with Allah (hablun min Allah) and his social horizontal relations with his fellow man (hablun min al-nas). Thus, in effect the primary goals of education include spiritual, moral, social, intellectual, and physical development with specific goals.

There is no conflict between societal and individual aims because there is unity of purpose. Just as knowledge is a reflection of man, ideally the curricular framework of an Islamic educational institution, particularly at the tertiary level, should reflect knowledge. Just as man is of a dual nature - having a body and a spirit - so also the curriculum should possess a center or a core consisting of revealed knowledge ('ilm alnaqliyah), which fulfills the spiritual needs of the individual, and acquired knowledge ('ilm alnaqliyah), which fulfills the physical and intellectual needs necessary for societal development radiating from it. Both knowledges, fard 'ayn and fard kifayah, are essential for happiness in this world and the next. The balance between them must be preserved. Being the core of the curriculum, fard 'ayn (revealed knowledge) will be required of all students. To fulfill the requirement of fard kifayah acquired knowledge.

Islamization of the Curriculum

It demonstrates how the curriculum design is important for the moral and social well-being of individuals as well as societies. Having asserted that, the paper argues that curriculum design depends fundamentally on a well-defined philosophy of education. Without a philosophy of education that can give moral purpose to both individuals as well as societies, it will be difficult to identify a core element that can anchor the curriculum design. The paper then proceeds to identify the fundamental elements of an Islamic education philosophy and from it elicits the core concerns of an Islamic education curriculum. The paper also discusses several strategies to integrate revealed knowledge and acquired sciences for Muslim universities and schools.

It has been acknowledged by educators throughout the world that education serves a dual purpose, one for the individuals and one for society. Through proper education, an individual's potentials - physical, intellectual, moral, spiritual, and emotional are drawn out, cultivated, and developed. In this sense, Socrates referred to a teacher as a midwife because his or her role is to draw out something already innate in a child. Of course, what is drawn out and how soon depends very much on the skills and ability of the teacher. Education also serves another important role, which is to transmit and transform the cultural values, and legacy of a particular society. Education is said to be playing a conservative role when it merely transmits the prevailing cultural values and beliefs from one generation to the next. It is also capable of playing a more radical role when it attempts to reform society. In general, education plays both a conservative and a radical role in the progress of civilization.

Education is a lifelong process. A famous tradition of the Prophet Muhammad exhorts believers to "seek knowledge from the cradle to the grave." Just recently, modern medicine has shown that a child can also receive external stimuli even when he/she is still an embryo. Thus, the potential of learning begins as early as a few months after conception. Education is of three types: informal, formal, and non formal. The home is the most important institution of informal education. In it, learning takes place in an unstructured and indirect manner. It is the first "school," and the mother is the first "teacher." School is the most important institution of learning for formal education. In it, learning experiences are structured and organized systematically to achieve specific learning outcomes. In formal education, the school curriculum and the school teachers are very important facilitators of learning.

In addition, learning occurs non formally, which means that education is provided through institutions or organizations other than the formal school, for example, adult literacy classes.

Education covers a broad spectrum of issues. Therefore, it is not surprising that the Muslim Ummah have been consistently reminded and cautioned by its scholars that the state of its education seems to be the root of its problems. Some scholars have reasoned that as a discipline, education consists of five sub disciplines, namely, curriculum, counseling, management, instruction, and evaluation. This chapter is an attempt to examine curriculum, which is one of these sub disciplines. Curriculum is so important that it has been named the queen of educational sciences. Curriculum is a reflection of the educational philosophy of the institution concerned, in fact, the mechanism by which its goals are attained.

Problems in Muslim Educational Institution

As a consequence of the Western influence, the university curriculums in Muslim countries are still compartmentalized into the various divisions of natural sciences, social sciences, applied sciences, humanities, and religious sciences, without having any core fundamental knowledge to bind them together and give them unity. Each division maintains a watertight separation from the other divisions, thereby depriving all sciences of the foundational basis in faith. Without the guided intellect, there is every opportunity for man to become arrogant and ungrateful to his Creator, leading to transgression of natural laws and finally to environmental and personal destruction. This contradicts man's mandate as khalifah (vice regency) on earth.

Similarly, because of compartmentalization, the faculty of religious studies is deprived of knowledge in the humanities and in the natural and social sciences, which are necessary for it to be a meaningful guide in contemporary life. Man's activities in this life determine his station in the

Hereafter. There is every danger of man becoming narrow in thought and the door of ijtihad (personal reasoning) closing, resulting in the fiqh (jurisprudence) becoming restricted in scope and meaning. Concentration on religious studies alone will not ensure man of other knowledges and skills necessary to confront the challenges of living, even the challenge of preserving faith, life, and property. This situation is not only true for the universities but also for the school system. Religious studies alone lead to an imbalance and an unintegrated educational system.

In reality, the curricular framework proposed above is not reflected in most Muslim educational institutions. Institutions in Muslim countries tend to subscribe to a curricular framework borrowed wholesale or partially from the West. In most cases such models are secular, do not possess a core or a center, and do not reflect the true nature of man or knowledge. Ironically, even American universities that subscribe to the general education curriculum, which has the purpose of producing the good man (that is, the man who makes right choices) have a core curriculum. This core curriculum requires courses from each discipline: (1) literature and the arts, (2) history, (3) social and philosophical analysis, (4) science and mathematics and (5) foreign languages and cultures.

The curriculum has the goal of producing an educated man who is able to think and write effectively; to have a critical appreciation of the ways in which one gains knowledge and understands the universe, society and himself; to be informed of other cultures and other times; to have some understanding and experience concerning moral and ethical problems; and to have attained some depth in a field of knowledge. Thus, in a sense, Western curricula are better rounded than Islamic curricula. Even if there is a core, as in the case with most universities in Malaysia, it is based on pragmatic rather than intellectual or religious considerations. Probably the only exception is the International Islamic University, Malaysia, which designates some courses on Islamic Revealed Knowledge to be core courses and therefore, required of all students, whether they specialize in economics, law, engineering, education, architecture, or medicine.

Today, the selection of subject matter for the curriculum, especially in higher education, is obviously driven by utilitarian and pragmatic aims rather than by Islamic educational goals. The goal of fostering national development and of producing a good citizen has overridden that of human development and producing a good man. That the Malaysian Ministry of Education has overemphasized the applied sciences over the social sciences and humanities, as evident in the call for the 60:40 ratio for natural and applied sciences to social science and humanities in Malaysian universities, is a manifestation of national emphasis over individual development.

Similarly, the establishment of specialized universities such as the University of Petroleum, the University of Telecommunications, the University of Energy, and (recently) the University of Industry in Malaysia is a reflection of the confusion and misunderstanding over the concept of a university, which, as the name implies, is concerned with the universals, the whole (jami'ah), and less with the particulars (kulliyy). Again, national economic development overrides holistic human development. The notion of the university as merely a factory producing products for national development was acutely felt when a directive was issued by the Malaysian higher educational authority to shorten the length of study from four to three years as a step to accelerate the production of manpower for national development.

It is common knowledge that the content of the curriculum, that is, courses or subjects offered in Muslim educational institutions from the elementary to the tertiary levels, particularly in the acquired sciences - is borrowed from the Western, secular worldview. Thus the knowledge taught is devoid of religious values; even if it is not, it is filled instead with values that are frequently incompatible with the beliefs and values of the Islamic faith. Thus, in the long term, Muslim children are indoctrinated with alien values, primarily the idea of dualism of body and spirit, of truth, humanism, secularism, and tragedy.

The curriculum has also not provided accurate and adequate learning experiences for the children in order to attain the educational objectives, aside from intellectual and physical development. The curriculum tends toward intellectual development at all levels of education, although studies on psychology and moral development have shown that good moral habits and character are inculcated at an early age. Piaget concluded from his studies that the stage of formal operation in which the cognitive ability is more mature only begins to form at the age of about eleven or close to the age of biological puberty. The book All I Need to Know I Learned in Kindergarten illustrates the fact that for most of us, good moral habits and good character were developed in the first five years of life. Unfortunately, our curriculum designers have not been able to integrate the findings of these studies and philosophical reasoning into their plans.

Fortunately, most Muslim educational institutions provide Islamic religious instruction. Sometimes, however, the approach is rather theoretical and neglects the practical. For example, although a school might teach its students the importance of the five daily prayers, the procedures of performing them, their appropriate times, and so on, the school's formal and hidden curricula do not encourage their performance; no specific schedule or arrangement is specified in the school timetable, nor, in some cases, are the facilities provided.

Performing the prayer is left to the student's initiative. This could be good in an effort to teach responsibility and independence, but in most cases it discourages a student from praying, because he has to ask for permission from his teacher to leave the class for prayer. This is very crucial for those attending the afternoon sessions since they have to account for salat alzuhr (noon prayer) and 'asar (afternoon prayer) in school. The hidden curriculum seems to teach that moral virtues are only preached, not practiced.

The fact that our curriculum is gender blind is another manifestation of Western liberal influence. The curriculum shows no appreciation of the different needs of the learners by gender and roles. Both sexes have been treated "equally." Had the Qur'an and Sunnah been our reference point, female modesty and roles would have been emphasized in the curriculum, as would have been the male roles as the family breadwinners and protectors of women. The impending rise in social illnesses, one of the major contributors of which is the disintegrating family, has still not alarmed our policy makers. Therefore it would not be surprising if Toffler's prophecy on the new non-nuclear or non-extended family of the Third Wave (the Information Technology Age) will also hold true for that of Muslim nations.

Educational Evaluation

As a consequence of the Western influence, the university curriculums in Muslim countries are still compartmentalized into the various divisions of natural sciences, social sciences, applied sciences, humanities, and religious sciences, without having any core fundamental knowledge to bind them together and give them unity.

Each division maintains a watertight separation from the other divisions, thereby depriving all sciences of the foundational basis in faith. Without the guided intellect, there is every opportunity for man to become arrogant and ungrateful to his Creator, leading to transgression of natural laws and finally to environmental and personal destruction. This contradicts man's mandate as khalifah, or vicegerent, on earth.

Similarly, because of compartmentalization, the faculty of religious studies is deprived of knowledge in the humanities and in the natural and social sciences, which are necessary for it to be a meaningful guide in contemporary life. Man's activities in this life determine his station in the Hereafter. There is every danger of man becoming narrow in thought and the door of ijtihad (personal reasoning) closing, resulting in the fiqh becoming restricted in scope and meaning. Concentration on religious studies alone will not ensure man of other knowledges and skills necessary to confront the challenges of living, even the challenge of preserving faith, life, and property. This situation is not only true for the universities but also for the school system. Religious studies alone lead to an imbalance and an unintegrated educational system.

In reality, the curricular framework proposed above is not reflected in most Muslim educational institutions. Institutions in Muslim countries tend to subscribe to a curricular framework borrowed wholesale or partially from the West. In most cases such models are secular, do not possess a core or a center, and do not reflect the true nature of man or knowledge. Ironically, even American universities that subscribe to the general education curriculum, which has the purpose of producing the good man (that is, the man who makes right choices) have a core curriculum. This core curriculum requires courses from each discipline: (1) literature and the arts, (2) history, (3) social and philosophical analysis, (4) science and mathematics, and (5) foreign languages and cultures.

The curriculum has the goal of producing an educated man who is able to think and write effectively; to have a critical appreciation of the ways in which one gains knowledge and understands the universe, society and himself; to be informed of other cultures and other times; to have some understanding and experience concerning moral and ethical problems; and to have attained some depth in a field of knowledge. Thus, in a sense, Western curricula are better well-rounded than Islamic curricula.

Even if there is a core, as in the case with most universities in Malaysia, it is based on pragmatic rather than intellectual or religious considerations. Probably the only exception is the International Islamic University, Malaysia, which designates some courses on Islamic Revealed Knowledge to be core courses and therefore, required of all students, whether they specialize in economics, law, engineering, education, architecture, or medicine.

Today, the selection of subject matter for the curriculum, especially in higher education, is obviously driven by utilitarian and pragmatic aims rather than by Islamic educational goals. The goal of fostering national development and of producing a good citizen has overridden that of human development and producing a good man. That the Malaysian Ministry of Education has overemphasized the applied sciences over the social sciences and humanities, as evident in the call for the 60:40 ratio for natural and applied sciences to social science and humanities in Malaysian universities, is a manifestation of national emphasis over individual development.

Similarly, the establishment of specialized universities such as the University of Petroleum, the University of Telecommunications, the University of Energy, and (recently) the University of Industry in Malaysia is a reflection of the confusion and misunderstanding over the concept of a university, which, as the name implies, is concerned with the universals, the whole (jami'ah), and less with the particulars (kulliyy). Again, national economic development overrides holistic human development. The notion of the university as merely a factory producing products for national development was acutely felt when a directive was issued by the Malaysian higher educational authority to shorten the length of study from four to three years as a step to accelerate the production of manpower for national development.

3

Sociology of Education

The sociology of education is the study of how public institutions and individual experiences affect education and its outcome. It is most concerned with the public schooling systems of modern industrial societies, including the expansion of higher, further, adult, and continuing education. Education has always been seen as a fundamentally optimistic human endeavour characterised by aspirations for progress and betterment. It is understood by many to be a means of overcoming handicaps, achieving greater equality and acquiring wealth and status. Education is perceived as a place where children can develop according to their unique needs and potential. It is also perceived as one of the best means of achieving greater social equality. Many would say that the purpose of education should be to develop every individual to their full potential and give them a chance to achieve as much in life as their natural abilities allow. Few would argue that any education system accomplishes this goal perfectly. Some take a particularly negative view, arguing that the education system is designed with the intention of causing the social reproduction of inequality.

A systematic sociology of education began with Émile Durkheim's work on moral education as a basis for organic solidarity and that by Max Weber, on the Chinese literati as an instrument of political control. It was after the Second World War, however, that the subject received renewed interest around the world: from technological functionalism in the US, egalitarian reform of opportunity in Europe, and human-capital theory in economics. These all implied that, with industrialization, the need for a technologically-skilled labour force undermines class distinctions and other ascriptive systems of stratification, and that education promotes social mobility. However, statistical and field research across numerous societies showed a persistent link between an individual's social class and achievement, and suggested that education could only achieve limited social mobility. Sociological studies showed how schooling patterns reflected, rather than challenged, class stratification and racial and sexual discrimination. After the general collapse of functionalism from the late 1960s onwards, the idea of education as an unmitigated good was even more profoundly challenged. Neo-Marxists argued that school education simply produced a docile labour-force essential to late-capitalist class relations.

Sociology of Education is a philosophical as well as a sociological concept, denoting ideologies, curricula, and pedagogical techniques of the inculcation and management of knowledge and the social reproduction of personalities and cultures. In practice, the sociology of education is mostly concerned with schooling, and especially the mass schooling systems of modern industrial societies, including the expansion of higher, further, adult, and continuing education. School organization and pedagogy has drawn upon at least four competing educational philosophies: élitist or Platonic; open or encyclopaedic; vocational; and civic (as exemplified by American pragmatist education for democracy and the polytechnic school systems of Marxist state socialism). Sociologists argue that the power structure and needs of individual societies determine which of these is emphasized.

Systematic sociology of education can be traced to Émile Durkheim's pioneering studies of moral education as a basis for organic solidarity and Max Weber's analysis of the Chinese literati as an apparatus of political control. But the first major expansion of the subject after the Second World War was associated with technological functionalism in America, egalitarian reform of opportunity in Europe, and human-capital theory in economics. These all asserted a causal linkage between amounts of schooling and the economic advancement of both individuals and societies. They also implied that, with industrialization, the need for technologically educated labour progressively undermines class and other ascriptive systems of stratification, and that educational credentialism promotes social mobility.

However, statistical and field research in numerous societies uncovered a persistent link between social class origins and achievement, and suggested that only limited social mobility occurred through schooling. As a result, intense controversy developed over the determinants of the educability of groups disadvantaged by class and ethnic background. Sociological studies pointed to a wide range of material, cultural, and cognitive factors likely to depress intellectual development. Other work showed how patterns of schooling reflected, rather than challenged, class stratification and racial and sexual discrimination.

That school learning is an unmitigated good was even more profoundly challenged with the general collapse of functionalism from the late 1960s onwards. Neo-Marxists argued that school education simply produced a docile labour-force essential to late-capitalist class relations. Advocates of deschooling argued that, for the world's poor, schools merely created institutional dependence on professional educators. In particular, the deschoolers drew on a growing research literature revealing numerous counter-productive effects of human-capital-inspired development programmes for the Third World. An analogous challenge, combining research and ideology, was mounted against human-capital compensatory programmes for the urban poor of the industrialized West.

Phenomenological and interactionist perspectives emphasized several important dimensions of knowledge management through schooling: in school classroom interaction; by the professionalizing of the teaching process; through the bureaucratization of school organization; and, at the cultural level, where the links between the sociology of education and the sociology of knowledge are more immediately visible.

Vedic Education

The Pratishakhyas are some of the supplementary literature of the Vedas. Pratishakhyas are those texts, which discuss the pronunciation of syllables, the syntax and inflexions in different Vedas in detail. Different schools of thought came into existence which was founded by sages to come to a consensus in different tones of syllables and to perpetrate their thoughts and traditions. He who learns to recite the Vedas from one school of thought is said to belong to that respective tradition. It is at this time that the Gotra Pravar branch was incepted. After a long time to protect the respective customs and to commemorate it Pratishakhya texts were written. The two things covered in these texts are education and Grammar.

Until sometime back all the PratiShakhyas of all the branches of Vedas were being followed and adhered to. But now, Rik Pratishakhya created by Shaunak of the Shakal branch of Yajurveda, Vajasaneya Pratishakya of Vajasenya branch, author by Katyayana. Sama Pratishakhya authored by Pushpamuni of Samaveda, Atharva Pratishakhya of Atharvaveda or Shaunikiya Chaturadhyayi are only available. There are 3 chapters, 6 patals and 103 Kandikas in Shaunak's Rik Pratishakya. Another text which is a supplementary text named 'Upalekha Sutra' is also seen. Firstly it was Vishnu Putra who had written its commentary. Seeing this Uvratacharya wrote a comprehensive commentary on it.

One can see discussions of Atreya, Sthavir, Kaudinya,

Bharadwaj, Valmiki, Agniveshya (Agni Veshyayan) in the Taitereya Praatishakhya. But one does not come across discussions related to Taitereya Aranyaka or Taitereya Brahmana in either of the chapters, the commentaries of Atreya, Marisheya and Vararuchi which are not available now. Seeing these old commentaries, Kartikeya wrote a comprehensive commentary named 'Tribhashya'.

There are 8 chapters in Katyayana's Vajasenaya Pratishakhya. The first chapter discusses the Noun, the second 'Tones of Syllables' and from the third to the fifth, 'Sanskaras' are discussed. The different pronunciations of the verb are discussed in the sixth and seventh chapter while in the eighth chapter 'rules related to recitation of Vedas' are discussed. One can come across different opinions and discussions of Shakyayan, Shakarya, Gargya, Kashyap, Dalamya, Jatukarna, Shaunak, Upashivi, Kanva and Madhyadin in this text. In the first chapter one can also see the explanations related to Vedas and commentaries. The Sama PratiShakhyas comprises of 10 chapters. In the first two chapters there is a brief discussion related to the Sama Samuhu (compilation of mantras) i.e. Dashratra, Samvatsar, Ekaha, Aheena, Satra, Prayashchitta, Kshudra, Parvanusara and Stotruja.

In the third and the fourth chapter of the Pratishakhya procedural advises/sermons are given related to Shrut Arha Bhava and Prakriti Bhava in the Sama. The fifth chapter discusses the Vriddha and Avriddha Bhava. The sixth chapter discusses where the Sama Bhakti Samuha (incantations) should be sung and where they should not be sung. The eighth chapter throws light on the extinct Vedic texts and changes taken place in syllables at different places. The Bhavakathan (meanings) is discussed in the 9th chapter while the 10th chapter enumerates the decisions (Krishtakrishta) and the salient features. There are 2 Atharva PratiShakhyas which have come into light.

One of them is Shaunakiya Chaturadhyayika in which

following 6 points have been discussed:

- The objective of this text, introduction and features.
- Vowels and consonants, Uddatradi Laxan, Pragridya, Alphabets, structure/syntax, compound syllables, Yama, Abhinidhana, Nasikya, Swar Bhakti Sfotan, Karshana and index of syllables.
- Samhita Prakarana.
- Krama Nirnaya.
- Pada Nirnaya.
- Self-study and its necessity.

Some of the Sutras from the Pratishakhyas are very old and ancient while some of them are composed after Panini's Sutras. Pandit Satyavrat is of the view that *Sama Pratishakhya* created by Pushpa is much older than *Panini Sutras*. In fact it is older than the oldest known philosophy of Mimansa because:

Tatha Cha Samagaa Abdhuhu Vriddham Tanavymaaha Bhavati

This quotation from the Sama Pratishakhya is quoted and interspersed in the 'locative case' Mala (chain) of the Mimansa philosphy. Some scholars opine that the author of Vajasaneya Pratishakya, Katyayana and the author of *Panini Sutra,* Vartikkar Katyayana both are one. In the same way as he has criticized Panini in the Vartik, as well as in the Pratishakhya. This confirms that *Panini Sutra* is older than Vajasaneya Pratishakhya.

Pratishakhya mostly comprises of pedagogical contents and the quantity of Grammar is very less in comparison. In fact there is hardly any detailed metaphors of Grammar in the PratiShakhyas although one can see scientific analysis of all this in the Shaunikiya Shiksha at length. Teaching has been an important part of the Vedas which compre-hensively discuss the pronunciation of syllables, tones and vowel marks etc. a lot of emphasis has been laid on the pronunciation by the Vedic sages. Pronunciation is of utmost importance in the

Shrutis but the significance of the recitation of the mantras is something different altogether.

Dushtaha shabdaha swarto varnato va mithya prayukto na tvam artha maha |

Sa vaga vajro yajmanam hinasti yathendra shatruhu swarto aparaa dhaata ||

which means that when the syllables or the vowels/ consonants develop defects or are polluted due to inappropriate pronunciation and diction and do not convey the anticipated meaning then it assumes the form of a sentence composed by the most 'incompatible and misleading' words that destroy the person. Alike the defect in the tone of the word 'Indrashastra' accrued in the murder of Vritra.

When Indra killed Vishwarupa then Sad Trashta began a ritual. In this ritual one had to recite the mantra "Indrashastro Vivardhasva" whose anticipated meaning was 'Want a child who shall be the enemy of Indra.' Here there is a difference between the compound formations Bahubrihi and Tatpurusha. When this incantation was used to destroy Indra then the last words is recited in a high pitch but out of ignorance Twashta recited the first word in the high pitch, through which the meaning construed or comprehended was "We want a child towards whom, Indra is hostile."

Accordingly the child born to Twashta was killed by Devraj Indra. In the ancient times, the Shaunakiya Shiksha was treated with equal respect on par with the Vedas. Panini has quoted the view point of the author of Shabdendu Shekhar who has praised Shaunakiya Shiksha and has opined that it is equally beautiful as the Vedas as "shaunakadibhya sha chandisi" | The Shabdendu Shekhar comments on the Panini Sutra 'Chandasi Kim?' Shaunakiya Shiksha is the last chapter in the Vedas. Hence one can construe that the basic aim of Shiksha is the perfect and impeccable pronunciation of the Vedas.

Applied philosophy involves the application of

philosophical principles and concepts to the practical affairs of the human condition. Philosophers have written widely on such topics as science, law, politics, religion, history, and education. They have sought to have an influence on the definitions, ideas, methods, and theories of these human pursuits. In this essay we will take a brief look at one example of applied philosophy and illustrate how general philosophical principles and concepts come into play. The example we will use is philosophy of education. Philosophers of education have approached their subject in many different ways. One course may restrict itself to studying a single philosophy of education, while another course may be a survey of the various philosophies that have been presented, with an eye to discovering their similarities and differences.

Since we are only interested in considering philosophy of education as an example of applied philosophy, we will take the latter view for a starting point. Within American education, many philosophers have identified at least three broad philosophies of education: Essentialism, Perennialism, and Experimentalism. Essentialism has sometimes been further divided into Idealism and Realism, and Experimentalism has been divided into Progressivism and Reconstructionism. Additionally, some philosophers of education recognize an Existentialist approach to education as well. This latter philosophy of education will be ignored here because I don't think it has matured into a consistent and influential philosophy of education at this time.

Now, just because philosophers of education have formulated a few categories of educational philosophies does not mean that one or more of these philosophies can be said to "the" philosophy of education which prevails in American schools. The fact of the matter is, I suspect, that in the real world of American schooling, no one philosophy of education is really dominant and our education system is rather eclectic, borrowing something from each of the differing philosophies. It is true that the philosophy of education called Experimentalism (in both its Progressivist and Reconstructionist varieties) has had a profound influence on the direction of American education for most of the early days of the twentieth century, but its influence has been tempered by the traditional views of Essentialism and Perennialism.

The academic discipline known as philosophy of education deals with what I call third-order questions or problems. Third-order questions are the province of an applied philosophy. First-order questions (such as what is real? What is truth? What is man?) are fundamentally metaphysical and epistemological questions and lay the foundation for the development of normative philosophy, which asks what I call second-order questions (such as what is good? What is beauty? What is the best way to organize society?). Disciplines which deal with third-order questions (philosophy of law, philosophy of science, etc.) are dependent on the principles and concepts formulated within descriptive philosophy (metaphysics, epistemology) and normative philosophy (axiology, ethics, politics, and aesthetics).

What sort of questions and problems does philosophy of education deal with as a member of the category known as applied philosophy? Let me just mention a few general ones with the understanding that more detailed questions are possible but not essential for our purposes in this essay. Let me, then, ask four general questions which are important to the philosopher of education. The first question asks: How should American culture support and control education? The second question asks: How and what should our young people learn? The third question asks: How much and what kinds of academic freedom can we justify? And, finally, the fourth question asks: How should the community is related to the school?

How one answers these four general questions usually provides a clue as to which philosophy of education is most acceptable to the respondent. Furthermore, since these third-order questions are directly related to first- and second-order questions, an acute observer can probably determine what sort of general philosophy is subscribed to by the respondent; for example, whether one is a metaphysical idealist or a metaphysical realist, and whether one is an epistemological subjectivist or objectivist, and where one ought to stand on ethical and political issues. Keep in mind, however, that people are rarely consistent in their philosophic beliefs and all we can really say is that if they accept certain basic principles and concepts as "true," they ought to then accept the secondary and tertiary principles and concepts which follow from them as "true."

This is not usually the case unless one has spent a great of time "checking one's premises," as Ayn Rand has said on so many occasions. A consistent and coherent philosophy of life, in any total sense, is very difficult to achieve and most of us are subject to mistakes, inconsistencies, and so forth, as well as being influenced by our emotions and present circumstances. Keeping in mind what has been said above, let me now briefly sketch out what sort of philosophy of education would most likely be acceptable to a person who held certain general philosophical principles and concepts, using the categories of Idealism, Realism, Perennialism, and Experimentalism as a guide.

The Idealist believes in a world of Mind (metaphysics) and in truth as Idea (epistemology). Furthermore, ethics is the imitation of the Absolute Self and aesthetics is the reflection of the Ideal. From this very general philosophical position, the Idealist would tend to view the Learner as a microscopic mind, the Teacher as a paradigmatic self, the Curriculum as the subject matter of symbol and idea (emphasizing literature, history, etc.), the Teaching Method as absorbing Ideas, and the Social Policy of the school as conserving the heritage of Western civilization.

The Realist believes in a world of Things or Beings (metaphysics) and in truth as an Observable Fact.

Furthermore, ethics is the law of nature or Natural Law and aesthetics is the reflection of Nature. From this very general philosophical position, the Realist would tend to view the Learner as a sense mechanism, the Teacher as a demonstrator, the Curriculum as the subject matter of the physical world (emphasizing mathematics, science, etc.), the Teaching Method as mastering facts and information, and the Social Policy of the school as transmitting the settled knowledge of Western civilization. The Perennialist will generally fall into one of two camps, secular or theistic. The differences between these two camps are small but significant.

The secular Perennialist believes in a world of Reason (metaphysics) and in truth as Reason. Furthermore, ethics is the Rational Act and aesthetics is a matter of Creative Intuition. From this very general philosophical position, the secular Perennialist would tend to view the Learner as a rational being, the Teacher as a mental disciplinarian, the Curriculum as the subject matter of the intellect and spirit (mathematics, languages, logic, Great Books, etc.), the Teaching Method as training the intellect, and the Social Policy as transmitting the great ideas of Western civilization.

The theistic Perennialist believes in a world of Reason, Being, and God (metaphysics) and in truth as Reason and Intuition. Furthermore, ethics is the Rational Act and aesthetics is a matter of Creative Intuition. From this very general philosophical position, the secular Perennialist would tend to view the Learner as a rational and spiritual being, the Teacher as a mental disciplinarian and spiritual leader, the Curriculum as the subject matter of the intellect and spirit (mathematics, languages, logic, Great Books, Dogma, etc.), the Teaching Method as training the intellect, and the Social Policy as transmitting the great ideas, both secular and religious, of Western civilization.

The Experimentalist (adhering to progressivism or reconstructionism) believes in a world of Experience (metaphysics) and in truth as What Works (pragmatism).

Furthermore, ethics is a matter of the Public Test (moral relativism) and aesthetics is a matter of Public Taste. From this very general philosophical position, the Experimentalist, Progressivist, or Reconstructionist would tend to view the Learner as an experiencing organism, the Teacher as a research-project director, the Curriculum as the subject matter of social experience (emphasizing social studies, projects, problems, etc.), the Teaching Method as problem-solving, and the Social Policy as teaching how to manage change or, in the Reconstructionist position, as teaching how to reconstruct the social order.

A few more educational implications may be drawn in regard to the philosophies of education noted above. When it comes to specific methods of teaching, the Idealist tends to promote the lecture and discussion method, the Realist tends to favor demonstration and recitation, the Perennialist likes the lecture, the controlled discussion, and formal drill and, in the case of the theistic Perennialist, "readying the spirit" and the catechetical method, and the Experimentalist or Progressivist or Reconstructionist much prefers the group problem-solving-project methodology.

Regarding character education, the Idealist supports the imitating of exemplars and heroes, the Realist prefers training in rules of conduct, and the Perennialist tends to promote the disciplining of behaviour to reason, while the Experimentalist, Progressivist, and Reconstructionist insist on promoting character education by making group decisions in the light of the consequences of those decisions. Finally, when it comes to developing taste, the Idealist would teach good taste by studying the masterworks of civilization, the Realist would do so by studying design in nature, the Perennialist by finding beauty in reason, and the Experimentalist, Progressivist, and Reconstructionist by having students participate in art projects. All human societies, past and present, have had a vested interest in education; and some wits have claimed that teaching (at its best an educational activity) is the second oldest profession.

Philosophical realism

Contemporary philosophical realism is the belief in a reality that is completely ontologically independent of our conceptual schemes, linguistic practices, beliefs, etc. Philosophers who profess realism also typically believe that truth consists in a belief's correspondence to reality. We may speak of realism with respect to other minds, the past, the future, universals, mathematical entities (such as natural numbers), moral categories, the material world, or even thought. Realists tend to believe that whatever we believe now is only an approximation of reality and that every new observation brings us closer to understanding reality. Realism is contrasted with anti-realism.

Despite the seeming straightforwardness of the realist position, in the history of philosophy there has been continuous debate about what is real. In addition, there has been significant evolution in what is meant by the term "real". The oldest use of the term comes from medieval interpretations and adaptations of Greek philosophy. In this medieval scholastic philosophy, however, "realism" meant something different — indeed, in some ways almost opposite — from what it means today. In medieval philosophy, realism is contrasted with "conceptualism" and "nominalism". The opposition of realism and nominalism developed out of debates over the problem of universals. Universals are terms or properties that can be applied to many things, rather than denoting a single specific individual—for example, red, beauty, five, or dog, as opposed to "Socrates" or "Athens".

Realism in this context holds that universals really exist, independently and somehow prior to the world; it is associated with Plato. Conceptualism holds that they exist, but only in the mind, Moderate Realism holds that they exist, but only insofar as they are instantiated in specific things; they do not exist separately from the specific thing. Nominalism holds that universals do not "exist" at all; they are no more than words we use to describe specific objects, they do not name anything. This particular dispute over realism is largely moot in contemporary philosophy, and has been for centuries. In its Kantian sense, realism is contrasted with idealism'. In a contemporary sense, realism is contrasted with anti-realism, primarily in the philosophy of science.

Idealism

Idealism is the philosophical theory which maintains that the ultimate nature of reality is based on mind or ideas. It holds that the so-called external or "real world" is inseparable from mind, consciousness, or perception. In the philosophy of perception, idealism is contrasted with realism in which the external world is said to have a so-called absolute existence prior to, and independent of, knowledge and consciousness. Epistemological idealists (such as Kant), it is claimed, might insist that the only things which can be directly known for certain are just ideas (abstraction).

In the philosophy of mind, idealism is contrasted with materialism in which the ultimate nature of reality is based on physical substances. Idealism and materialism are both theories of monism as opposed to dualism and pluralism. Idealism also refers to a tradition in Western thought which represents things in an ideal form, or as they ought to be rather than as they really are, in the fields of ethics, morality, aesthetics, and value.

Western Philosophy

Idealism is a philosophical movement in Western thought, and names a number of philosophical positions with sometimes quite different tendencies and implications in politics and ethics, for instance; although in general, at least in popular culture, philosophical idealism is associated with Plato and the school of platonism.

Pragmatism

Pragmatism is the philosophy of considering practical consequences or real effects to be vital components of meaning and truth. Pragmatism is generally considered to have originated in the late nineteenth century with Charles Peirce, who first stated the pragmatic maxim. It came to fruition in the early twentieth-century philosophies of William James and John Dewey and, in a more unorthodox manner, in the works of George Santayana. Other important aspects of pragmatism include anti-Cartesianism, radical empiricism, instrumentalism, anti-realism, verificationism, conceptual relativity, a denial of the fact-value distinction, a high regard for science, and fallibilism.

Pragmatism began enjoying renewed attention from the 1950s on, because a new school of philosophy put forth a revised pragmatism which criticized the logical positivism that had dominated philosophy in the United States and Britain since the 1930s, notably in the work of analytic philosophers like W. V. O. Quine and Wilfrid Sellars.

The concept of naturalized epistemology was further developed and widely publicized by Richard Rorty, whose later work grew closer to continental philosophy and is often considered relativistic by its critics. Contemporary pragmatism is still divided between work that is strictly within the analytic tradition, and a more relativistic strand in the wake of Rorty, and lastly neoclassical pragmatism (which includes philosophers such as Susan Haack) that stays closer to the work of Peirce, James, and Dewey.

Origins

As a philosophical movement, pragmatism originated in the United States in the late 1800s. The thought and works of Charles Sanders Peirce and William James (both members of The Metaphysical Club) as well as John Dewey and George Herbert Mead figured most prominently in its overall direction. The term pragmatism was first used in print by James, who credited Peirce with coining the term during the early 1870s. Prompted by James' use of the term and its attribution to him, Peirce began writing and lecturing on pragmatism to make clear his own interpretation. Peirce eventually coined the new name pragmaticism to mark what he regarded as the original idea, for clarity's sake and possibly (but not certainly) because he disagreed with James. He claimed the term was so ugly; nobody would be tempted to steal it.

James and Peirce were inspired by the crucial links among belief, conduct, and disposition by saying a belief is a proposition on which a person is prepared to act. Inspiration for the pragmatists include Francis Bacon who coined the phrase "knowledge is power", David Hume for his naturalistic account of knowledge and action, Thomas Reid for his direct realism, Immanuel Kant for his idealism and from whom Peirce derives the name "pragmatism", Georg Hegel for his introduction of temporality into philosophy, and J.S. Mill for his nominalism and empiricism.

Pragmatist epistemology

The epistemology of early pragmatism was heavily influenced by Darwinian thinking. Pragmatism was not the first to see the relevance of evolution for theories of knowledge: the same rationale had for example convinced Schopenhauer we should adopt biological idealism because what's useful to an organism to believe might differ wildly from what is actually true. Pragmatism differs from this idealist account because it challenges the assumption that knowledge and action are two separate spheres, and there exists an absolute or transcendental truth above and beyond the sort of inquiry organisms use to cope with life. Pragmatism, in short, provides what might be termed an ecological account of knowledge: inquiry is construed as a means by which organisms can get a grip on their environment.

'Real' and 'true' are labels that have a function in inquiry and cannot be understood outside of that context. It is not realist in a traditional robust sense of realism (what Hilary Putnam would later call metaphysical realism), but it is realist in that it acknowledges an external world which must be dealt with. A philosopher's general tendency is to push all views into either the idealist or realist camp, as well as William James' occasional penchant for eloquence at the expense of public understanding, resulted in the widespread but false characterization of pragmatism as a form of subjectivism or idealism.

Pragmatism in other fields of philosophy

While pragmatism started out simply as a criterion of meaning, it quickly expanded to become a full-fledged epistemology with wide-ranging implications for the entire philosophical field. Pragmatists who work in these fields share a common inspiration, but their work is diverse and there are no received views.

Education on Western Philosophy

The term western philosophy actually refers to the philosophical line of thoughts the western or the Occidental world. This is particularly opposed to the Eastern Oriental philosophies and other varieties of philosophies that exist in the world. From historical perspective, it may be said that it all began with the referring to the western civilization that had its beginning in Greece which saw the advent of the Greek philosophy. The beginning of basic Education on Western Philosophy, actually started in the ancient Greece. The whole concept of Western Philosophy was related with the ideas about universal knowledge that claimed in mathematics, astronomy, natural philosophy, music.

According to the available historical data, the western philosophy had its onset as an intention and not as development process of method or technology. One of the interesting factors that is related with Education on Western Philosophy began as a quest for working on universe model that began with the Greeks getting in sync with astronomical techniques at that particular point in time. In the contemporary times, western philosophy actually refers to the main contemporary main traditions; these are like Analytic philosophy and continental philosophy. Availing western philosophy education is all the more interesting because it has been strongly influenced by the western religion as well, spreading in several of the branches like science, and politics, and the philosophies of the Abrahamic religions (Jewish philosophy, Christian philosophy, and Islamic philosophy), among the many more.

Some of the central concepts and the elements are actually regarded to be linked with science and politics which also belong to the branches of western philosophy. In the present context, the distinction of the western philosophy and the other western disciplines is based on certain fundamental, classical, and universal frame of thinking. It is because of the involvement of several elements in this particular field of study, opting to get through the educational courses of western philosophy has become quite common in the world. So don't be surprised if you happen to find some of your friends opting out for the courses in the well known institutions in the world.

Again this has become all the easier with the advent of technology and the web doing the rounds among the youngsters who desire to pursue the course simply out of pure interest. Some of the most popular divisions that you can expect from Education on Western Philosophy, comprises of philosophy of mind, philosophy of science, philosophy of nature that is philosophy of biology and philosophy of physics, philosophy of law, and philosophy of art which is aesthetics.

A minor in philosophy is both a practical endeavor and a life-enriching experience. For many, the liberal arts college experience will, unfortunately, be the only place where thinking for the sake of thinking is supported and encouraged. But with a philosophy minor, graduates will be more likely to keep thinking once they leave academia, and bring their ideas to fruition in whatever field they choose. Not only will they understand why education matters, but they themselves will matter in the world. The philosophy minor at Western State College of Colorado was specifically designed to complement any major that Western offers. Given that philosophy as a discipline allows individuals to see the world from varied perspectives and helps to provide rational approaches to evaluate ideas, a minor in philosophy deepens the value of a liberal arts education itself by providing the tools needed to understand and appreciate the relationship among the fields of study available at Western.

For those considering graduate school, a minor in philosophy helps sharpen verbal and analytical skills needed for the GREs, LSATs, and GMATs. Most importantly, however, philosophy provides exposure to the theoretical discourse in which graduate work engages. Outside of academia, a philosophy minor helps develop real-world, professional skills. A background in philosophy enhances communication, argument, and critical thinking skills. Those with experience in philosophy are better able to understand and classify the content of information presented to them, and are not easily swayed by opinions disguised as facts. Philosophy also helps individuals to understand key issues in decision-making and problem-solving situations. It enhances research, investigation, design, and planning skills.

Being well-versed in philosophy enhances the ability to see situations from multiple perspectives, and better define the parameters of the task at hand. All of these skills are "transferable," meaning that they are not career-specific. Current trends indicate that over a current college graduate's lifetime, he or she will hold several jobs in several different fields. Thus, having skills that can move with an individual through any career shifts becomes vital to "real world" success. Reasoning, researching, planning, and communication are essential to problem solving and clearly presenting ideas. Whether planning to go into a traditional or non traditional career, a background in philosophy will enhance the knowledge gained in an individual's specific field of study, and allow the broadest range possible in terms of later career opportunities.

Sociology of education: concept and origin

After the Second World War it gained entity as separate subject of knowledge. Technological advancement and engagement of human capital(work force) in industrialization America and Europe gave rise to the social mobility .Now it is easier to move up to the upper strata of society gaining technical skills, knowledge. People who were farmer earlier became worker in factories. In that period social mobility was at top gear. And sociologist began to think that education promotes social mobility and undermines the class stratification.

It gained interest and lot of sociological studies done on the subject. Statistical and field research across numerous societies showed a persistent link between an individual's social class and achievement, and suggested that education could only achieve limited social mobility. Sociological studies showed how schooling patterns reflected, rather than challenged, class stratification and racial and sexual discrimination. But sociology of education is a branch of study and very helpful in finding the relation between sociology and education.

The sociology of education is the study of how social institutions and forces affect educational processes and outcomes, and vice versa. By many, education is understood to be a means of overcoming handicaps, achieving greater equality and acquiring wealth and status for all. Learners may be motivated by aspirations for progress and betterment. Education is perceived as a place where children can develop according to their unique needs and potentialities. The purpose of education is to develop every individual to their full potential.

Relation between sociology and education

The relation between sociology and education has always been a subject of debate. One concept says education is meant to overcome the inequalities of society whereas the other says the prime function of education is to promote the equilibrium status of the society i.e. it tries to maintains equality/inequality whatever state is prevalent in the society. The sociologist who favours second theory says that education is a social effort hence it runs the way society wants. And society moves in the direction the dominant group of society wants. According to them the second theory is a propagated myth by the promoter of first theory.

The first theory is said positive and second is leveled as negative thought. Although there is conflict which theory is most relevant; one thing is crystal clear that education is social effort and it reflects rather than directs society. If education is said to directs society it is true only because there is a social force favouring this. Both the theory has a role to play in defining the relation between sociology and education. This relation plays a great role in learning outcome. So it is a matter of great interest for the people like you; who is directly linked to educational institutions.

The Concept of Education in Social and Cultural Context

The objectives were (i) to study the concept of education, (ii) to study the concept of education in the light of the main schools of philosophical thought, (iii) to study the historical evolution of the concept of education, (iv) to study socio-cultural conditions prevailing in the different parts of the world in the context of education, and (v) to study the influence of socio-cultural conditions upon the concept of education. The historical method was followed. The data were collected from primary and secondary sources. The analysis of the definition of education by various thinkers of Greece and Rome, of the middle ages, renaissance and reformation periods and the modem period was carried out.

Further, for the collection of data regarding social-cultural conditions prevailing during the different ages, books on social, cultural and political history were consulted. In the light of social and cultural conditions as well as schools of philosophical thought, definitions of education were interpreted. The major conclusions were:

1. There was a link of thought throughout the ages in the concept of education.
2. The concept of education was influenced by the different schools of thought, viz., idealism, naturalism, realism, pragmatism, reconstructionism, existentialism and analytical philosophy.
3. The thinkers had thought on education keeping in mind the prevailing needs of the society, but in the middle ages thinkers and their definitions of education were strongly influenced by the idealism and religious goals of life and education
4. In the modern age the cultural base of education had changed to a pragmatic view and definitions were more or less influenced either by pragamatism or existentialism.
5. A sociological base was apparent in modem definitions of education.
6. In modem times some thinkers were attempting to analyse the process of education instead of defining the term education.
7. The analytical approach to the clarification of the concept and the language in which the concept was defined was apparent in the modern age.

4

Philosophy of Indian Education

Philosophy has been defined as "an analysis of the grounds of and concepts expressing fundamental beliefs." Philosophy provides the "why" we do things just like methodology determines "how" we do things. Our philosophy provides overall guidelines that provide a basis for our actions. Thus, the set of beliefs or ideas we hold are of vital importance because they provide a framework or guidelines for our later actions. I imagine a question that goes through your mind right now is, "Why do we need a separate philosophy for Indian education?" You might be thinking that there is no real difference in a philosophy for Indian students and students in the general population. You might hold, with some justification, the belief that all education is concerned with the needs of students.

If you have these questions, I want to assure you that you are absolutely correct—up to a point. However, it is my contention that each person serving Indian students, either totally or partially, needs to come up with or develop a philosophy of Indian education. This feeling is held because this serves to accentuate the fact that Indian students have cultural differences which affect the development of potential and have problems and disadvantages which, in many ways, cause them to stand aside from the general population. These disadvantages and differences exist to such an extent that if "equal education" for Indian students is the goal of the education program, special handling is required—and a set of beliefs or ideas for such handling is necessary. While this is my contention, let me be quick to say that in a broad context, I, too, believe that the needs of children in general are the same, but sometimes there exists a real difference in the degree of need. I feel that this is true of Indian students.

Thus, this is a justification for a set of beliefs or philosophy of Indian education. Such a philosophy will fit all students, but they will particularly fit the major problems Indian people face in today's world. Also, such a philosophy could be drawn up in 100 different forms, but, desirably it should be brief so that it is intellectually digestible and becomes a part of our thinking process and can be remembered rather easily. This is vital to us who are specifically concerned with the education of Indian students.

Here is a set of beliefs or a proposed philosophy of Indian education:

1. Education should provide the Indian student with all basic scholastic tools essential to the pursuit of learning in the modern world. This would, of course, include the ability to read, write, and to compute—or the three R's; but there is an important addition. The addition is a good, solid foundation in English capability essential to learning in today's world. We cannot escape the need for special attention to English capability. It illustrates that special "something" that Indian students need.
2. Education should provide him with a profound understanding that leads to a deep appreciation of himself, his society, and the world in which he lives. This belief is expressed by design and not by accident. The Indian student may have a background which leads to an undesirable self-image or a self-image that is not up to par. If he cannot see his background as a part of a

proper self-image, then education has failed in its task. Actually, he may have been better off to have not been exposed to it. We must prepare students to become what they will—we must give the student a chance to decide. In doing this, we must recognize the scriptural admonition, "Remember the quarry from which you were dug, the rock from whence ye were hewn," as it applies to the heritage of Indian students.

3. Education should provide the Indian student with the development of his ability to think critically and plan effectively within his environment. Why is this important? Because this fits into the last developmental task which is to develop his own set of beliefs or philosophy of life. It is another way of saying that education should not only provide him with knowledge but should develop his wisdom to use it. It further ties into the school of the future where conflicts must be resolved as a part of the educative process.
4. Education should encourage his creativity. It should develop his taste for fine things in regard to art and music. It should cultivate his talents in this regard. All should realize, however, that his talent might take a different turn from the established norm because of a different cultural background. By all means, let us all be wise enough to recognize the unusual child and encourage his creativity in whatever form it takes.
5. Education should prepare him for successful living. Indeed, it should give him a skill or many skills which would enable him to find success in a vocation, profession or avocation. It should prepare him for utilizing occupational opportunities which will provide him with the livelihood for living the "good life" as he has defined it.
6. Education for the Indian child should profoundly involve his parents and his tribe for direction, for coordination and for support.

Combined with the above, the serious attempts being

made at some schools to help transmit a small part of the cultural heritage of the Indian child should be enlarged and extended. This is needed to even a greater degree for the education of the Indian child than would appear to be needed in considering the education of his counterpart in the general population. This is true because in the latter, it is well accepted that the school is a cultural transmission instrument. A minority student in a majority society may have fewer social institutions which are supportive of his culture. Thus, an additional burden for the minority culture falls on the school.

Indian Control of Indian Education

The philosophy of Indian control of Indian education has its roots in Saskatchewan. Over the past two decades, Saskatchewan Indian leaders have recognized education as a priority and as a result have become pioneers in the field throughout North America. In 1969, the Federation of Saskatchewan Indians undertook the first major education development, the Education Task Force. At that time, Chief Dave Ahenakew mandated his executive director Sol Sanderson to conduct the task force. The task force was headed by Rodney Soonias and developed a comprehensive statement of the state of Indian education in Saskatchewan. The two volume report became the watershed for Indian control of Indian education and prior to that the Department of Indian Affairs had been busy imposing a system of integrated schools on the bands and transferring federal schools in the north to provincial control.

As a result of the pressure created by the report, school which had been transferred in the north returned to federal responsibility in 1973. In 1972, the National Indian Brotherhood education committee chaired by Clive Linklater, developed a statement on Indian control of Indian education. This statement went forward and in 1973 was endorsed by the Canadian Government. The minister of

Indian Affairs at that time was Jean Cretian and George Manuel was the leader of the National Indian Brotherhood.

In 1972, the Saskatchewan Indian Cultural College was established and Ken Goodwill became the first director. The College went on to develop a series of programs and became the hub of the Indian education developments that would continue on into the next decade. It nurtured the developmental work which evolved into Indian controlled school programs and post-secondary institutions. Also at that time, things began to happen at the local level. In 1973, the James Smith Band withdrew its students from Kinistino School and assumed control over education. Also at that time, similar education centres developed at Thunderchild and Little Pine Reserves.

In 1974, the Indian Cultural College began professional training which was to evolve into the Indian Federated College. The first program was an Indian social work program with an academic link to the school of social work at the University of Regina. Also that summer, training for teachers began at the Prince Albert Student Residence. Ida Wasacase headed up the professional development program. As Indian education developed, more and more people became employed in the field and professional and para-professional associations were formed under the authority of the FSIN. The organizations were the Indian Language Instructors Association, the Indian Guidance Counsellors Association, Child Care Workers Association, and the Indian Associate Teachers Association.

The following summer in 1975, summer school training programs were offered to approximately 220 students in three locations, Little Pine Reserve, Prince Albert Indian Residential School and the Qu'Appelle Indian Student Residence. In 1976, the Indian Federated College was established at the University of Regina and the Indian Community College was established in Saskatoon. Both of these institutions were direct spin-offs from the

Saskatchewan Indian Cultural College. Ida Wasacase was the first director of the Federated College and Tony Sparvier was the first director of the Community College.

The summer school program that year offered courses for approximately 200 at the Prince Albert Indian Residential School, Saskatoon and the Qu'Appelle Indian Residential School. Also at that time, on reserve teacher education programs were started with students living on reserve and taking classes on reserve. Teacher training programs were in place at the James Smith Reserve, the Little Pine Reserve and at Stanley Mission which is part of the La Ronge Band. Among the numerous bands who took control of their schools, the first were Red Earth, Montreal Lake, Sturgeon Lake and James Smith.

As education developments continued at the local, District and Regional level, it became apparent to the chiefs that they must come forward with more policy on Indian control of Indian education and institutions. In 1980 the chiefs gave a mandate to the FSIN to research and bring forward an Indian Education Act for consideration by the Legislative Assembly. This led to the establishment of the interim Saskatchewan Indian Education Commission. At this time, on reserve teacher education programs continued this time at Red Earth and the Beardy's Reserves. In 1982, the Federation of Saskatchewan Indian Nations Convention was developed and accepted by the Chiefs Assembly and also that year, the constitution acts sections 25 and 35 (1) recognized and entrenched the treaties and special status of Indians in Canada.

In 1985, the FSIN Convention Act was passed into law by the Legislative Assembly. Also that year, the FSIN passed into law, the financial management Act, the Personnel Management Act and the Code of Ethics for executive and employees was ratified by the FSIN legislative assembly. In 1985, the Saskatchewan Indian Institute of Technologies, formerly the Saskatchewan Indian Community College, established a satellite college system which included welding at the Kakawestahaw Reserve in the Yorkton District; Plumbing and Heating at Muskeg Lake Reserve in the Saskatoon District; and Recreation Technology in the Qu'Appelle Indian Education Centre.

The Thunderchild Technical Institute was established and, along with the National Indian Forestry Institute established by the Meadow Lake Tribal Council; both established a working relationship with the Saskatchewan Indian Institute of Technologies (SIIT). In 1986, the S.I.I.T. Act was passed through third reading by the Legislative Assembly of the Federation of Saskatchewan Indian Nations. Also, the Saskatchewan Indian Federated College Act was tabled for amendments for third reading. Both the Saskatchewan Indian Cultural College Act and the FSIN Education Act passed through first reading.

In 1987, the FSIN Indian Education Act passed through second and third reading. The results for Indian Control of Indian Education in Saskatchewan have been monumental. Over the past twenty years, many individuals have been involved in developing Indian education. Currently, the FSIN operates three institutions, the Indian Cultural Centre, the Indian Federated College, and the Institute of Techno-logies. Each institution has a separate board appointed directly or indirectly by the chiefs of Saskatchewan. The SIIT board consists of the district representatives; the SIFC board consists of district appointments along with members from the University of Regina, the University of Saskatchewan, the Province of Saskatchewan and the department of Indian Affairs. The Cultural Centre has a board consisting of district and agency appointments. Members of the Senate of the FSIN are also included on all the boards.

The Indian Cultural Centre continues to be a developmental institution in support of Indian control of Indian education at all levels. The Indian Federated College has developed a wide range of programs and has turned out numerous graduates over the past decade. The Indian Institute of Technologies Act is now a fully developed community college with satellite institutions throughout the province. It too, has turned out a vast amount of trained technicians. The future for Indian control of Indian education in Saskatchewan is limited only by the imagination of the people involved. We still have many areas to be developed and we still have a rapidly growing population that needs to be serviced. The future for Indian education in Saskatchewan remains bright.

Education on Indian Philosophy

Philosophy is that discipline which deals with the science of living or more appropriately, the ethics of what exists and what are the essential natures of it. It also deals with what is known as epistemology or genuine knowledge. Logic is an important branch of philosophy which deals with reasoning. Different philosophers have different ideas about the nature of reasoning but they are unanimous about the subject matter of philosophy. So, the Education on Indian Philosophy deals with all these aspects in respect to India. Indian philosophy is a popular domain in the education system of India and abroad. Many people like to pursue Education on Indian Philosophy who are from abroad and in order to study this, they often come down to India to gather the knowledge in more appropriate way and to relate their teachings with actual experiences.

Apart from gathering knowledge from particular institutions, you can also pursue Education on Indian Philosophy through online materials from the respective sites or the study materials of different college and universities. The online courses have affiliation with different institutes and so, you can also achieve degree either in bachelor's course or master's course through Internet itself. You can also go through these websites to gather knowledge and to apply these thoughts in your daily lives. The aims and objectives of Education on Indian Philosophy are as follow. It identifies the remarkable features of Indian Philosophy along with the differentiation in between the orthodox and unorthodox schools.

These courses also deal with interpreting the implications of Education on Indian Philosophy along with the implications of teacher education, which emphasizes on the teaching of philosophy. The epistemological objectives are discussed in the following lines. It teaches hot to sensitize with different phenomena and processes and to relate the different concepts with personal observations and experiences. Philosophy also teaches how to agree or disagree to a particular context. The philosophers can also appreciate any view in world with their power to agree or disagree. It also teaches how to choose individual response to the whole world. It has been seen that most of the Education on Indian Philosophy deals with acquiring knowledge on the basis of theories. Only learning is not enough if the persons cannot relate it in their daily lives. The most common dilemma of everyone is to determine whether an action is right or wrong. Through Education on Indian Philosophy you will be able to determine this. Philosophy also gives stress on totality, which means to understand every action with its totality and not to be studied in isolation.

Research in Philosophy of Education

Any serious attempt at a comprehensive review analysis and appraisal of research trends in a field like the philosophy of education, given its contentious nature, should be guided by certain basic reference criteria: How well do the research studies conducted under the rubric 'philosophy of education' represent the domain of this field of inquiry? How adequately do they reflect its spirit and method(s)? And, how far are they socially relevant and useful? Each of these interrogatives will be examined in some detail here. In the process, the state of the art of this field will be expounded and the general trends indicated by the researches conducted thus far analysed. This will be followed by a trend analysis and appraisal of the new research studies included in the present survey, a brief note on recent developments in the field and an exploration of possible research is- sues of contemporary relevance.

The Domain of 'Philosophy of Education'

If anyone uninitiated into academic scholarship in philosophy of education scans through the titles of the hundred and odd research studies thus far conducted under this banner he will, in all likelihood, get the impression that all there is to philosophy of education research is to 'study' the 'educational philosophy' or the educational thoughts and contribution of this or that thinker (generally one venerated in history) or scriptural text, either individually or in a comparative frame. So complete is the domination of this type of research that it has almost come to define this area. More than 7 5 per cent of the research output is accounted for by studies of this kind.

For the purpose of analysis, researches in philosophy of education can be divided into three classes: (i) 'critical' or simply 'study' of the educational philosophy, educational thoughts/ideas/contributions of individual thinkers, individually or in comparison with others, (ii) exploration of epics, historical periods, religious and philosophical systems for their educational philosophy, ideas etc., and (iii) thematic and conceptual studies. Almost half the researches fall under the first category with the rest divided between the second and third. Looking at the same thing in a different way, hardly 25 per cent of the researches have their focus on problems and issues cutting across philosophical schools and personalities; all the rest concern themselves with the study of the educational philosophy of thinkers and systems, quite a few of them being repetitive.

Gandhi, Tagore, Vivekananda, Upanishadic education

and Basic Education alone account for as many as 33 studies Others who figure under this category include Nehru, Bhave, Aurobindo, Dayananda, Bhaurao Patil, Azad, Tilak, Waliullah, Tulsi, Shankara, Thiruvalluvar, Besant, Narayana Guru, Kalelkar, J. Krishnamurthy, Ramakrishna and Gopabandhu Das. Amongst the Western philosophers/educational thinkers studied, are Deway, Kilpatrick, Rousseau, Freud, Adler, Jung, Read, Russell, Green, Bosanquet, Whitehead, Bergson. The philosophical and religious systems of the past that have been explored for their educational contributions include vedic, upanishadic, Jain and Buddhistic; the Sankhya-yoga schools; the smritis, *Gita, Ramayana, Mahabharata, Koran, and Guru Granth Sahib*. While some researches have employed the 'ism' framework of idealism, naturalism, existentialism and pragmatism, others have dealt with philosophy of education itself as a single over arching theme like, 'Evolution of Philosophy of Education in India', 'Fundamentals of Educational Philosophy', 'Educational Thoughts of Indian Thinkers', and 'Recent Philosophies of Education in India'.

As regards the third category, concepts and educational ideas that have become the focal points of research include freedom, ideology, explanation, human nature, personality, national integration, life-long education, distance education, equality of educational opportunity, and educational theory. How representative is this range of topics of the domain of inquiry, and how adequately does it reflect its characteristic concerns? Answering such questions would obviously entail an inquiry into the very conception of the nature and scope of this field, into the meaning of 'philosophy of education' itself.

It is not the intention here to enter into a detailed discussion on the meaning and scope of philosophy of education. Much has been said and written on the issue but differences persist. Nor is it intended to stipulate any 'definition' of philosophy of education or prescribe rules of procedure for 'doing' it. One is too well aware of the hazards involved in any such attempt and the futility of any search for an objective, universally acceptable definition of philosophy. The purpose of the sketchy discussion on the nature of philosophy which follows is only to indicate broadly the spectrum of issues and problems that have engaged the attention of philosophers, past and present, world-wide. Hopefully, such an exercise would also make one aware of the rich research possibilities of the field.

An approach to such an undertaking that suggests itself is to consider philosophy of education as the application of philosophy to education-its goals, processes, concepts, theories, institutions. 'Philosophy' here refers both to its tools and techniques and also the 'knowledge' gained through their application. It may be, as the logical analysts maintain, that philosophy does not produce any knowledge of a positive kind that is. But one also cannot deny that philosophical effort does result in some sort of wisdom which is not restricted to conceptual enlightenment alone. Historically, philosophy has expressed itself in several modes- speculative, normative and critical. On the speculative plane, philosophers have concerned themselves with sweeping general inquiries into what lies beyond immediate human experience-into the nature of the noumenal world, existence of God, relationship between matter and spirit and so on-to present a synoptic view of the universe and man's relationship with it.

The resulting world-views, however, had their basis not on uncritical thinking, fantasizing or unanalysed feeling, but were rooted in sustained, disciplined, systematic analysis of experience in its diverse manifestations science, art, literature, religion, politics. In the sphere of education, the metaphysical philosophers have contributed grand visions of education and educational utopias for their realization. The educational ideals and prescriptions of Tagore, Gandhi and Aurobindo, for example, were anchored in their metaphysical views about man, his possibilities and his destiny. Normative philosophy is concerned with the establishment of norms, standards and guidelines, for the conduct of human affairs. Values, both moral and aesthetic, become the chief concern here. The normative philosopher says what human dispositions are excellences and worthy of cultivation and why they are to be considered as such, adducing metaphysical justification if required.

Education essentially being a process of transmission of what is considered as good and worthwhile (knowledge, skills, values, attitudes, behaviour patterns), normative educational philosophy has primarily concerned itself with inquiries into the ethical dimensions of the ends and means of education. As critical analysis, philosophy of education becomes a meta- level activity of clarification and criticism of concepts, theories, and arguments appearing in the primary, on-going activity of 'education'. The predominant mode today in philosophy (and in philosophy of education) is the critical, analytical mode. The analytical philosophers engage in formal tasks such as elucidation of educational concepts, appraisal of the logical status of educational statements and validations of educational theories. They conceive their task as one of understanding and illuminating the language and discourse of education.

To equate philosophy with any one mode, therefore, would be dogmatic and a gross misrepresentation of its nature as it has unfolded in history. Nor would it be proper to think that these modes operate exclusively. No philosopher can be described as a 'pure' metaphysical, critical or normative philosopher. On the contrary, philosophizing activity is a blend of several modes albeit in different proportions. A normative prescription, for example, may require metaphysical justification. Despite the predominantly critical temper of modem times, it would not be improper, therefore, to assign to philosophy a much wider role than mere language or concept analysis, a role that would include legitimate constructive and normative functions also. Philosophy of education would, in that case, in addition to being a second order activity of analysis, also accommodate integration of such analysis with socio-historical and normative studies of education.

Such a comprehensive view of philosophy of education would indicate a wide range of research problems and issues than mere study of an educational thinker or system in a general, holistic way. Philosophy of education should raise important issues having relevance for education and tackle them philosophically-offering arguments, clarifying concepts, putting forward metaphysical views with intellectual support and offering grounds for normative assertions. It should provide a frame of reference for orienting ourselves, for gaining a sense of direction in education, a set of standards for the validation of our aims and values, justifying our curricular activities in terms of intrinsic and instrumental criteria and enlightening us about concepts like democracy, equality, secularism, freedom and authority as they operate in education. As meta-level reflection, especially, philosophy of education offers a variety of topics for the researcher.

In almost every aspect of education, its conception and meaning, aims, content and process-holds out possibilities for logical and conceptual examination. Apart from these, there are also philosophical insights to be gained about the relationship of education itself with other spheres of human activity, social, political, economic, and religious. Educa-tional discourse is highly complex in nature and cuts across the empirical, a priori and normative forms of inquiry. Clarification of concepts, analysis and appraisal of arguments, statements and theories, synthesis and integration of such understanding with substantive issues of the educational process and practices—curriculum, systems of schooling, the process of learning and teaching, school management, educational institutions and normative guide lines on aims, curriculum, methods, institutions and teachers-can all be legitimate objects of philosophical inquiry in education. Looking at the nature and kind of research efforts and outputs against the background of this territorial vastness of philosophy of education, it is difficult to withhold the judgement that the area remains largely uncharted.

Methods of Philosophical Inquiry

Even more important, perhaps, than the subject (topic) of research is the issue of method, although the distinction between the two may not always be clear cut. Philosophy of education essentially is an activity or a method, a disciplined, systematic way of thinking about a problem leading to illumination of conceptual meaning and understanding and appraisal of issues of educational policy and practice. Research should exhibit this spirit of the method and meet its exacting requirements: semantic clarity and meaningfulness, consistency and rigor of thought, consciousness of assumptions and methodological awareness. The question is, how well do our research studies stand up to these requirements.

That research in philosophy of education suffers from lack of methodological rigor and generally poor quality (apart from scanty output) has been pointed out on several occasions by reviewers of research in this area. The trend report in the Second Survey in this series noted that much of what goes on in the name of philosophical research is actually historical or descriptive research without the norms and rigor expected in these types of researches; the researches are mostly at an informational level, stopping short- of employing higher techniques of philosophical inquiry; they are mere compilations of ideas not extending beyond a first-level interpretation; they are repetitive, without indicating where the new contribution lies or increasing depth of under- standing or adopting any new line of approach; the 'critical methods' employed in some of the studies appear to take a simple commonsense approach without the rigor befitting philosophical criticism; some research endeavors in this area appear to have been prompted more out of the desire to escape the stringent methodological requirements of the other research areas.

Since the publication of this report more studies have appeared some of which were included in the Third Survey, but the overall picture that emerges does not warrant any substantial review of the earlier appraisal. 'Philosophy of education' researches continue to suffer from methodological anemic and absence of the enterprise necessary to break away from the beaten track. This is no place to go into the cause of this state of affairs. Yet, no proper evaluation of the quality of researches, especially from the methodological point of view, can be made without an acquaintance, at least, with the general factors that have made 'philosophy of education' what it has come to be today.

Philosophy of education, in the first place, is one of the later additions to the field of educational studies and a tradition of research in this field is yet to be established. It is only recently that it has come to acquire academic respectability and to be recognized as a branch of applied philosophy. Historically, its roots the in the unsophisticated amateur philosophizing engaged in by practical educationists whose primary interests were the improvement of educational practices. What is articulated today as philosophy of education (or, more commonly, 'educational philosophy') is actually a creature of teachers' training colleges and university departments of education?

This view has not gone beyond looking upon philosophy of education as the study of 'isms' and their `educational implications'. On this view, philosophy of education is the application to education of the speculative theses-metaphysical, epistemological, axiological of the different philosophical schools to derive directives and recommendations on educational alms, curriculum and methodology. As far as its teaching is concerned, it is offered as one of the foundation courses, either by itself or in combination with sociological foundations of education, usually at the M. Ed. level. At the first degree level, the current trend is to subsume some of its content under a general course on education. When it comes to actual curriculum transaction, things become more difficult. Neither the teachers nor the students, for the most part, possess sufficient prerequisite acquaintance with the methods of philosophical inquiry and logic. The result: all miscellaneous, undifferentiated discourse on educational aims, content and methodology gets peddled as philosophy of education. Certainly these are not conditions conducive to the nurturing of academic scholarship in the philosophy of education.

Be that as it may; it has already been pointed out that Study of the Educational Philosophy of type studies dominate research activity in this field. There is no doubt that such study is a worthy philosophical pursuit. But what precisely it means to study the educational philosophy of and what specifically it involves in terms of the intellectual tasks to be performed in such an undertaking, are by no means clear or obvious. The meaning one gives to 'study of the educational philosophy of naturally depends on one's conception of the nature and scope of 'philosophy of education'. But whatever be the philosophical model one chooses analytic, speculative or normative- mere collection and compilation of ideas and thoughts of a thinker would not amount to doing philosophy in the true sense of the term.

To organize the ideas in terms of philosophical principles, to examine their philosophical presuppositions and assumptions and to synthesize the different ideas into a coherent system, are some of the tasks involved in the study of the educational philosophy of an individual or a practice. Whether it is the study of Basic Education or the educational theories of Tagore, essentially the philosopher of education is expected to present a consistent and coherent account of the ideas, their basic assumptions, their validity and appraisal, with reference to a set of norms and values. Such systematic, rigorous philosophical study, unfortunately, is more an exception than the rule. Again, if it is the appraisal of an educational philosophy, the framework or criteria with reference to which the evaluation is carried out should be clearly set out.

It is also disquieting that the researcher sees an educational philosopher in anyone who has had something or other to say about education and hypostatizes an educational philosophy where none exists. A mere collection of stray sayings on education does not make an educational philosophy. It requires much more sustained, systematic thinking on educational matters, the firm foundation of a philosophy of life, knowledge and value, and a conscious, committed articulation of one's position on the means and ends of education. A welcome trend is the increase in the number of researches with focus on themes-concepts, problems, principles, keeping personalities and institutions only in a perspective. Such endeavors can prove philosophically more satisfying and rewarding too. This is not to say that thematic research would automatically pass the test of quality. Even a theme, say, national integration or life-long education, may be handled only superficially. There is no foolproof stopping of such a possibility. Nevertheless, the challenge of philosophical exploration of ideas and themes should not go unaccepted.

The Nature of Philosophical Inquiry

The question of method is a crucial one in philosophy of education, especially for research. It is sometimes asked whether 'research' can be applied to philosophical types of studies at all. 'Research' no doubt has acquired its particular connotation by being applied to studies of the empirical type. But in the broad sense of disciplined inquiry, there is no reason why it should not be applied to studies of the philosophic type as well. This is purely a semantic question. There should not be any objection to talking about philosophical research as long as one is clear about the logic of the particular form/forms of inquiry through which the research problem is Studied and the kind of 'knowledge' that it leads to. The methods question in philosophy of education assumes importance because educational problems can be researched from several disciplinary perspectives education being the kind of interdisciplinary area that it is. The aims, ideals and values of education, for example, could be looked into, apart from the philosophical, also from the sociological, historical and psychological angles.

The value system of a society can be sociologically described and explained. The goals of an educational system can be studied as they evolve historically. The study of attitudes towards Gandhi and philosophy would essentially be a psychological rather than a philosophical undertaking. The subject of enquiry alone therefore, does not entitle a research to be deemed philosophical. What characterizes philosophical research is the level and depth of critical analysis, the probing into the basic assumptions, concept elucidation, synthesis of views, justification of normative assumptions and prescriptions. Much of the difficulty in method stems from the undifferentiated conception of educational studies and loosely referring to all miscellaneous talk about education that cannot be classified as belonging to sociology, psychology or any of the other fields of inquiry as philosophy of education. The discourse is sometimes empirical (several studies on philosophy of education have surveys, attitude measurement and other empirical activities as part of their research), and at other times historical.

Scholarly pursuit of a field of study is based on respecting the logical and epistemological distinctions that separate the different forms of inquiry-empirical, conceptual, historical, descriptive, and experimental-and violation of this ground rule will certainly not enhance the cause of knowledge in any field. This, however, should not be taken to mean that empirical, historical findings are irrelevant to philosophy of education far from it. No worthwhile philosophizing about educational issues would ever be possible in the absence of knowledge of relevant empirical findings. The point being made is that the philosopher of education qua philosopher should not put on the robes of a historian or a scientist, although he can peruse knowledge from these fields for his own work as philosopher.

There are as has already been noted, a variety of tasks that are associated with philosophy of education synthetic, analytical, speculative-synoptic, critical-constructive, and normative-evaluative. Historically, however, it came to be interpreted as a system of beliefs on reality, knowledge and value and their 'educational implications'. Researches based on the 'systems' model have taken the form of searching for articulated 'isms' in an educational thinker or system, for example pragmatism in Gandhi's educational thoughts or naturalism in Tagore or idealistic trends in Vedic education. The research subject is approached here within the framework of a philosophical school. Alternatively, a particular philosophical system-Buddhism, *Gita, Upanishads*, Sankhya, and Jainism has been explored for its educational principles and prescriptions.

Progress in philosophical thought inspired by a variety of factors has projected to the forefront a view of philosophy that puts its analytical-critical function at the centre. Philosophy of education on this view is the activity of analysis, clarification and criticism exercised on the concepts, statements and theories of education. The analytical movement has been one of the most influential in the history of philosophy and it represents the contemporary spirit in both philosophy and philosophy of education, it will not be out of place here, therefore, to explain the approach in some detail. The analytical philosopher of education, to start with, accepts and respects the epistemological distinctions that characterize different forms of inquiry-empirical, a priori, and normative. He then clearly demarcates the logical and conceptual issues relating to the subject of his study which alone are his concern qua philosopher.

This can be illustrated with reference to an educational issue of great contemporary relevance, viz., and equality of educational opportunity. This problem can be studied from various stands points-historical, sociological, economic, psychological-as, in fact, it has. Now what does philosophical research into such a down to-earth problem mean? Obviously, it does not mean accumulation of factual data bearing on the problem (although this does not mean, as has already been ob- served, that the philosopher of education can afford to be ignorant of empirical findings from these fields). On the contrary, what it means is that he addresses himself to certain basic questions pertaining to the subject which clearly fall outside the purview of observational and experimental methods. What then, are these questions?

First, there are conceptual issues to be clarified. 'Equality of educational opportunity' is a notoriously vague and complex concept. Empirical knowledge in this field cannot even begin unless the logical and conceptual issues like What do equality and equality of opportunity mean and What constitutes an "equal educational opportunity" T, are first analysed and clarified. It is the task of philosophical research to make explicit the hidden dimensions of this concept and their logical implications. Secondly, equality of educational opportunity like most other educational problems is largely a normative problem. Judgements on it, therefore, necessarily involve value assertions and discussions on it are often hortatory.

These cannot be settled by appealing to empirical considerations alone. They need the rigour of philosophical inquiry. Further, a rational justification as to why equality of educational opportunity should be accepted as a value or an excellence should come from philosophy. Finally, the ideal of equality of educational opportunity has given rise to a number of controversies regarding the several aspects of our education like merit based admissions, the common school system, nurturing of talent in special institutions, the institution of Navodaya Vidyalayas, reservations and quotas in institutions of higher learning, affirmative action and compensatory education programmes, to cite only a few. Many of these controversies derive their- force, partly at least, from a lack of conceptual clarity.

The 'analytic guillotine' helps us to see our way clearly through these controversies and this is an essential first step in their resolution. It is also the task of research to identify the point of the controversy, to examine the different points of view and the arguments advanced in support (or against) them, to test for conceptual confusion and fallacies in reasoning, to make an appraisal of programmes and practices with reference to how well they satisfy the criteria of equality of educational opportunity and to work out a reconciliation and synthesis. Granting then that there are distinctly philosophical questions in education-logical and conceptual, normative and speculative-how does one go about one's task? What, in other words, are the different tasks involved in doing philosophy and how are these to be performed? The import of these questions is not to call for the complete description of a 'method', arranged in a logical and operational sequence. Such a rule-of-thumb method, frankly, does not exist.

Nor would it be desirable, philosophically, to be prescriptive and deterministic in these matters. Nevertheless, examination of the work of philosophers of education, especially those whose work is based on the analysis of 'ordinary language' does indicate the existence of distinct ways of thinking and tackling problems: analysis of concepts, appraisal of arguments, and validation of theories. One may discover in this the hazy contours of a 'method' for those who wish to embark upon research in this field. As the burden of this presentation is to dispel the notion that philosophy of education research has no guidelines or a rigorous method, an attempt has been made here to make explicit the mechanics of this method in terms of operations and tasks involved while dealing with different aspects of education.

Social Relevance and Usefulness of Philosophy of Education

Of what significance can philosophical research in

education be to the educational practitioner and theoretician? What, in other words, is the use of a philosophy of education? It cannot be denied that philosophical research should justify itself, apart from its intrinsic worth as an intellectual excellence to be pursued for its own sake, also by its practical utility to the educational policy maker and practitioner. That philosophy of education can be useful in this sense also can be argued. In the first place, policy decisions on education, by the very nature of the enterprise cannot be based solely on the factual findings of the concerned empirical fields of investigation like psychology, sociology and management sciences. They also need philosophical inputs to make explicit the whole range and depth of the meaning of the issue at stake, its ramifications and logical implications, to clarify the kinds of decisions that have to be faced in dealing with them. One would also look to philosophy to deal with value disputes in educational issues and also for rational justification of the goal, ideal or value being pursued. Further, to deal effectively with educational controversies, one needs the philosophical temperament and rigor of thought to lay bare conceptual confusions, hidden assumptions and fallacies of reasoning.

If philosophy of education is to perform its instrumental function effectively, research endeavor should be directed primarily on those problems of educational policy and practice as are of 'here and now' concern. The Indian educational scene today is characterized with dissensions and debates raging around issue like national goals of education, democratization of education, issues of curriculum, new educational technologies, and covering all stages and sectors of education pre-school, primary, secondary, higher, technical and professional. But, going by the researches conducted thus far, philosophy of education appears to be deeply obsessed with the past and have very little to do with ongoing happenings. One gets the feeling that only events and personalities deep in the past are worthy of philosophical pursuit. If the objects of philosophical inquiry are limited to ancient lore alone, philosophy to that extent moves away from living reality, weakens its link with emerging policy concerns and becomes just an academic exercise.

Of course, one can justify such research on the ground of searching in history for insights which may help in the understanding of the present and, possibly, its betterment. When carried out in that spirit, research into the past certainly can fulfill one of its important purposes. But this is not to say that one should look for enlightenment to the past alone, taking what 'was' as a reservoir of such wisdom. The point is that philosophy of education research will have functional value only when its concerns emerge from events and problems that are experienced here and now. It is in this context that thematic and problem oriented type of research studies acquires great significance. Sadly, there have not been enough of them. This need not come as a surprise. In a way, the state of researches in philosophy of education reflects the state of its parent discipline, philosophy. General philosophy has also come under fire for its lack of direction, social relevance and originality, a situation that is paradoxical considering our very rich philosophical legacy.

This, however, can be no consolation for philosophy of education. The point of drawing this comparison is to reiterate that philosophy of education, being a branch of applied philosophy, gets its sustenance also from general philosophy. Unfortunately, there has been very little communication between philosophers and educationists and philosophy of education remains deprived of the nourishment that it should, under more favorable circumstances, get from such interaction. The absence of interest on the part of philosophers in the problems of education appears odd, considering the vitality of current educational debate in the wake of recent developments like the announcement of a new National Policy of Education, the appointment of the National Commissions on Teachers, the publication of the discussion document, Challenge of Education (1985), to cite only a few. Again, discussions currently going on value-orientation of education, university autonomy and academic freedom and such other issues have not involved philosophers to the extent one would wish. Understandably, therefore, philosophy of education has not emerged as a vibrant, intellectual activity.

The Indianization Question

In the context of the general demand for social relevance, there is a cry from many quarters for the Indianization of courses and curricula. It has been pointed out that much of what is taught (and, as a corollary, researched) derives its inspiration and has its basis in borrowed Western models of thinking. The relevance of such knowledge and modes of thinking to the understanding of issues in Indian education, arising in a unique socio-philosophic-cultural context is not in any case apparent. The Programme of Action (1986) has observed that there is too much emphasis in textbooks on Western ideas and teachers under training do not get exposed adequately to Indian philosophical and psychological concepts of education. All this may be true. But the demand for Indianization has to be carefully understood and assessed if its genuine intentions are to be realized.

In the first place, one has to think of how far one can stretch the meaning of 'Indianization'. Indian philosophical thinking enjoys a distinctiveness with its emphasis on reason, intuition, analytical and synthetic thinking. Definitely these should inform the approaches to the understanding of Indian educational issues. At the same time, Indianization should not be taken to mean refusal to take due note of recent developments in the area of philosophy of education elsewhere solely on the basis of philosophical prejudices. Such a stance would be narrow and chauvinistic. Different socio-cultural contexts bring different educational problems and issues into focus and in different intensities. Indianization should be manifested in the kind of the distinctly Indian concerns that it deals with and not in the refusal to adopt this or that approach solely because the approach is not of Indian origin.

Researches conducted thus far have, of course, concerned themselves with distinctively Indian issues, the study of the educational philosophy of Indian thinkers and Indian systems of education, Indian scriptures and religious systems. Some of these are set in a comparative framework, generally with a model from the English speaking West-Gandhi and Dewey, Tagore and Whitehead, for example. There are also researches whose exclusive focus is on individual Western thinkers like Russell, Read or Kilpatrick. More popular, however, are researches which have adopted the framework of Western philosophical schools like Pragmatism, Existentialism or Idealism, These researches have attempted to understand the educational thought of Indian educationists and educational systems with the help of philosophical theories on reality, knowledge and value associated with the different isms'. It would be interesting to explore these very educational themes and systems from the point of view of Indian philosophical thinking as articulated in its several schools. This, however, has not been attempted in sufficient measure.

Trends Indicated in the New Researches

After these general observations on the trends indicated in philosophy of education researches as a whole, attention may now be turned to the 39 additional research studies abstracted in the present volume. In terms of their research themes, barring a few exceptions, they continue on the trodden path: critical/comparative study of this or that educational thinker or philosopher or this or that educational ideology, school or system (many of them recurring from the past) like Plato, Aurobindo, Annie Besant, Gandhi, J. Krishnamurthy, Vivekananda, the Sikh Gurus, Tagore, Kalelkar, Gopabandhu Das, Dewey, the Gita, the Koran,

Vaidic Shiksha, Varnashrama Vyavastha, Ramakrishna Mission. Some titles, happily, indicate the aspect of the subject that is singled out for treatment, viz., Integral Yoga of Aurobindo, Free Progress System of Aurobindo International Centre, Art as a medium of education in Tagore, Narayana Guru as a social educator, and synthetic spiritualism of Sri Ramakrishna.

A refreshing development is the shifting of attention from individuals and systems to the critical study of ideas and concepts: creativity, freedom, human nature, explanation, ideology, distance education. While the philosophy done on these concepts and themes may still lack the requisite vigor and exacting standards, it is at least a good sign and a happy portent of things to come that the gaze of the researchers has turned to issues and themes that are both philosophically significant and educationally relevant.

Studies Focusing on Individual Thinkers

Abhyankar (1982), (1987), Bhattacharya (1981), Das (1986), Gupta (1985), Kaur (1983), Rai (1986), Pathake (1986), Vaid (1971), Vyas (1986) and Misra (1986) have studied the educational thoughts/contributions/ philosophy of J. Krishnamurthy, Tagore, Gopabandhu Das, Vivekananda, the Sikh Gurus, Malaviya, Kalelkar and Annie Besant. The methods they have employed have been variously described as historical, library research, descriptive, analytical, comparative, and content analysis. They have used for their study literature available in the form of books, primary and secondary sources, personal interviews, visits to institutions, old records, commentaries, speeches and writings.

Both Abhyankar and Vyas have studied J. Krishnamurthy's educational philosophy. While Abhyankar claims to 'evolve educational theory' from Krishnamurthy's speeches and writings and to 'study the implications and impact of his thoughts on educational practices and life', Vyas aims at simply 'highlighting J.Krishnamurthy's thoughts on education from a larger perspective'. Such studies lack a suitable frame of reference. No coherent, consistent theory of education can emerge from their findings. It is difficult to understand and present a rational interpretation of a mystic's thoughts on education and any attempt towards such a goal should at least produce valuable insights into his thinking if not a comprehensive and convincing interpretation of it.

Bhattacharya's study on Tagore aims at bringing out a coherent structure of Tagore's educational thoughts, to search for an equation between his life, literature and education, and to compare his educational principles and practices with those of Western and Indian thinkers. Das has sketched the profile of Pandit Gopabandhu Das as a nationalist educator. Gupta has studied the educational thoughts of Swami Vivekananda and examined their usefulness for the reorganization of our present educational system. Misra's research subject also is Vivekananda (critical study of educational philosophy and teaching method of.....) and his objectives also are more or less similar. The value of such studies would be enhanced if approached from the standpoint of a philosophical theory-metaphysical, epistemological or ethical-or a coherent educational theory. The same observation applies to Kaur's study of the educational philosophy of Sikh Gurus and Rai's Madan Mohan Malaviya ke Shaikshik Vicharo ka Adhyayan. Critical study of educational philosophy should not stop at the level of description (of what the Sikh Gurus or Malaviya say on the different aspects of education) but must analyses interpret and evaluate their sayings with reference to a philosophical and educational framework.

Pathake's study of the educational thinking of Kalelkar gives indications of such an effort. Under-taking content analysis, he has examined Kalelkar's thoughts with reference to such criteria of linguistic analysis as logical coherence, meaningfulness, verbosity and contradictions. He has also employed as critical frames of reference Peters' criteria of education, O'Connor's aims of education and James's criteria on curriculum for the evaluation of Kalelkar's educational philosophy. Vaid's study of educational philosophy educational experiments and the contribution to Indian education of Annie Besant covers the main tenets of her educational thought, their psychological and philosophical bases and their assessment in a comparative frame with other Western educational thinkers.

Studies in Comparative Perspective

Although the comparative dimension has been brought in some of the above-mentioned studies, only six have stated comparison as their main focus. In all these cases, excepting one, what is being compared is stated as educational philosophy, ideas or doctrines, all omnibus ex- pressions that lack specificity. Lalitha (1967) has analysed the similarities and differences in the educational philosophies of Gandhi and Dewey and evaluated them with respect to the present-day educational system. Pandey (1985) has compared educational philosophy propounded in the Gita and Koran and highlighted the practicability of the ideas given in these scriptures in the present context. Singh (1983) has compared the educational doctrines covering meaning and aims of education, curriculum, teacher, methods and so on of Plato and Aurobindo. Sinha (1984) has made a comparative study of Tagore and Whitehead's ideas on education, employing the technique of content analysis. Vaid (1985) has compared the educational philosophies of Annie Besant and Gandhi.

Comparative studies prove to be of great value when the focus of comparison is a specific aspect of the educational philosophy of the thinkers that is of concern to the theory and practice of education. This could be an educational or philosophical concept like 'education', 'teaching', 'creativity', 'discipline', 'learning', or a theme like 'women's education', 'educational equality', 'nationalism in education'. The focusing of comparison on some such specific aspect would also give the research a depth and rigor which would be lacking if the comparison is kept at a general and superficial level.

Singh's (1984) comparative study of the concept of human nature propounded by educational theorists and revealed by psychological studies suggests a good effort in this regard. His identification of criteria for the selection of educational theorists and specific aspects for comparison indicate the conscious systematic application of the philosophical and comparative method to his research. He has also stated the purpose of the comparative exercise undertaken by him as constructing a unified picture of human nature and building up an integrated view of human nature on the basis of the meeting ground between educationists' and psychologists' findings on human nature.

Specific Aspects of Educational Philosophy

Certain studies have singled out an aspect of the educational philosophy of an individual thinker or a religious scripture. Abhyankar in his study of Vivekananda's educational thought has focused on the value education motif. He has employed the theoretical-empirical model for the analysis and interpretation of data. The focus, however, seems to have been diffused in execution due to failure to exercise controls. Sun's study of Aurobindo concentrates on his Integral Yoga and its educational implications. The objectives of his study have again been diffused by bringing in the comparative dimension with Gandhi, Tagore and Radhakrishnan. Pereira has studied Narayan Guru as a social educator with a clear framework for analysis. Paul has focused his attention on art as a medium of education in Tagore. His objectives confirm the central focus of the study. Das highlights the synthetic spiritualism of Sri Ramakrishna 'through historical and philosophical perspective'. Kesari has studied the Gita as Learning Process with reference to modem education.

Study of Educational Practices/Systems

Tiwari has examined the ancient Indian Varnashrama

educational system and its utility in the modem age. Raval has studied the philosophical beliefs of Buddhism, drawn educational aims from them and also the educational ideals advocated by the Buddha. Dube has chosen for his study the educational philosophy of the Smriti period. Awasthi's main objectives were to study the theory and practice of the Vedic system of education and suggest their implications for modern Indian education. Saxena has studied the educational philosophy of British Idealism with special reference to Green and Bosanquet. Dave has conducted an investigation into the new dimensions of Basic Education.

His objects were to investigate the causes of decay of Basic Education and search for new modes that would make it meaningful. He has employed the survey- questionnaire method to collect his data. This is essentially a descriptive study. Sanyal (1986) has studied the Ramakrishna Mission and its impact on contemporary Indian education but she has employed the historical method and literature survey. Patel (1983) has studied the psychological foundation of the Free Progress System in the Aurobindo International Centre of Education by employing survey techniques.

Thematic Research Studies

Research in philosophy of education holds exciting prospects for those who approach themes and issues, philosophical or educational that contributes towards deepening our understanding of educational theory and practice, rather than personalities or systems. The task involved is undoubtedly exacting and challenging as befits philosophical research and to undertake such a task one should be well armed with the techniques of philosophical inquiry. It is heartening that this challenge is being accepted by more and more researchers. Deenammal in her thesis, 'Ideology and Education', has attempted to study the meaning of ideology and its interaction with educational policy in different kinds of societies and cultures and the relevance of Idealistic, Marxist, democratic and Gandhi an ideologies for contemporary Indian education. This is a case of Ph.D. research in philosophy having education as one of its major concerns. Devi has made a critical study of the concept of creativity in philosophy with special reference to Bergson, Whitehead and Aurobindo.

This is a research study in pure philosophy and its relevance to educational theory and practice is therefore not indicated. Elanjimannil in his research, 'An Explanation of Explanation' has attempted to synthesize all the findings on explanation. He has adopted the 'transcendental variety of rational analysis covering both the retrospective and on-the-experience analysis'. Such researches which attempt to deepen understanding of pedagogical processes by explaining their epistemological rationale are welcome. There are two studies on the concept of freedom, another important concept in education. Jain has tried to analyse the concept of freedom and education given by various philosophers and establish relationship among them. There has classified the philosophers into types, organized their thoughts and critically analysed and evaluated them.

This, again, is a research from general philosophy focusing on education. Singh has studied the development of the concept of freedom in education since Rousseau in a historical prospective. Indra Devi's study is entitled 'Philosophical Analysis of the Concept of Distance Education and Its Implications on the Emerging Non-formal Systems of Education with special reference to Teacher Education'. Her study was designed partly as a philosophical enquiry and partly as an empirical study. Ray has identified the objective of education in the light of expectations of the people and also its effectiveness in removing social ills like untouchability and the dowry system. Bhargava has made a critical study of the attitudes of adolescents towards Gandhian philosophy and its relationship with intelligence, socioeconomic status and achievement. Both these studies can however be classed as empirical researches.

Sharma has made a critical study of the nature and development of human personality in ancient Indian thought. He has examined philosophical principles of different schools of thought having a bearing on the concept of personality, critically analysed their positions and constructed an integrated view of human personality 'truly reflective of Indian approach to human life and its ideals'. The objectives, methodology and findings of the research study reveal scholarly effort of a high order. Mathur in her *Approaches to Educational Theory: A Philosophical Probe,* has attempted to achieve several objectives, leading up to the under- standing of educational theory and the philosophical influences on its development. The study exhibits methodological rigor and sophistication, but due to its sweep, the research findings appear broad and general. Desai has studied the 'evolution of the concept of education in social and cultural context'. The objectives of this study also are too sweeping ('to study socio-cultural conditions prevailing in the different parts of the world in the context of education') and as a consequence the research findings read as broad generalizations.

A word may not be out of place here regarding reporting of philosophical findings. Philosophical wisdom gained out of research activity may comprise increased and deepened understanding of, fresh insights into or new points of view on educational issues and problems. It may also include normative judgments and prescriptions for educational action. The reporting should therefore employ the proper philosophical idiom and be at a level of generality and abstraction befitting philosophical research and not be trivial or commonplace.

Hermeneutics and Phenomenology

In the English speaking-west, philosophy of education underwent a transformation during the middle of this century in the wake of the emergence of the analytical movement. Analysis itself was the upshot of the philosophical 'revolution' inspired by the works of Russell, Moore and Wittgenstein earlier. The past decades have seen hectic analytical activity and philosophy of education has been enriched by a variety of invaluable contributions: analysis and clarification of concepts like 'education', 'teaching', 'learning', 'play', 'discipline', 'moral education', 'equality', 'educational theory', epistemological inquiries into the basis of curriculum, and justification of curricular choices, to cite only a few.

Presently, philosophy of education appears to be set for another mutation. Recent developments in the fields of philosophy of science and sociology of knowledge, especially those dealing with the methodological aspects of scientific inquiry, have sparked off a controversy on the nature, scope and function of theories and philosophies in education. With reference to the logical status of the social sciences, it is asked whether it is right to base educational research on the positivistic model of scientific inquiry, with its aim as explanation leading to prediction and technology. Education, it is argued, is to be looked upon as a humanistic enterprise dealing with unique, non-repeatable circumstances and aiming at the illumination of intentions and purposes leading to hermeneutical understanding. Hermeneutics refers to the theory and practice of interpretation and understanding in different kinds of human contexts. Although it includes several lines of thought, its main point, as far as educational research is concerned, is the understanding of various cultures, groups, individuals, conditions and life-styles and detecting the meaning underlying specific educational practices.

Another major development in educational research to which philosophy of education has contributed in no small measure is the emergence of qualitative methods like ethnographic research. This research, with its basis in the phenomenological philosophy of continental Europe, consists essentially of a description of events that occur within the life of a group, with special regard to the social structure and the behaviour of individuals with respect to their group membership, and an interpretation of the meaning of these for the culture of the group. Yet another rival paradigm to the conceptual analysis model of philosophy of education is neo-Marxism. The neo-Marxists, mostly writers in the social sciences, claim that reality is socially constructed and that a ruling class exploits the rest, especially through education, by a 'structured' misrepresentation of reality. Philosophy of education, they argue, should, through analysis, lay bare where this exploitation is occurring.

5

Research Topics for Philosophy of Education

A host of areas in Indian education are crying out for philosophical analysis and enlightenment. With the nation having adopted a new National Educational Policy, a vigorous debate on its different ideas, theories and recommendations has been triggered off. Much is being said and written about the orientation and goals of national education, the concept of a national system of education, the notion of education for equality, child centred education, life-long education, general education, Navodaya Schools, National Curriculum, the goals of higher education, vocationalization of education, the teacher and the teaching profession-its accountability, appraisal and professional ethics. These are just the kinds of issues which provide philosophy of education the opportunity to inform the current discussions with the needed philosophical light and pave the way for the emergence of clear-headed and sound programmes of practical action.

In addition to these, one may also mention many other socially relevant topics for philosophical research like, elucidation of the concepts of 'secular education', 'national integration', 'peace education', 'liberal education', 'education for all', 'educational quality', 'creativity', 'common school system'; the concept and practice of value education: can schools teach values? Are there uniquely Indian values appraisal and justification of educational policies and practices; positive discrimination and compensatory education; talent search examination; reservations and quotas in institutions of higher learning; merit based admissions. With such an impressive array of research issues: available for those who wish to venture into this field one hopes that future research output in philosophy of education will distinguish itself by its extensiveness, superior quality and social relevance.

A Comprehensive, In-depth and Critical Analysis of Swami Vivekananda's Educational Thought and its Philosophical Foundations with Special Focus on Value Education in the Context of Nuclear and Space Age' Global 'Value Crisis' and the Need for Value Education in India Today, The objectives of the study were (i) to analyse and organize Vivekananda's educational thoughts, (ii) to trace the roots of Vivekananda's educational thought embedded in ancient Indian philosophical works, (iii) to assess the need for value education in India today, and (iv) to analyse Vivekananda's viewpoints concerning 'Value Education' in the context of the modem global value crisis and cry for morality.

The present study involved combination of the documentary survey and the analytical method of research. It used the theoretical- empirical model for analysis and interpretation of data. Data were gathered from primary and secondary sources concerning Vivekananda's life, works and educational thought, and global value crisis. The findings of the study were:

1. Vivekananda's educational thought was primarily based on Advaita Vedanta which was conducive to philosophical eclecticism.
2. In spite of the occasional and fragmentary nature of the expression of Vivekananda's educational viewpoints, the basic underlying theme of self-realization was predominant throughout his speeches and writings concerning education.
3. Indian philosophy in general and Advaita Vedanta in

particular, have considerable relevance to and affinity with modem nuclear physics.

4. Many aspects of Vivekananda's educational thought reveal the influence of the ideal features of the gurukul and monastic systems of ancient Indian education.
5. Vivekananda stood for a synthesis of Adi Shankaracharya's intellect and Buddha's heart.
6. Vivekananda was more of a 'Hindu revivalist' rather than a reformist.
7. He, however, positively and emphatically preferred internal evolvement as a more effective solution to socio-religious problems than external imposition of reforms.
8. Vivekananda's educational thinking was not primarily and directly geared towards prescribing immediate solutions to the varied and specific political and socioeconomic problems confronting contemporary India.
9. His first, foremost and deepest educational concern was the propagation of the teachings of Advaita Vedanta which, he firmly believed, offered fundamental, durable and long range solutions to all the fundamental problems confronting not only India but all humanity. Hence, the contemporary political and socioeconomic problems in India had relatively little direct influence on Vivekananda's educational thought.
10. Some of the educational ideas advocated by Vivekandanda appear to be potentially and futuristically in tune with certain trends and developments in the field of education in India today.
11. There is a vital and urgent need for value education at all levels of schooling in India today.
12. Throughout his speeches and writings concerning education, Vivekananda's emphasis is on the inculcation of specific external values like love, self-realization, brotherhood, service, responsibility, sympathy, non-violence, dutifulness, tolerance, freedom, and courage, and self-reliance, dignity of labour, honesty, truth and fearlessness.

J. Krishnamurti's Philosophy of Education

The major objectives were (i) to evolve educational theory from J. Krishnamurti's speeches and writings, (ii) to find out the implications of his philosophy for education, (iii) to study his approach to life-situations, problems and their solutions, and deeper understanding of the process of education, (iv) to study the thoughts and experiences of some of the thinkers of international reputation of the contemporary period, in order to understand J. Krishnamurti's original contribution to philosophical thought, and (v) to study the impact of his thoughts on educational practices and life.

The historical method and library study were adopted for this study. The general nature of the method and the approach was study and evaluation of the available literature, personal interview of some of the scholars/ followers of J. Krishnamurti in India, visits to the institutions run by the Krishnamurti Foundation, India, and attending some talks in India by J. Krishnamurti. The major findings were:

1. J. Krishnamurti regards education as of prime significance in the communication of that which is central to the transformation of the human mind and the creation of a new culture. 'Self-knowledge' is considered to be the most important aim of education.
2. In J. Krishnamurti's approach, great emphasis is laid on the question of relationship. According to him, the learner must be educated to establish a right relationship with things, persons and ideas, because thus alone can one be happy.
3. The twin status of private and public life splits the personality of man and creates and sustains contradiction within him.
4. J. Krishnamurti's approach to education is through the transformation of the teacher. But a transformed teacher in terms of his approach is not an idealistic teacher. He

is one who has an extraordinarily pliable mind so that he does not act from the accumulated experiences of the past, but from the immediate perception of the present, from the comprehension of 'what is'.

5. J. Krishnamurti refuses any sort of speculation. Understanding of the transcendental being is possible only after the comprehension of the conditioned existence.
6. J. Krishnamurti considers the action of will as incomplete and superficial and it is at the psychological level. Its basis is effort, i.e. conflict, and thus it breeds more conflicts.
7. J. Krishnamurti suggests a new way of living, of living intelligently without identification, without the self-seeking resistance which is the struggle for existence, without the effort to be something, without seeking fulfillment in idea, in a sensation.

Rabindra Siksha Darsaner Samiksha

The main objectives were (i) to bring out a coherent structure of the thinking of Tagore on education, analysing his significant writings on education, (ii) to trace the underlying educational principles of Tagore as manifested in his educational experimentation at Santiniketan, (iii) to search for an equation between his life, literature and educational thoughts, and (iv) to make a comparative study of his educational principles and practices with those of western thinkers like Plato. Rousseau, Froebel, Dewey and Indian thinkers like Vivekananda, Gandhi and Aurobindo.

The data were collected from rare primary sources and old records and standard works on Tagore from Viswa-Bharati, Santiniketan, libraries in Calcutta and personal treasures of eminent litterateurs who came in contact with Tagore. The design was descriptive, analytical and locale was the city of Calcutta. The main findings were:

1. Educational thoughts of Tagore possess links with creative endeavours of other Bengali litterateurs, philosophers and social thinkers of the 19th century.

2. His educational thoughts contain the essence of his poetry, religious ideas and perception of truth.
3. His educational thoughts contain fulness, totality, freedom and joy and, on the other hand, emphasize social consciousness and ethical considerations.
4. According to Tagore, every scheme of education should aim at cultivation (sadhana) of humanism through the fullest development of body, intellect and soul.
5. Teacher and students should feel together the beauty of the nature outside and of the sentiments within.
6. The festivals in school are one of the best modalities of education.
7. The syllabus should contain literature, science, social science and visual and performing arts.
8. The mother-tongue should be the prime vehicle of expression in the teaching-learning process at all stages of education.
9. Tagore's educational ideas are in tune with both western and eastern educators: above all, the synthesis of the two is found in his international perspective of education, which he called the religion of man.

Educational Philosophy of Sri Aurobindo

The purposes of this study were to inquire into the fundamentals of philosophy of education, to visualise the philosophy of education suitable to meet the demands of our age, to systematize Sri Aurobindo's philosophy of education, and to evaluate and examine it in the light of contemporary Indian and western philosophies of education. The objectives of the present work were (i) to present a systematic outline of the philosophy of education in the thought of Sri Aurobindo, (ii) to work out the salient features of educational philosophy of Sri Aurobindo, (iii) to show how far the educational thought of Sri Aurobindo indicated the outline of a future philosophy of education, and (iv) to assess Aurobindo's contribution in transforming the character of Indian education through a critical analysis of the challenging views which were expressed in the manifold creations and compilations of this great thinker.

The historical methods, along with construction through criticism, were followed in the present investigation. A few primary and secondary sources were scanned, scrutinized and studied. Some of these were also subjected to careful internal and external criticism. Primary sources of data were the original works of Sri Aurobindo, and secondary sources were works of other writers and published work on Aurobindo, and actual study and critical examination of the practical working of Sri Aurobindo's system of education in Pondicherry and Delhi.

The major findings of the study were:

1. The educational ideas and ideals of Sri Aurobindo were the out come of the emerging period of renaissance in India.
2. The concept of internal education aimed at all-round development of personality and realization of self through the development of physical, vital, mental and psychic faculties.
3. The psychological and sociological bases of Aurobindo's scheme of education were integral because he envisaged all-round development of personality and at the same time gave equal importance to the individual, to the community and to humanity. His scheme of education found no conflict in individual, national and universal aims and principles.
4. Physical education, according to him, was to be based on logic exercises.
5. In the integral scheme of education neither the educator nor the educand was solely important; rather both were unified in a common bond. According to him, the teacher was the helper and the guide of the child. The education he advocated provided full freedom to the individual growth of the education. His free progress

system of education was based on subjective evaluation by the teachers.

6. He tried to modernize education in India by integrating old values with new values.
7. His philosophy of education was a happy synthesis of idealism, spiritualism, naturalism, realism, individualism and socialism.
8. According to him, accelerated evolution from man to the supra-mental being was through the practice of integral yoga and the evolution of super mind.
9. According to him, realization of national soul and reorganisation of collective national life-laws, education and all other activities-aimed at freedom, truth and maximum good of all and each nation.

Comparison with Modern Trends of Thinking

The objectives of the study were (i) to trace educational thoughts, practices and disciplines in Vedic and non-Vedic Sanskrit literature, (ii) to compare the ancient Indian educational system with pragmatism, naturalism, Tagore's idealism and existentialism, and (iii) to investigate the extent to which educational values in ancient Sanskrit literature were useful and practicable in today's secondary school education. The study was a kind of survey with a historical perspective. The tools used were, (i) a pilot questionnaire, (ii) a final questionnaire, and (iii) an interview schedule constructed by the researcher.

The following were some of the findings:

1. The ultimate aim of education was self-realization.
2. The cooperation between teacher and taught was considered important for knowledge of the self and its relation with ultimate reality.
3. Philosophy and religion, knowledge and character, arts and crafts, were integral parts of the guiding principles of Indian life.
4. Women had equal status in education with men.

5. The teacher enjoyed full freedom in educational administration.
6. The consideration of human welfare transcended all geographical and regional boundaries.
7. Social welfare was an equally important objective as individual welfare.
8. Yagnya was considered a great symbol of sacrifice.
9. Education was considered as an operational form of the culture.
10. Scientific and adhyatmic ideals were perfectly coordinated.

Pandit Gopabandhu Das

The main aim of the research was to study the contributions of Gopabandhu Das, a pioneer nationalist of Orissa, in the field of education. Historical, analytical and comparative methods were adopted. Both primary and secondary sources were used. The major findings were that Gopabandhu Das was an eminent educationist. He made innovations in the field of education which have been followed by others in other periods. His contributions in education were significant, particularly relating to education outside the classroom, craft education and physical education. These entire he combined in the Satyabadi system of education.

Synthetic Spiritualism of Sri Ramakrishna

The main aim of the study was to highlight the synthetic spiritualism of Sri Ramakrishna through history and philosophical perspective. The analytical-critical method was followed. Data were collected from various sources, mainly literature. Some of the major conclusions were:

1. Sri Ramakrishna was neither a historian nor a material theorist, but his teachings had deep philosophical and historical implications.
2. His spiritual ideas could never be kept confined to a

particular dogma. This made for an over all synthesis of religions and also a revolution in the philosophical world.

3. Sri Ramakrishna's ultimate reality was impersonal in nature but was revealed as Sakti or consciousness in the cosmic manifestation of the world. His message was synthetic in nature.

   He was not only a spiritualist but also a materialist in the best spiritual sense of the term. According to him, there was no basic difference between science and spirituality. The spirit of the infinite runs through the entire cosmic union. Mind is everything. Spirituality flows in multifarious ways. Interaction and contradiction of world cosmos with mind only germinate new meanings and insights. Universal cosmic play ultimately leads to fathomless void. It is the Infinite or Transcendental stage of Universal Cosmic play.

4. Sri Ramakrishna did not leave anything systematic on language. He solved the wrangling of vedantic schools over the nature of God.

Ideology and Education

The objectives of the study were (i) to study the meaning, nature and definition of educational policy and its relationship with ideology, (ii) to study the interaction between ideology and educational policy in three different societies, viz., Russia, Japan and Turkey, (iii) to examine the interaction between ideology and educational policy in some agrarian and industrial cultures, viz., India, China and the USA, and (iv) to study the four basic approaches (Idealistic, Marxist, Democratic and Gandhian) to education and their relevance to contemporary India.

The methodology followed was philosophical as well as comparative. It was philosophical in the sense that ideologies prevailing in a particular era were critically analysed and evaluated with reference to education. It was also comparative as ideologies and education systems of various countries like Russia, Japan, China, the USA and India were identified and compared. The materials and literature used were those related to the ideologies of Marx, Dewey and Gandhi, along with materials on the educational systems of different countries. There is always an interaction between social reality and ideology. The historical, cultural and social conditions of a man influence him in accepting a particular ideology.

1. People in the same conditions and having the same needs and aspirations automatically group together and hold the same ideology and, with its help, try to conserve and change society. The dominant group, with its ideology, generally influenced the society.
2. An educational policy is a method of action decided upon by an individual, group or government as the best among the available alternatives, in the light of given conditions, to educate the children and youth of the community. Educational policy is mainly concerned with objectives and means of implementing them. Based on the types of ideology adopted and different possible approaches, educational policy can be classified accordingly.
3. Peter the Great of Russia did not succeed to the extent he wanted to in westernizing Russia, but Meiji leaders were successful in their efforts to modernize Japan. Similarly, Lenin was able to lay the foundation for a communist society in Russia, but Kamal failed in his attempt to westernize Turkey. The reason for all these lay with the education policies and ideologies adopted in each case. While the ideologies of the successful matched the educational policy adopted by them, the ideologies of the unsuccessful did not.
4. There has been an interaction of religious ideologies in India with the educational system right from the early Vedic period. There had been a great gulf between the educations of the upper castes on the one hand and that of the toiling masses on the other. This was the reason for the neglect of science and rational technology in India.

5. The present Indian education is the outcome of the ideas of few distinguished Indians, viz., the Orientalists (Dayananda), the Anglicists (Rammohan), and those who stressed science and technology (Viswesvaraya).
6. The Chinese traditional culture, its educational system, content and form of examination and educational practices were mostly shaped by Confucianism.
7. In the formative periods, American education was a compound of British and continental cultures and also a synthesis of classical, Puritan and republican ideas. Major figures like Benjamin Franklin, Georage Washin-gton and Thomas Jefferson helped American education to acquire a democratic bent.
8. India today needs just not liberal education, but profe-ssional expertise in engineering, technology and medi-cine. The Platonic scheme did not pay much attention to this aspect.
9. Marx laid great stress on the necessity to abolish the distinction between manual labour and intellectual work. This idea has a greater relevance to India where there is a gulf between unskilled labour and skilled labour, between technicians at the lower level and engineers and technologists at the higher levels, between practical sciences (engineering, medicine, etc.) and theoretical disciplines (physics, chemistry, etc.).
10. The continental size of India, its constitution, its political institutions, the degree of industrialization, its university and school system and the urge of the population to have an improved standard of living, all these have greater relevance to the Dewey ideology of democratic and technological society where the dignity of physical labour and need for everyone to become productive is emphasized.
11. In case of the educational ideas of Gandhi, the most relevant idea was dignity of labour.

    But Gandhi's ideas lose relevance when considered in the light of the fact that Indian education has not only to be secular but geared to the industrial and defence needs of the country. Science, engineering and technology, at all levels, have to receive every possible encouragement. India needs industrialization in a big way to raise standards of living. All these aspects of education had not been advocated in Gandhian ideology.

The Essence of Indian Philosophy

The finest element of the culture and civilization is regarded as the philosophy of a country. The various principles of Indian Philosophy originated and developed in India. Each school of thought has separate identity and was born in Indian cultural atmosphere. Each has its own distinctive feature of Indian culture and recognized certain ideas, which bore the distinctive perception of Indian culture. Thus, the different systems present in a diversity of views, they reveal a common perspective. The most underlying point of agreement is that all the sects regard philosophy as a practical necessity.

The aim of philosophical schools in India is not merely the satisfaction of intellectual curiosity, but mainly the acquisition of an enlightened life. The task of Indian philosophy, therefore, did not end in mere theoretical speculation; it must show its application of life. Every system of Indian philosophy excepting the Carvakas is moved to philosophical speculation by a spiritual concern at the sight of sorrows and evils in the world and in life. This spiritual dissatisfaction at the present order of things has actuated Indian thinkers to philosophical speculations. This is, in other words, the so-called pessimism of Indian Philosophy. But Indian philosophy is not pessimistic, because Indian philosophy does never end in pessimism. All the systems of Indian philosophy believe in the existence of universal moral order.

The faith in an eternal moral order sustains human beings in their struggle against sorrows and sufferings, in their onward march towards the ideal of future happiness. Intimately connected with the faith in an eternal moral order is the general tendency of the Indian thinkers to regard the world as a moral stage in which the individual identities are performers with diverse costumes in the form of physical bodies, sense-organs, etc. Another view held in common by all Indian Philosophers, except the Carvakas, is that ignorance of reality is the root cause of our bondage and sufferings. In order to attain liberation from these sufferings, a true knowledge of the real nature of the world and the self is essential. All Indian thinkers are unanimous in their opinion that liberation cannot be attained without dispelling ignorance.

Indian thinkers have felt the necessity of continued meditation and self-control as the pre-ıequisites to right knowledge. This Indian philosophy is not ascetic or rigoristic in character. It is a philosophy of self-realization or perfection where all the tendencies and impulses are kept in harmony under the control of reason. Finally, all the systems of Indian Philosophy, except the Carvakas, accept the idea of liberation or moksa as the highest end of life. Though the Indian thinkers differ among themselves with regard to the positive nature of liberation, yet they agree in regarding it as a state of total extinction of all sufferings.

Bergson, Whitehead and Sri Aurobindo

The objectives of the study were (i) to find out if creativity was the general scheme of reality, (ii) to find out if creativity was linked with different concepts of this universe, that is, with becoming, cosmic evolution, consciousness, organic evolution and teleology, (iii) to trace the historical background of creativity both in Indian and in Western thought, with special reference to the Vedas, Upanishads, Plato and Plotinus, (iv) to locate the concept of creativity in Bergson's ideas, (v) to investigate how Whitehead contributed to the concept of creativity, (vi) to identify the concept of creativity in the ideas of Sri Aurobindo, and (vii) to analyse various theories of creative evolution developed by S. Alexander, L. Morgan and James Ward.

The methodology adopted was philosophical, historical and comparative. The study was philosophical in the sense that ideas of various personalities were organized, critically analysed and evaluated. It was historical because the development of the concept of creativity from various sources had been traced. Further, it was comparative as commonness between the ideas and theories of various persons on the concept of creativity had been identified and critically evaluated. Content analysis was used both as a tool and technique to analyse the educational ideas of Tagore and Whitehead. Content analysis consisted of documentary analysis and thematic analysis. For content analysis, primary as well as secondary sources were used. The material was also examined to find out its suitability for the proposed research by way of internal and external criticism.

Some of the findings of the study were:

1. Creativity constitutes the very basis of reality.
2. Creativity has been conceived by various thinkers as an exercise of nonfigurative powers of the whole psyche involving all its substance, the play of its entire energy. The creative action is more than cerebral, more than visceral, involving more than mind and heart, intellect and emotions. It augments the structure of human vision by introducing some new, vital configuration of ideas or from among those available to organize experience.
3. Creativity was the power to evolve a pattern that remained omnipotent insofar as it touched the details of actualization. Creativity was a widely recognized ideal for every human being.
4. Both east and west emphasized that what was creative about spiritual experience was not its psychological accompaniments but the inward change which manifested itself in the fruits of the spirit-peace, JOY and loving suffering. A new type of life emerged with a higher correspondence between one's self and the ultimate sources of reality. New qualities of mind and character were called forth out of ordinary men and women, qualities which manifested the Divine in them.
5. Bergson's concepts élan-vital had led to a revolutionary

syndical that would restore a purified social life by insisting that social change in any class of people could be achieved only by the force of their own associations, through means that would evolve so as to suit their particular needs. In the theory of science, he had inspired a new 'positivism' that criticized scientific data in a vigorous and original way and showed how much arbitrariness there was in our methods of measurement of magnitudes.

6. Whitehead introduced an omnibus principle called creativity, which was a sort of universal blanket to cover all logical branches that his philosophy had created. Whitehead's emphasis on the organic character of natural systems and his attempt to bring physics and biology closer together had a good deal in common with the Gestalt approach to mind and nature.
7. Some emergentists advocated the theory of levels according to which evolution proceeded by the method of creative synthesis and life and mind came of a certain kind of organization of non-living elements. These new qualities could not be inferred by merely adding together the qualities of elements taking part in the organization. At each new level of reality, new powers, new capacities and new qualities emerged. Life appeared at one of these levels. Along with it emerged a series of new qualities such as growth, assimilation, irritability, adaptability and reproduction. Mind was the result of still more highly complex organizations. This was called creative evolution or emergent evolution whose pioneers were Bergson, Alexander, Morgan and Ward.
8. Sri Aurobindo's evolution admitted mechanism and emergence, determinism and freedom. The creator was the super mind and it was a power of Sachchidananda. Hence the process of evolution was free, self-imposed and self-determined by Sachchidananda. The world was not the result of blind chance but a self-manifestation of the ultimate. Nature's processes appeared to us to be mechanical merely because the purpose was under disguise. Nothing was created from outside.

9. Creativity constitutes the very basis or foundation of reality. It was the creative purpose which steered and guided cosmic evolution and natural evolution. Creativity in human civilization was the expression of creation, which was at the root of nature and reality.
10. Man's future is in the hands of two creative agencies, his biological evolution and his psychological evolution. Genetic and natural environmental forces continued to influence the development of man. Psychological control dominates the direction of human evolution. Man's personal potential is biological, but he is freely And creatively designed. His future depended upon his understanding and attitudes towards reality. Man would be creative and free in projecting his future only if he could at one and the same time realistically immerse himself in the history of his age and culture, discover trans-historical meaning and affirm divine communication.
11. Bergson, Sri Aurobindo and Whitehead are quite close to each other as far as the process of creativity is concerned.

Thoughts of Swami Vivekananda

The investigation was designed to study the educational thoughts of Swami Vivekananda and to examine their usefulness for the reorganization of the educational system. The material consulted consisted of original writings of Swami Vivekananda and commentaries on them by different educationists. From his study the researcher concluded:

1. Swami Vivekananda laid stress on physical and mental development of students.
2. Education should be preparation for life.
3. Education should develop a feeling of nationalism and international understanding.
4. Education should lead to development of character.
5. Education should be free and compulsory.
6. Mother-tongue should be the medium of instruction.

7. Education should make students self-dependent.
8. There should be no state control over education.
9. There should be equality of educational opportunity for all.
10. Education should be according to the aptitudes of the students.
11. Education should provide motivation for attainment of Nirvan.
12. Curriculum should include religious education, Vedantic education, physical training, philosophy, geography, history, science, technical subjects, vocational training, art, music, home science, etc.

The findings imply: (1) Suitable changes should be made in our school curriculum. (2) Stress should be laid on Indian culture and the Indian value system. (3) Education should aim at fulfilling the needs of present-day Indian society. (4) Stress should be laid on improvement of the place of teachers in the society. (5) Education should be free and compulsory for all. (6) There should be separate schools for boys and girls. (7) Stress should be laid on programmes for adult education.

Educational Orientation of Non-orthodox Schools of Indian Philosophy

The main objective was to elucidate unorthodox Indian educational philosophy. The unorthodox Indian schools of philosophy covered were Charvak, Jainism and Buddhism. The study was mainly analytic. With the help of some primary and secondary sources, some concepts were deduced. Besides, some descriptive research was also done, using the survey method. The views of students, teachers and laymen related to Jainism and Buddhism and the Acharyas were collected through and interview schedule from a sample consisting of 176 individuals. The statistical technique used was percentage. The main findings were:

1. The various concepts of Charvak, Jainism and Budd-

hism could be successfully used for solving the various problems of education regarding discipline, teachers, teaching, student personality, adjustment, educational environment, teacher student relations, etc.

2. Some concepts of Charvak, Jainism and Buddhism were relevant in ancient Indian culture only but not relevant in the present situation.
3. All the three unorthodox schools of philosophy did not contribute equally to education.
4. The best use of the concepts of Charvak, Buddhism and Jainism would be possible only by adopting a synthetic approach.

Concept of Freedom and its Relation to Education

The major purpose of this study was to analyse the concept of freedom and education given by various philosophers and then relate these in order to establish relationship among them. It was an analytical philosophical study in which an attempt was made to analyse the concept of education and the notion of freedom from various angles. The main philosophers studied were Bereiter, Dewey, Engels, Fraser, Freire, Hollins, Huxley, Kohlberg, Lock, Peters, Rousseau, Rusk, Scheffler, Skinner, Torrence, Whitehead, White and Wilson. Their thoughts were organized, critically analysed and evaluated in relevance to freedom and education.

The study revealed:

1. Philosophers involved in reflections on education fell into three types, viz., logical analysts, psychologist-philosophers and metaphysical philosophers. The contribution of analysts was that they set out a complete range of possible meanings so as to minimize the possibility of misunderstandings arising out of individualist and socialisationist views. The psychologists saw education as a process which only in- tended the child to be happy and adjusted rather than one which confronted the child with ethical and intellectual problems. The metaphysicists saw education as training of mind and

raised value questions like: What were the skills that need to be generated? What were the priorities and methods of training that needed to be accepted?

2. Freedom had been treated by philosophers as a value which bestowed the final dignity of man and pointed to the direction in which man could reach out to a superior order of existence. Further freedom was not obtained in experience but enjoyed only because, (a) self-consciousness was the minimal condition of freedom, (b) as long as there was an indeterminism (chaotic or chance situation) or determination by others, the condition of freedom could not be said to obtain, (c) freedom only existed with reference to others, where shareability and universality existed together.
3. Almost all philosophers agreed that education had to be viewed as deliberate involvement with processes which helped the actualization of freedom.
4. Education and freedom were related because (a) all activity of human beings involved faith-the faith that there were other men who were concerned with man; (b) the concrete experience of freedom with each step in education not only proved that all education was a movement in freedom but also demarcated the appearance of freedom from education; (c) language and literacy were basic for experiencing love, humility, faith and hope which were nothing but minimal conditions for freedom; (d) rationality was the total tool through which interaction with the world and other people was possible. To acquire the rational approach to a problem, education was most needed. Further, the rationality came by participating in deeper cooperative consciousness; (e) a self-conscious critico-creative approach was the fulfilling movement in the human phenomenon, could not be achieved by semi- possible dimensions of thought and action.
5. Freedom, humans, who could be made human only

through education. 6. The correct method for a movement in freedom could neither be liberation propaganda nor a psychological condition. The correct method was in conscientisation, which in turn would involve love, faith, humility and hope, together with a critical spirit. 7. Dialogical situations would in a true sense be educational situations where each step would be rewarded in itself and, above all, is a step in freedom.

The study has its implications for the methodology of teaching in educational institutions. The teachers need to create dialogue conditions in the classroom. They need to avoid two hazards in the classroom situation; one is lectures by the teacher and the other is non critical participation of students

The Educational Philosophy of Sikh Gurus

The main objective of the investigation was to study in perspective of the evolution of the educational philosophy of the Sikh gurus from Guru Nanak to Guru Gobind Singh. The relevant data and evidence were gathered from the writings of the gurus and by reviewing the political, religious, social and cultural and economic conditions of the times in which the gurus lived. The study revealed that according to the philosophy of the gurus:

1. Education is self-realization in all its powers and potentialities.
2. Reading without understanding and realization is useless.
3. Education is a dynamic force in the life of an individual influencing his physical, mental, emotional, social and spiritual development.
4. The main aims of education are individual development, social development and preparation for a life for action.
5. Contents of education include religious education, study of biographies, teaching of mother-tongue, calligraphy, arithmetic and bookkeeping, manual labour, arts and

crafts, music and poetry, training in arms, study of history and politics.

6. To educate adults the non-formal methods of teaching are required like kirtan, katha, celebration of festivals, discussion and debates, traveling, etc.
7. To educate children, methods required are oral-cum-memorization, use of poetry and song, recitation, and play.
8. The teacher is he who has realized the True Lord and is a seeker of truth.
9. The teacher prepares the disciples for God. Realization and acquisition of real knowledge is possible through His guidance.
10. Beside the teacher the other teachers are God, Self, Word, Guru-Granth Sahib and the Sangat of Gurus.
11. Intellectual, social, moral and spiritual development is possible only when there is a conscious endeavour on the part of the education to discipline his life.
12. A disciple is one who follows the discipline of the gurus and is a fully dedicated soul and seeker of truth.
13. Woman has her role in the preservation and proper functioning of society as mother, wife, sister and daughter.
14. Female education consists of reading and writing of Gurmukhi and study of the Holy Granth.
15. The method of evaluation consists of correction by the teacher while the student recites or repeats.

The Gita as Learning Process with reference to Modern Education

Objectives of the study were (i) to study concepts relating to Individual Self, Absolute Self, material world, education for material welfare, fearlessness, and the process of education, and (ii) to analyse the teaching-learning process relating to the fundamental causes of all human problems, the ultimate goal of life, the activity method, acquisition of wisdom, concentration and purification of the mind, development of ethical, moral and human values, development of personality and national integration, all with relevance to modern education.

The study was philosophical where various books written about the *Gita* and the *Gita* itself were critically studied and analysed with special reference to concepts relating to the individual self and the absolute self.The findings of the study were:

1. The *Gita* is a textbook of the teaching-learning process to educate man in the development of the Inner Man.
2. Education policy and its system were meant to develop the inner man and his human character.
3. The *Gita* is a text-book of action on the philosophy of life for development of the whole personality, material as well as spiritual.
4. The *Gita* gives the right meaning of education, conveying that education is life and life is education. S. Gita's metaphysics (Brahma vidya) and its teaching- learning process (Yoga sastra) are for the development of the total personality for the realization of Truth. Avidya (education for material welfare) and vidya (education for the realization of the self), both make education complete.
5. The learning process of the Gita helps man to develop an integrated personality-victory of the spirit over nature.
6. The *Gita* is a textbook for bringing awareness in man towards (a) the principle of life, (b) the purpose of life, and (c) the process of life.

The Educational Philosophies of Gandhi and Dewey

The objectives of the study were (i) to analyse the similarities and differences in the educational philosophies of Gandhi and Dewey, and (ii) to evaluate the ideas of Gandhi and Dewey with respect to the present-day educational system. The methodology of research adopted was philosophical as well as comparative. It was philosophical in the sense that investigation of the ideas of Gandhi and Dewey was organized, critically analysed and evaluated. It was comparative as ideas common between Gandhi and Dewey were identified and critically evaluated. Content analysis was used which consisted of documentary analysis and thematic analysis.

The findings of the study were:

1. Gandhi was born in Hindu family and was a product of the freedom struggle, while Dewey was born a Protestant Christian and belonged to an industrialized, independent and democratic America. These circumstances had their impact on their philosophies.
2. Further, Gandhi was influenced by Tolstoy, Ruskin and the Gita; Dewey by Hegelian idealism and William James's pragmatism.
3. Gandhi and Dewey differed in their conception of truth. Gandhi identified truth with God, while Dewey regar--ded truth as temporal and pragmatic. But both agreed that knowledge was acquired and not innate.
4. For Gandhi, seeking the good and the absolute was the ultimate aim of life. Dewey did not postulate any such aim.
5. Gandhi formulated his theory of education, taking as his ideal what he believed to be the ancient Indian way of life and education, while Dewey took as his guiding lights democracy, science and progress.
6. Gandhi viewed education as a liberating process, that is, education trained man in mental discipline whereby he would gain the power to think and act freely. Dewey viewed education as a part of life, that is, by experie-ncing life man got educated.
7. Both Gandhi and Dewey stressed the individual and social aims of education. But they differed in their respective approaches to these aims. For Gandhi,

education was an instrument wherewith the individual could be molded into a truthful and non-violent citizen. He differed from Dewey in placing a heavy responsibility on education by conceiving it as the formative force which moulded the mind and character of different individuals in the same way. The fundamental note of difference in their approaches was that Dewey encouraged the development of individual characteristics while Gandhi advocated the conversion and convergence of all individual traits into the three cardinal virtues of his conception—Truth, Beauty and Goodness.

8. Gandhi's ideal society was conformist, agrarian and traditional while Dewey's was progressive, industrial and scientific. But both of them agreed that education was for life and the process of learning was continuous and life long.
9. Gandhi did not approve of any role for the state in education, whereas for Dewey democratic government existed merely to serve the people.
10. Whereas Gandhi expected the state to provide primary education till such time as each village attained self-sufficiency and conducted its own education, Dewey believed that it was enough if the state gave a helping hand to institutions and individuals.
11. For Gandhi religion was connected with education but Dewey was against inclusion of religion in curricula. Dewey's contention was that schools had to bring together individuals speaking different languages, belonging to different nationalities, creeds and traditions, while Gandhi believed in increasing the understanding of different creeds through study of them.
12. Gandhi and Dewey strongly advocated the utilization of sensory organs in the process of education. The craft-centred Basic School of Gandhi's conception had a resemblance to Dewey's Laboratory School where learning by doing was encouraged.
13. Both Gandhi and Dewey agreed that the teacher's

personality counted a great deal. The pupil did not distinguish the teacher from the subject he taught. Gandhi differed from Dewey in advising teachers to abide by the ideas and policies accepted by society.

14. The philosophies of both were understood by only a handful of people. In the case of Gandhi, as long as he was alive, there were many who enthusiastically followed his suggestions. But soon after his death Basic Education lost its appeal. In the case of Dewey, despite vehement criticism of his progressive education, it held the ground for well over a quarter of century in American school history. His theory of 'learning by doing' brought a great revolution in Western education.
15. Dewey's conception of truth seemed to be more tenable and realistic than Gandhi's. The history of science and current experimental science were more in tune with the former than the latter.
16. Dewey's ideal democratic society was ever progressive and it was industrially and technologically oriented. But Gandhi's ideas seemed to be less tenable in this age of science.

The Basic Principles of Indian Educational Philosophy

The main purpose of the present investigation was to study critically the basic principles of Indian educational philosophy. The study followed the critical and analytical method. Firstly, the basic principles of different systems of Indian philosophy, viz., Jainism, Buddhism, Sankhya, Nyaya and Vedanta, and the basic principles of the philosophy of modern Indian thinkers, viz., Swami Vivekananda, Sri Aurobindo, Rabindranath Tagore and M.K. Gandhi were collected systematically, consulting both primary and secondary sources. In the second phase, the views of these philosophical systems and thinkers on educational theory and practice including aims and objectives, the nature of the student. The role of the teacher, teaching methods, curriculum, discipline and school were collected and analysed.

The study revealed:

1. According to Jainism, education was that which provided real life to the individual and was for the betterment of the society as well as the individual. In this system of educational philosophy, the individuality of the pupil acquired much importance in the teaching-learning process.
2. Buddhism was found to have taken a middle path between spiritualism and pragmatism while advocating its curriculum. Importance was attached to moral values in the educational philosophy of Buddhism. The physical development of the individual and learning by honest means were advocated by this system of educational philosophy.
3. Child development visualized in Sankhya educational philosophy had strong psychological bases. This educational philosophy was found to be similar to the democratic philosophy of education, attaching special importance to individuality. There was a happy synthesis of spiritualism and pragmatism in its curriculum and method of teaching.
4. The analysis of the thinking process in the Nyaya system was particularly similar to that of modem psychology. There was a synthesis of direct and indirect methods of teaching in Nyaya educational philosophy.
5. Self- realization was the ultimate aim of Vedantic educational philosophy. The relationship between educator and education described in Vedanta was found ideal for every society and for all periods.
6. The educational philosophy of Swami Vivekananda was based upon humanism. According to him, education aimed at the development of universal brotherhood among individuals. Through education, he sought the establishment of humanism in the society. To him,

knowledge, action and devotion (bhakti) were related to one another.

7. Sri Aurobindo's educational philosophy was a synthesis of Sankhya and Vedanta. To him, education was for the development, modification and transformation of consciousness in human beings.
8. The educational philosophy of Rabindranath Tagore was a curious blend of essentialism, naturalism, pragmatism, humanism and realism.
9. Gandhian educational philosophy was based on Karma Yoga. According to him, character-building was the aim of education. Being influenced by the idealistic thought of Indian culture, Gandhi was found to be opposed to western materialism.

Contemporary Indian Philosophy of Education and its Prospects

The major objective of this was to study the nature of contemporary Indian philosophy of education, so as to provide a suitable base on which to build a new educational system to meet the demands not only of today but also of tomorrow.

The major observations were:

1. All educators and philosophers have to interpret abstract philosophy in operational terms, so that individual and groups can achieve satisfaction in a given environment. In a developing society, the operational objective of education is the creation of personalities who can handle quasi-static situations and who can handle the required changes in society and achieve the desired degree of satisfaction. This operational change in the objective of education must be scrutinized by educators. The basic psychological elements-the energetic, well-informed and well adjusted image of an educated gentleman-an extrovert and forward-looking dynamic personality-are urgently required for a democratic industrial society.

2. One has to ascertain the nature of man or discover the philosophy of man. After knowing the original nature of man, one will be able to direct man on the right lines towards perfection and encourage him along the way. The motto should be suggestive and helping but not interfering. In other words, the task of education is to prepare man not only for rational efficiency, not only for world solidarity, but also to make the individual feel that he has within himself something deeper than intellect, which is his 'original nature'. The basic truth concerning human nature is two-fold. Originally, and at his deepest core, man has divine potentiality, but as an individual soul he is a bundle of instincts, emotions, desires and inclinations. He inherits various sorts of Sanskaras from his previous lives, which constitute his law of being or Swabhava, which is unalterable, yet can be exhausted gradually by his present satawik karmas.
3. The student of today cannot discriminate between right and wrong, because the need-achievements of our younger generation are very high but they are very tamasik in action. To get rid of this obstacle is impossible without developing reasoning power or perfect mental function. The student must have courage to take up the right type of knowledge and apply it fearlessly in the interest of posterity. If such an education is given, the direct result will be that it will be self- supporting.
4. To make the educational system a healthy, rational system, one should not allow it to be controlled by Western or outdated Indian concepts which are no longer useful. We must introduce the original meaning of the concept in a befitting manner contextually. For example, the often-quoted maxim, 'Sa Vidiya Ya Vimuktye', will be the base of our educational philosophy but it will be used in its wider and original meaning. 'Sa Vidiya Ya Vimuktye' means that is education that leads towards mukti. But, unfortunately, the meaning of mukti has been narrowed down to the

liberation of soul only, whereas its true meaning is 'If man is to acquire freedom in every field of his life-process, he must acquire economic and political freedom, freedom from superstition, ignorance, prejudice and many other forms of bondage which obstruct his advancement'.

5. The educational system ought to be built on a solid foundation of educational philosophy which could not be other than a naturo- idealistic one, because the child is partly a spiritual being and partly a natural being. This means, man is an integrated whole of spirit and matter, he is an animal being which lives in the natural environment; at the same time he outgrows animality.
6. The researcher has discussed the nature of the contemporary philosophy of education keeping in view the fact that the ideal can only be achieved through the actual. No flowers of ideals bloom in the sky.

Approaches to Educational Theory

The objectives of this study were (i) to explicate and understand the various issues involved in any philosophical attempt at formulation of educational theory, and (ii) to try to maintain the rigour of coherent and consistent reasoning which philosophy demands. The study being philosophical, it followed different methods of inquiry at different stages such as (i) the synthetic method which involved demonstration and exposition of causal relations, (ii) the method of inquiry into the origin of ideas, (iii) the Socratic method of analysis, (iv) the intuitive method, and (v) the reflective method of introspection. Further, in order to identify and examine the approaches which might lead to better understanding of 'education theory', the philosophical literature was examined. The literature included primary as well as secondary sources like original documents and critical notes of eminent scholars.

The findings of the study were:

1. In the West the philosophers had been engaged in three

kinds of activity, viz., speculative, normative and analytical.

2. Educational philosophy came to bear upon it a distinction through education as a process of human development and education as a discipline or field of study.
3. Philosophy of education meant philosophy of the process of educating or philosophy of the discipline of education.
4. In the highly scientific West, the process of education was studied through the manifest practices of instruction and learning in the social institution called 'school'. The processes were studied by persons belonging to the various disciplines of sociology, psychology, economics, etc.
5. The discipline of education was seen to be in need of analysis. This was concerned with analysing the concepts of the factual sciences of education, e.g. intelligence, growth, etc.
6. It was seen that the fragmented view of both philosophy and of education in the West had led to a skepticism which proclaimed that philosophy was not what education needed; what it needed was a theory as generated by the factual sciences of sociology, psychology, etc.
7. In the Indian context the philosophy was seen as the practical way of life. Its role was seen as one of nurturing and nourishing the spirit.
8. The different systems of Indian philosophy were moksha or liberation- centred. The liberation which the Hindu philosophers sought, unlike Marxist liberation, was not material. It had a spiritual content so far it was concerned with self-realization. The practical way to 'good' living must form the inspiration for any theorizing about the 'education' of man. 'Educational theory' must not fall prey to the tendency to be theoretical and intellectual.
9. From the exposition of the history of philosophy in

India and the West, the philosophy of the West could be characterized as being theoretical, whereas philosophy in India is practical.

10. Modem educational theory in the West was moving away from philosophy, and was looking from practical guidance from the social and behavioural sciences.
11. The question of framing any educational theory, at no stage appeared as a felt need on the Indian scene, because Indian thinkers were inspired by deeper, more intriguing issues that kept complicating the Indian scene.
12. Life was conceived by Indian thinkers as continuity, and therefore, the principles that governed a man's life were deduced in terms of eternity.

Educational Ideals as Depicted in Buddhistic Philosophy

The objectives of the study were (i) to study the philosophical beliefs pertaining to metaphysical, epistemological and axiological realms of the Buddhistic philosophy and their relevance to education, (ii) to study the different educational ideals as advocated by the Buddha, and (iii) to derive educational aims from the Buddhistic metaphysics, epistemology and axiology.

The historical method was followed. The researcher used primary and secondary sources for data collection. The primary sources included original literature of Buddhism produced and edited by the followers of the Buddha in languages like Pali, Sanskrit and the same translated into English and other Indian languages, biographies of the Buddha, magazines, periodicals, reports, etc. The secondary sources included books written by eastern and western writers which contained elaborations, interpretations and presentations of the teaching of Lord Buddha, bibliographies, abstracts of books, journals, etc.

The collected data were analysed into three main

categories, namely metaphysical, epistemological and axiological beliefs of Buddhistic philosophy. The educational ideals were derived from the metaphysical, epistemological and axiological beliefs of Buddhistic philosophy.

Some of the major findings were:

1. Sixty-four values were identified out of which the maximum number of values pertained to the categories of spiritual and moral-ethical values.
2. The hierarchy of value categories was spiritual values, moral-ethical values, physical-organic values, social values, educational values, intellectual values, economic values, political values, biological values, aesthetic values and cultural values. No values in aesthetic and cultural categories were found. The spiritual and moral values dominated amongst all other value categories.
3. In all, 60 ideals were derived. The maximum number of ideals pertained to the axiological category.
4. The Buddhist concept of the good life consisted of observing discipline, namely, abstaining from stealing, from doing wrong which related to sensual desires, from lying, slandering, bitter speech and idle babbling.
5. According to Buddhist philosophy, the concept of education was to train the student in religion, morality, wisdom and meditation and to equip him with intellectual and spiritual powers. It also incorporated certain ingredients such as regard for the subject of learning, simple living and high thinking, love for manual work, self-help, community life, maintaining sincerity and discipline, humility, respect to elders and veneration to teachers.
6. The aims of Buddhistic education as they emerged were to enable the pupils to realize the ultimate truth, to help them in acquiring arhatship and to attain the ultimate aim of human life, that is nirvana or moksha, to make them aware about the realities of life, to enable

them to eliminate ignorance and acquire knowledge and wisdom, to make them understand the law of karma, to make them sharpen their faculties of intellect, discrimination and decision-making, to help them develop good moral character, to cultivate a scientific attitude in learning and living, to develop their ability for logical reasoning, argumentation and dialectics, to inculcate universal ideals of love, compassion, brotherhood, friendship, welfare and peace.

7. The curriculum was spread over three stages of education, namely, early stage, middle stage and higher stage. The general course of instruction included initial training in listening, speech, reading and writing, simple mathematics and language at an early stage; other auxiliary sciences, mathematics, language, physical education and social sciences at the middle stage; philosophy, religion, logic, psychology and humanities at the higher stage.
8. The methods of teaching were lecture, discussion, debate, assignment, project, raising doubts and seeking clarification, etc.

Identification of Indian Objectives of Education with special reference to West Bengal

The major objectives of the research were (i) to identify the real objectives of education in India in the light of the expectations of the people, (ii) to identify the expectations of the people from education, (iii) to find out the impediments in the way of satisfaction of such expectations, and (iv) to formulate strategies to be adopted for fulfilment of these expectations.

The study was divided into two phases: (i) study of the effectiveness of education in removing social ills like untouchability and the dowry system; (ii) identification of expectations of people (both elite and uneducated) from education. The sources of data were documents and records.

The findings of the research were:

1. It indicated that education had a significant role in West Bengal in removing social ills like untouchability, but its influence in removing the dowry system was not significant.
2. It was felt that unless a young man was inclined to marry a particular young woman and vice-versa, everybody was directly or indirectly in favour of dowry or at least was neutral in his stand and education had failed to do any worthwhile service to stop this undesirable practice.
3. Even the educated youth, both males and females, were not clearly opposed to dowry.
4. Even the majority of educated girls expected their parents to give them a reasonably good amount at the time of their marriage.
5. Education had, however, an indirect role in de-emphasizing dowry by making possible a large number of self-arranged marriages between brides and grooms who came close to each other through the process of education.
6. In the case of educated women in salaried jobs, the demand for dowry was much less. It seemed that, to remove the dowry system in the state of West Bengal excluding the tribes in the hills, a possible way was to make young women economically productive and oriented to jobs through a special type of education.
7. The expectations of the people from education were (a) good salaried service or employment, (b) good income even in the absence of employment, (c) honour, status and dignity in the society, (d) security for the future, (e) a good life partner, (f) enjoyment of civic and democratic rights, (g) efficient service to the community, (h) loyalty to superiors and the nation, (i) growth of a rational attitude on every aspect of life, and (j) development of democratic, social, ethical and spiritual values.

The Rama Krishna Mission and its Impact on Contemporary Indian Education

The study aimed at bringing out the problems people faced at the time of the appearance of Rama Krishna Paramhans and highlighting his special endowments and his contribution in the field of education. The investigator employed the historical method and consulted the relevant literature published by the Rama Krishna Mission and commentaries by various religious reformers and educationists.

The main findings of the study were:

1. Rama Krishna emphasized that man possessed divine qualities and efforts should be made to develop these qualities.
2. Stress should be laid on the divinity of labour.
3. Stress should be laid on preservation of Indian culture.
4. School curriculum should develop cognitive, connective and aesthetic abilities.
5. Scientific and technical development should not be neglected.
6. School curriculum should include knowledge of health and hygiene, general understanding of community as well as social life of the people,
7. There should be close cooperation between the teachers and the students.
8. Stress should be laid on both the theoretical and practical aspects of science.
9. Education should lead to development of sincerity and honesty.
10. Stress should be laid on conversation, story-telling and demonstration as methods of teaching.
11. Schools should plan activities for constructive work for the welfare of the society.
12. Rama krishna laid stress on synthesis of East and West.

13. Though basically a religious organization, the Rama Krishna Mission's social role is equally important.
14. In spite of limitations of funds and scarcity of dedicated workers, the Rama Krishna Mission is rendering significant educational services to the country.

The Nature and Development of Human Personality in Ancient Indian Thought

The objectives of the study were (i) to identify the enunciation of philosophical principles that conceptualized human personality in the various systems of ancient Indian thought, (ii) to undertake an exposition of the various constituents of human personality in each system, (iii) to assess the concept of human personality within a particular school of thought, (iv) to assess the framework of the process of development of human personality in a particular school of thought, (v) to critically analyse various positions regarding the nature and development of human personality held by different schools, their points of strength and weaknesses, (vi) to frame an integrated view of human personality, truly reflective of an Indian approach to human life and its ideals, and (vii) to evolve an integrated educational strategy for realization of human personality as envisaged in the system.

The study was philosophical-cum-historical. The primary sources used were aphormisms (Sutras) and important commentaries (Bhasyas) on the Indian schools of thought as given in the Vedas. The secondary sources were essays and works of eminent persons like S. Radhakrishnan, S.N. Dasgupta and others. The statements made about human personality in various processes of thoughts were analysed and compared with one another. In this way, various inferences were drawn through syllogism.

The findings of the study were:

1. Vedanta was the most profound exposition of the metaphysical basis of the world.
2. All in Brahma was pure existence, consciousness and

bliss. The phenomenal world was simply a seeming reality, i.e. something that appeared to be existing.

3. Man was not different from Brahma. Everything merged into the Brahma.
4. Advait approached Brahma through self-realization which was the result of knowledge of the difference between reality and appearance. There was an implied transcendence in action, not from action.
5. Ramanuja held that the highest could be achieved through jnana and bhakti as well as karma.
6. The composition of human personality in Vedanta was true to its metaphysical mainstay. Human personality had only empirical existence. Man's true personality was embedded in impersonality.
7. A remarkable feature of Vedanta was its ontology of human personality that reduced all dualistic and pluralistic entities to one ground source-the Brahma.
8. The highest ideal for Vedanta was Atma-Bodha-the self-realization which could be achieved by the removal of avidya and the veil of maya.
9. The beauty of human existence was achieved through a discipline which was preparatory in nature. The final realization was of course intuitive.
10. Vedanta recommended four disciplines for the fullest development of human personality: discriminative knowledge, renunciation, the longing for liberation, and ethical principles. These disciplines educated an individual to become qualified for the knowledge of the Divine.
11. The conception of human personality in the Indian systems provided immense strength to a philosophy of life which in turn should percolate into educational thought, policies and practices so as to produce persons with personalities and not machines manufactured on assembly lines.

Educational Thought of Dr Zakir Husain

The objective was to undertake a critical study of the educational thought of Dr Zakir Husain. The major observations of the study were:

1. There seems to be a general consensus that Dr Zakir Husain was an outstanding creative thinker on education in contemporary India. He wanted to disseminate the ideas of other great thinkers and also to ameliorate the state of education; therefore, he translated Plato, Russell, Edwin Cannon, Friedrich Lists, etc. into Urdu. He wrote beautiful animal and bird stories in traditional Indian and Greek literary styles to usher in an era of good literature for children. His stories particularly portray battles between virtue and vice. Obviously, Dr Zakir Husain always realized the urgency of educational reform and, therefore, deeply involved himself in evolving a scheme of national education. Thus, being a thoroughgoing educationist, his interest in education never faltered or wavered even for a while.
2. Dr Zakir Husain always felt the need to reconstruct education in order to meet the social and political aspirations of the people. He perceived a deep and living interrelationship between the school and the society, and, therefore, took into consideration not only the immediate needs of the emerging society, but also drew inspiration from the socio-cultural heritage while developing his educational ideas.
3. He was, however, quite sore at the way the socio-political situation in the country was taking shape for the worse during the first part of the twentieth century, especially when its colonial rulers sought to thwart the wheel of progress in a number of obvious ways, including communal riots, dragging India into world wars, the 'divide and rule' policy, etc. Dr Zakir Husain found the Western system of education narrow and

limited in its objectives, thin and anemic in content, and weak in the context of our national life. He made it a point to keep these considerations in view while weaving the fabric of his educational thought. He made inculcation of national values and spirit the main plank of his philosophy. His nationalism drew strength from the ideas of Abul Kalam Azad, Maulana Mohammad Ali, Sir Mohammad lqbal's poetry and other sources. To him, religion and nationalism could never be antithetical. A true Muslim, he believed, is he who served his country as religiously as he does his religion, lest he should feel ashamed of himself as being unworthy of the Creator.

4. In this search for Truth, Dr Zakir Husain was also greatly influenced by other thinkers also like Georg Kerschensteiner, Mahatma Gandhi, Edward Spranger, Pestalozzi, Froebel and Dewey. Yet the fact, however, is that Dr Zakir Husain was not simply an armchair philosopher never accepted any theory uncritically, before putting it on the anvil of practice, particular), for its suitability and workability in Indian conditions. Therefore, whether he taught in municipal night schools in Germany or at Jamia Millia Islamia, Dr Zakir Husain endeavored to construct a strong educational foundation for making his educational thought and ideas viable, applicable and down-to-earth, especially in Indian context.
5. Dr Zakir Husain's educational philosophy allows new ideas and knowledge to enter his mind from all directions in order to fit them all into the Indian scheme of things and culture. Therefore, though most of his ideas are not original as such, yet through the process of philosophical synthesis, he makes these assume such a form as makes them Indian in origin and Indian in culture. His synthetic approach is reflected in all his concepts. He achieves a practical harmony of purpose in his life as well as his ideas via the process of

philosophical synthesis; his life has itself been a synthesis of the old and new, traditional and modern, Eastern and Western, simplicity and grandeur, poverty and taste; and his ideas reflect a synthesis between individual and society, science and humanities, freedom and authority, ethics and technology, material and spiritual values, temporal and eternal, skilled efficiency and awakened conscience, achievement and conviction, knowledge and faith, etc. He made philosophical synthesis a potent factor of his educational philosophy.

6. The fundamental concepts of Dr Zakir Husain's philosophy pivot around certain basic educational postulates concerned with the aims of education, the nature of the education, the cultural goods and character-formation, among others.
7. He was not satisfied with any cut-and-dried curriculum. He believed that curriculum should not only be organic but should also be related to the real life of the education. He, therefore, fully appreciated the importance of curriculum development.
8. Like all other educational philosophers, Dr Zakir Husain too realized the importance of language. Realising that India was a multi-lingual society, he favored mother-tongue as the most effective medium of education at the primary stage, a regional language at the secondary stage and a modern Indian language at the higher stage.
9. Dr Zakir Husain attached a great deal of importance to educationally productive work.
10. He never considered a university degree or a school-leaving certificate to be an indication that one's education has come to an end.

The Development of the Concept of Freedom in Education since Rousseau

A historical study of the concept of freedom in the classics of the thinkers since Plato and more particularly since Rousseau, and its implications in education was undertaken here. The first chapter, based mainly on Sabine's The History of Political Thought, Erich Fromm's, The Fear of Freedom, and Paul Monroe's A Text Book in the History of Education, gives a summary of the idea of free will, independence and freedom up to the end of the 17th century. The discussion starts with Plato and other Greek thinkers, and then gives the position held by leaders of the reformation, Renaissance, Enlightenment and philosophical romanticism movements.

Basing the study mainly on Monroe, Rusk, Payne, Mayer and Asirvatham, Rousseau's concept of freedom is discussed in the second chapter. The concept of freedom in the modem phase is discussed in the third chapter. Ideas of philosophers contemporary to Rousseau are described as outlined by Mayer. The post French Revolution concepts of freedom as enunciated by Bentham, John Austin, Fitche, idealists like Bosanquet, T.H. Green, individualists such as Adams, Humboldt, H. Spencer, socialists like Karl Marx, anarchists like Proudhon, Fabianists like Sidney Oliver and communists like Engels are summarized, mainly on the basis of Mahajan and Sethi's Recent Political Thought. Freedom as conceived by revisionists democratic liberals, and fascists is also discussed.

Thereafter, the thoughts of Whitehead, John Dewey and Erich From, as well as those of Raja Ram Mohan Roy, Tagore, Aurobindo, Gandhi, and Isaiah Berlin are described. Chapter four is a discussion on freedom in education, and possibilities of avenues of freedom in educational endeavours. The issues covered are academic freedom, its rationality, conditions making for it, and academic freedom in relation to purposes of education as well as its relation with other freedoms. The relationship of intellectual freedom with authoritarian religion, and with the authority of the State are also discussed. Lastly, academic freedom and freedom to learn, the authority of the teacher, discipline, self-examination and freedom to be oneself, to choose, to grow, are also covered. In conclusion, it is stated that education is one of the most potent enterprises which can cherish the ideal of freedom in its processes and purposes and that this freedom can be strengthened only when people have faith in education.

The Concept of Human Nature Propounded by Educational Theorists and Revealed by Psychological Studies

The objectives of the study were (i) to compare the conception of human nature put forward by educational theorists with a view to constructing a unified picture of human nature on the basis of the results of the said comparison, (ii) to ascertain how far the conception of human nature put forth by the educational theorists were similar or dissimilar to what the psychological scientists have said on the matter, (iii) to build up an integrated view of human nature on thc basis of the meeting-ground between the educational theorists' conception of human nature and the findings of scientific psychology, and (iv) to put up some suggestions for framing educational theories and practices on the basis of the integrated view of human nature.

The methodology of research adopted in the study was philosophical and comparative. It was philosophical as ideas of different educational theorists on the concept of human nature were organized, critically analysed and evaluated. It was comparative as inter theorist comparisons relating to their conception of human nature were made. Further, the comparison of each theorist's conception of human nature with findings of studies conducted in the field of scientific psychology was also made.

In the light of the objectives of the study, some educational theorists were selected on the basis of particular criteria, such as (i) producing original work related to aspects of education; (ii) contributing to the aspect of epistemology;

(iii) showing unusual insight into theories of education; (iv) interpreting theories of education pertaining to his time; (v) bringing in some contemporary trend of thinking related to aspects of education; (vi) establishing an educational institution of unique character, leading eventually to the enrichment of the theory of education; (vii) contributing to the growth of the teaching profession by suggesting new and more appropriate lines; (viii) indicating new possibilities of man's transformation for the better through the process of education. On the basis of these criteria, the educational theorists included in the study were Plato, Aristotle, Locke, Rousseau, Pestalozzi, Herbert, Froebel, Dewey, Tagore, Gandhi, Sri Aurobindo and Makarenko. From the field of psychology, the findings of only those studies were utilized for the purpose which was relevant to the task of required comparisons.

The study revealed that the integrated view of human nature worked out on the basis of meeting-points between the educational theorists' conception of human nature and the findings of scientific psychology had the following features:

1. Man is natural and not a super natural being.
2. Man is a psycho-physical being, having an integration of mind and body.
3. Original human nature is not fixed; it is rather a process in the making.
4. Man is originally dynamic rather than passive or just reactive.
5. Man is both a determined and indetermined being.
6. Original human nature is pliable and has its unchanging aspects also.
7. Human nature is both universal and variable.
8. The roots of cognition, affection and connation originally inhere in the inherited material.
9. Human nature is unity. The cognitive, affective and conative elements of human's nature do not operate independently of one another. There is hardly any mental activity that can be called exclusively either

cognitive or affective or conative.

10. Original determinants of behaviour are physiological as well as psychological.
11. There is no significant difference in the psychological endowments of men and women.
12. Original human nature does not come in the form of any clear-cut capacities, dispositions or impulses. It rather comes in the form of undifferentiated capacities and vague impulses and dispositions.
13. There is no original human type.
14. Human nature is characterized by a rich variety of individual differences.
15. Individual differences in respect of cognitive capacities are chiefly determined by genetic factors.
16. Individual variations in regard to noncognitive characteristics of human personality are primarily the result of the divergences in the experience which human beings happen to undergo.
17. The nature of the child is qualitatively different from that of the adult.
18. The child's nature at each stage of his development has its own peculiar characteristics.
19. Right from the time of conception, human growth and human development are marked by continuity and gradualness.
20. Different stages of development are not sharply marked off from each other.
21. Each stage of development prepares the ground for the developments of the subsequent stage.
22. In the shaping of human nature, the role of heredity is creative and that of environment developmental.
23. While describing human nature, the approaches adopted by the educational theorists and by the scientific psychologists basically differ in terms of their end results, but they have not been found to be incompatible.

They rather complement each other. There is a very substantial identity between the unified view of human nature as it emerged from the similarities among the educational theorists. Further similarity also exists about the integrated view of human nature worked out on the basis of the meeting points between the educational theorists' conception of it and the findings of scientific psychology.

On the basis of the findings about human nature, some lines of theory-building were suggested for the would-be framers of educational theories. These were: (1) The framers of educational theories should not feel absolutely bound by the nature of original human potential, rather they should go by its possibilities. (2) Educational theories should be so constructed that they provide for the development of human potentialities of both lower and higher orders. (3) The framers of educational theories should provide for active and creative participation of pupils in all educational activities. (4) While constructing educational theories for the development of children, it is the nature of the child that needs to be closely kept in mind and not the nature of the adult.

The Educational Doctrines of Plato and Sri Aurobindo

The objectives of the present study were (i) to compare the views of Plato and Sri Aurobindo on the three underlying bases-philosophical, psychological and sociological, and the various components and issues of the educational process-meaning and aims, the curriculum, the teacher, teaching methods, the school, discipline, evaluation programmes and the education of women, and (ii) to assess the practicability and relevance of their educational ideas and schemes in the present context.

The relevant data and evidence were gathered using both primary and secondary sources. Various reports, magazines, etc. were also consulted. The study revealed:

1. Comparision of Plato and Aurobindo on their ontolo-

gical viewpoints shows a few striking similarities though there are divergences. Both dwell on philosophical speculation and analysis to change the present status of human beings and society, and are optimistic in their vision of the future.

2. Both conceive a continuum of the cognitive process. Plato lays too much emphasis on training to apprehend true knowledge whereas Aurobindo gives less weightage to training and more to evolution and transformation of being,
3. Both emphasize self-realization and perfection of being-eudaimonism and altruism, though their concepts of perfection are not strictly the same. Their views on aesthetics and ethics are governed by the higher principles of reality.
4. The psychological gleanings of Plato are inadequate because psychology covered a long distance after him, yet they are significant for educational practice. Aurobindo has developed an integral psychology based on his integral monism and yoga which is nothing but a practical psychology.
5. Regarding the relation of the individual to society, both have developed an organic theory, but Aurobindo does not pursue it too far. He wants to see individuals developing their individuality. Plato emphasizes too much the unity of the state. He therefore, propagates conformity whereas Aurobindo advocates reciprocity and mutuality.
6. For both, education is an unfolding, an educing of the human potential that is within. Aurobindo's treatment of education is deep, whereas Plato gives only gleanings, valuable flashes.
7. Plato's aim of education is to prepare good citizens and administrators for the state; Aurobindo's aim is to prepare men for integral perfection and divine living.
8. Through their curricular proposals both want to train the faculties of learners, so that they are able to actualize their potentialities. Plato, however, has devised a rigid

scheme whereas Aurobindo has not devised a plan, he has only hinted at certain provisions and principles on which an evolutionary curriculum could be devised.

9. Both recommend a close personal relationship between the teacher and the taught.
10. Both the philosophers appreciate the use of certain maxims of teaching from near to far, concrete to abstract, etc., and modes of learning-play, activity, imitation, narration, question- answer, team teaching, project and problem positing, etc. They do not develop a rigid system of learning but provide certain hints on which an up to date methodology can be evolved, attacking the problem from different angles.
11. Both visualize the school as a centre for preparing future citizens and developing higher consciousness. Plato favours state run schools; Aurobindo does note.
12. Problems of indiscipline, according to Aurobindo, are transitional phenomena. The strict thought control suggested by Plato does not find much support in Aurobindo but there is an inner censor in his educational provisions.
13. Plato prescribes external and final examination, whereas Aurobindo prescribes spontaneous and individual evaluation.
14. Neither has differentiated the education of women from that of men.
15. Both want to transform the society, its set up values and norms.
16. On the efforts level too, the two educators and their followers are quite sincere. Plato's ideas have seen a long span of more than two thousand years. They have been practised in different shapes and degrees in different countries. Aurobindo's ideas are getting recognition in several parts of India and other countries.
17. Keeping in view the modem educational thinking and

the present and future needs of mankind, the educational ideas of Plato and Aurobindo appear to be most relevant and practicable.

Tagore and Whitehead's Ideas on Education

The objectives of the inquiry were (i) to study the contribution of Tagore to education, (ii) to find out whether the ideas of Tagore could by systematically integrated to represent his theory of education, (iii) to investigate whether Whitehead had significant ideas relating to education which could be systematically organized into his theory of education, and (iv) to find out whether there were certain ideas common to both Tagore and Whitehead which could be developed into an educational theory.

The methodology of research adopted was philosophical, historical and comparative. The study was philosophical in the sense that the ideas of Tagore and Whitehead were organized, critically analysed and evaluated. It was historical because the roots of Tagore's and Whitehead's philosophy were traced to various sources. Further, it was comparative as common ideas between Tagore and Whitehead were identified and critically evaluated. Content analysis was used both as a tool and technique to analyse the educational ideas of Tagore and Whitehead. Content analysis consisted of documentary analysis and thematic analysis. For content analysis, primary as well as secondary sources were used. The material was also examined to find out its suitability for the proposed research by the way of internal and external criticism.

Some of the findings of the study were:

1. Tagore and Whitehead were contemporaries. Despite the fact that there was no direct contact between them, parallel ideas were found in their educational views. They recognized the supreme importance of reason while they theorized on education.

2. Both Tagore and Whitehead recognized that integration of Eastern and Western culture was possible, if both oriental and occidental people pinned their faith on reason.
3. Both thinkers laid stress on the cultivation of values through the educative process. In their view, life was a search for values, and success in life was the attainment of values. Values cannot be understood through scientific analysis and logical reasoning, but, rather, through intuitive comprehension.
4. Both Tagore and Whitehead recognized the fundamental importance of science and values in any educational programme, from the level of primary education up to the highest academic level of rigorous research. Both pinned their faith on empirical truth, which could be obtained through scientific research. Yet, both of them recognized the supreme importance of intrinsic and eternal values, which had sustained human existence for centuries. Creativity, love, happiness and peace were some of the perennial values, which humans all over the world had been cherishing from the very dawn of civilization.
5. Both Tagore and Whitehead recognized the importance of facts and values in any civilized society. In their view, empirical science gave us knowledge of facts and axiology gave us knowledge of values. An effective system of education integrated scientific facts with values. Humans dealt with actualities in life with the aid of scientifically established truths and ideals in human existence through moral vision, aesthetic refinement and religious intuition.
6. Both Tagore and Whitehead recognized that, although humans lived and moved about in the actual world, which was full of difficulties and hopes, they had a strong urge to transcend the hard actualities of life through passionate love for humanity, lasting peace on a global scale and communion with God through religious intuition.

7. The aim of education, according to both, was all-round development of personality. Both of them, therefore, emphasised the intellectual, aesthetic, moral and cultural development of the individual.
8. Both Tagore and Whitehead recognized the dignity, freedom and creative potentiality of all human beings. Both of them emphasized the basic goodness in all persons, which could be nurtured and sustained through education. The aim of education according to both was to develop the personality of the individual to the fullest possible extent along with the overall development of the society.
9. Both of them believed in allowing maximum possible freedom to learners during the process of learning. However, both Tagore and Whitehead recommended that there should be a proper balance between freedom and discipline.
10. Rigid, dull and stereotyped learning was criticized by them while favouring dynamism, change and flexibility in education. They were critical of bookish knowledge which led to uncritical acceptance of facts. Both of them lay due emphasis on development of imagination in pupils. Both laid stress on nurturing creative potentialities in young learners. Both believed that creativity thrived and flourished if it was nurtured and declined and withered if it was oppressed. Both laid emphasis on the environment of the educational institution which provided ample opportunity to learners for the development of their creative imagination. Both of them recognized that the process of education would be effective only if the creative potentialities in individuals found opportunities for self-actualisation. Both gave due emphasis to attainment of human excellence for the development of civilization.
11. Both Tagore and Whitehead laid stress on intimate contact of learners with nature. They recommended that the balance, rhythm and harmony in this universe

must not be disturbed. Both laid stress on education for ecological harmony, which was one of the main themes of contemporary civilization.

12. Both of them laid stress on the moral, aesthetic and humanistic aspects of education. They urged that a lasting world order should be ushered into existence through conflict resolution and building bonds of mutual understanding between different people.

13. The affinities in the viewpoints of Tagore and White-head existed because both were humanists, idealists and perfectionists.

6

Research in Economics of Education

Mid-term appraisals and periodic evaluations of the socioeconomic programmes have a tremendous advantage from the point of view of future programme formulation and development of future strategies. In the case of research, however, appraisals and reviews of current thinking should be considered with high degree of responsibility and caution. Research is essentially a gradual process. This is particularly true in the case of relatively newer disciplines like economics of education. For any new discipline there is likely to be an initial enthusiastic response and open-hearted welcome by re- searchers. This has been the experience within discipline of economics of education also. There is, however, only an occasional initiative and interest in the newer aspects. By and large, only the traditional themes in this field continue to attract researchers.

In the case of economics of education, there is yet another problem of mixed treatment from economists on the one hand, and educationists, on the other. Educationists, traditionally averse to considering the economic aspects of the sacred field of education, seem to have been initially overcome by the upsurge of interest among economists in this field. Though this is a welcome development, it also appears that there is still an element of suspicion and lack of fuller conviction among educationists about the utility of studying the economic aspects of education. Unless the educationists, on the one hand, and economists, sociologists and other social scientists, one the other, come together to examine different dimensions of education, the discipline of education will not be enriched and mutual suspicion of the two perspectives will continue. While, prior to the 1950s, education was the concern of only educationists, the mid- 1950s, the whole of the- 1960s and 1970s reflected the increasing awareness of the economic dimensions of education.

During the 1970s and 1980s, however, the sociological dimensions of education seemed to be coming out more and more clearly in a number of research studies. There seems to be a cyclical pattern of ebb and flow in the development of ideas relating to education. This is particularly true in the case of the economics of education. It is sometimes said that, during 1960s and 1970s, education belonged to economists, whereas during the late 1970s and 1980s, the importance of economics seems to have declined and this period is said to belong to sociologists. In the ultimate analysis, education does not simply belong to any one field. If it has to be considered as an effective agent to social change, education should be viewed from the point of view of many disciplines. It is in this background that we are attempting below a review of studies in the field of economics of education, with occasional references to the studies undertaken by non-economists on some of its aspects.

It is proposed to develop a thematic review instead of an author- based one. The major themes that have been selected are the following:

1. Education-economy interdependencies
2. Education and socioeconomic equality
3. Problems of educational finances
4. Planning and management in education

This thematic review is followed by a brief analysis of the

directions in which the discipline of economics of education is moving. This analysis also makes few cautionary observations, so that the discipline may take note of some of the basic maladies of its past growth and the pitfalls that must be avoided in charting its future course.

Interdependencies between economy and education

Ideally the economics of education should trace the two-way relationships, in a dynamic setting, between the educational sector and socioeconomic factors. Many writings in this field, however, have tried to trace the relationship between the two mainly from the angle of education as an agent of socioeconomic change. Policy prescriptions for the educational sector arising out of the study of two-way relationships are likely to be more meaningful than policy prescriptions based on the analysis of one-way relationships. It should be noted that the term, education, needs to be interpreted in a broad sense, to cover skill-generating activities and training, in addition to the usual literacy programmes and formal and non-formal educational activities.

A number of studies falling within this broad coverage have been reported which are concerned with the interdependencies between education and the socioeco-nomic factors. We present below a quick review of these studies under two broad heads namely, (a) the effect of education on the socioeconomic status of the individual and the national economy and policy suggestions for education arising out of these studies and (b) the implications of socioeconomic status for education and the concomitant policy implications for education.

a. From Education to Socio-economic Status

That education has a significant effect on farm productivity and farmers' earnings has been the subject of research studies in India and abroad over the past two decades. However, since farmers have exhibited some initial inhibition concerning sending their children to school and college, the conclusions of these research findings have not been able to substantially influence education policy in relation to farmers. If farmers are allergic to sending their children to school and college for regular, long-term courses, would they be interested in very short-term training? What will be the overall impact of such training on their life-style, attitude and functional knowledge? What should be the content of such training if optimum results are to be realized from it? These are some of the questions which need to be considered in order to make the link between education and the farm sector effective and meaningful. Panwar, on the basis of his study of short-duration agricultural training on farmers' earning, concludes that even five day training is likely to lead to a significant increase in the functional knowledge of farmers, significant changes in their attitude and farm practices and also on their earnings. Interestingly, other socioeconomic and personal factors like age, cost, size of holding, socioeconomic status, etc. do not have a significant effect on the gain in knowledge of the farmers due to the short' duration of training.

What is true of farmers may be true for industrial workers also. As the studies by Nagia and Pinto show in two different contexts, technical training and workers' education schemes have proved to be quite useful in increasing workers' productivity and their socio- economic status, though there is much to be desired in the way education and training are imparted, suggesting that there is a scope for significant improvement in these programmes. Interestingly, some of these studies have also hinted that formal education does not seem to be very necessary for making the training programme effective.

Education and training are likely to have a socioeconomic impact through their effect on the employability of the trained and educated persons. There is a general presumption that better-trained and educated persons have a higher probability of getting employment. Whether this presumption is factually true is open to question. A study of the employers' responses conducted in labour-market situations, metropolitan and *moffusil* revealed that employers do not assign much weightage to the degrees and certificates of the candidates who seek jobs in different concerns in these two employment markets. Added to this general phenomenon of the limited relevance of education, there is also the question of devaluation of education as is revealed by the above mentioned study and also from the review of Indian evidence in this context. Different levels and categories of education are increasingly devalued, indicating that, for doing the same job, higher and higher levels of education are employed, implying a redundancy of higher levels of education for the purpose of the job.

Also, unemployment among the educated is spreading far and wide, with a shift in the employment pattern from the primary to the secondary and tertiary sector. This in itself could be an indication of the limited usefulness of education so far as employment is concerned. Even where education is likely to have better nexus with employment, educational opportunities are not found to be adequate as is revealed from a micro study of the tea garden labourers of Assam. Similar is the state of affairs so far as educational development and manpower development in Marathwada are concerned. Does education offer any other gains for the economy apart from employment and earning advantages for the educated? Are educational revolution and technological revolution closely related? Does the developmental process get intensified and deepened with expansion in education? These are some very relevant questions. The answers may well bring about a renewed interest in education among economic planners.

Based upon data collected from 30,000 rural households in 245 randomly selected villages located in Tumkur district of Karnataka, the study by Moonis Raza, Ramchandran and Manvikar (1986) tried to ex- amine these questions. Though the conclusions were not categorical with regard to these questions, it appears that education does play a positive role with regard to the socioeconomic transformation of households and the country. Improvement in the status of women is obviously very closely related to their empowerment, both in terms of employment opportunities and education. Unfortunately, there is a problem here because the employment of women in developing countries is largely in the primary sector and their occupational status is very low. Their propensity to receive education is also very low. As a result, they have a low degree of educational empowerment and economic empowerment, leading to continuation of their low status in society. This was brought out from a study of the changing status of working women in Bihar.

Education is thus found to be a useful agent for improvement. In socioeconomic status so far as groups and communities suffering socioeconomic deprivation are concerned. Even in the case of the physically handicapped, education is found to be an investment, suggesting that, with education, such handicapped persons are made more productive economic agents in the society. That there is a close link between education and development was brought out by a study of education and economic development of Bangladesh. It was found that, so far as Bangladesh is concerned, there is an attempt to effectively integrate education with economic development so that the former contributes to the latter. In this background, and examination of education and manpower planning in the course of the Five Year Plans in India would provide a useful input for framing future policies of integrating educational and socioeconomic development. M.A Akhtar (1983) attempts a critical appraisal of educational and manpower planning in India during the Five Year Plans.

b. From Socio-economic Status to Education

As stated earlier, while education may have significant

implications for the socioeconomic processes, socioeconomic factors would also have significant implications for the educational sector. This reciprocal relationship between socioeconomic factors and education is considered one of the bases in manpower strategies and policies for educational development. Apart from the macro-goals of manpower planning, educational demand at the individual level may be significantly influenced by socioeconomic factors affecting the individual. That this is so is clearly brought out by the low propensities of the farmers and the socio-economically backward communities to send their children to school or college. Using the data for 772 boys and girls in different courses in Allahabad, the study by P. Kumar (1980) clearly brings out the significant role that the socio-economic status of the family, educational level of the father, occupational status, etc. play in the demand for education. Interestingly, apart from the economic advantages from education, the more important factors behind the desire to seek higher education were found to be non-economic in nature, such as attainment of knowledge, character building, eradication of social evils, etc. This indeed seems to redeem the country's emphasis on higher education.

These ideas about interlinkages between education and socioeconomic factors have a powerful policy implication namely, that in order to achieve socioeconomic equality there ought to be properly graded educational equality'. Obviously, in a country with extreme socio-economic inequalities, the policy of absolute educational equalities cannot lead to desirable results. In order to ensure that education is equitably distributed, it must be unequally distributed. This statement appears to be self-contradictory on the face of it. However, socioeconomic equality and educational equality demand unequal treatment of unequal at the hand of education. This brings us to the question of inequality in education in the socioeconomic context.

Education and Equality

To what extent does education contribute to

socioeconomic equality? Given the other socioeconomic variables, to what extent can equality in education be achieved by tackling the problems of inter-regional inequality in education? To what extent can the equilization policies be tagged on to the personal circumstances of the aspirants for education? Can such policies be formulated once and for all or should there be flexibility at regular intervals so far as the content, the focus and the emphasis on these policies are concerned? These are some of the major questions in the field linking education with the goal of equality.

There have been a number of studies with some of these issues as their focus. 'Inequality in education-A Socio-economic Perspective' by P.R. Panchamukhi and S. Shirwadkar (1987) presents a comprehensive review of the thinking in this field. Maya Shah (1981) brings out the importance of economic factors in explaining the variations in literacy rate in rural areas of Gujarat. Obviously, farm practices, irrigational facilities, land holdings, proximity to the urban areas, etc. have their own implications for literacy levels in rural areas. A study conducted by NIEPA concluded that the economic base of a region exerts a strong influence on the spread of literacy. T. Maitra (1981) concluded, on the basis of a survey of public education in West Bengal, that, despite serious efforts, public education in the rural areas of the state is far below the level obtaining in urban areas. This conclusion seems to be true for the country as a whole also.

Regional disparities in education need to be properly measured so that policies are effectively directed towards overcoming them. It is not proper to consider only one or two aspects of educational development in order to understand the status of a region so far as educational progress is concerned. Though the Finance Commission and the Planning Commission have methods of measuring educational development in region, there is scope to undertake rigorous methodological studies in this field. P.R.

Pamchamukhi (1970, 1983), J.B.G. Tilak (1981) and K.P. Jain (1981) developed some interesting methods of measuring regional disparities in educational development.

Community-specific and individual-specific policies for achieving educational equality have necessarily to be based upon a full understanding of a current profile of inter-personal and inter- community inequalities. N.D. Joshi (1985), A.S. Rajput (1985), B.M. Rajput (1985), and V. Trivedi (1987) have attempted to highlight some aspects of the role of the personal circumstances of the individuals so far as their educational backwardness is concerned. Poor socioeconomic conditions at home, a low degree of response and responsibility on the part of teachers towards the educational development of children of backward communities and with poor socioeconomic backgrounds, with a low degree of awareness of both their own educational backwardness and economic backwardness in the case of these communities, etc. were found to be responsible for continued social, cultural and educational backwardness of Adivasis in Kerala.

What is true in the case of linkages between socioeconomic factors and general educational attainment seems to be true in the case of performance in new subjects and courses also. Based upon a sample of 1000 students from various Central Schools, a study found that the socio-economic status of children affected their achievement in the important subject of mathematics. V. Trivedi (1987) concluded, on the basis of a study of 523 girls in colleges in Lucknow, that there is a significant relationship between academic achievement, parental attitude and socio-economic status. Students belonging to higher socio-economic status showed better academic achievements. Obviously, equal distribution of educational opportunities is a precondition for equal educational achievements. The question of 'equal' access and a reasonable supply of facilities to the deprived is obviously linked with general resource availability.

The resource question deserves an unconventional

approach in the background of the elusive goals of equity and equality. For example, the question of resources for education needs to be viewed not only from the point of view of the agencies supplying education but also from the point of view of the aspirants for education. Surprisingly, the question of educational finances has been considered by researchers as the one relating to only the former namely, finances for supplying education. Also, most of the studies seem to consider the question of educational finances as the one dealing with fees, government grants, donations, etc. Some of the more effective resources for education which are under the control of the education sector itself do not seem to have attracted the attention of researchers. Since the financial crisis for all the sectors of the economy in general and for the education sector in particular, is likely to grow deeper and deeper in the near future, such endogenous resources for education obviously become increasingly important.

One method of mobilizing resources from within the educational sector is by re-allotting educational expenditures and also by increasing the efficiency of their utilization. Effective utilization of the facilities within the educational sector is thus very closely linked with the objective of equity in education. This area of utilization of the facilities within the educational sector has remained practically a virgin field for research. There have been some governmental reports at the state level to indicate the extent of facilities available. However, for the purpose of examining the problem of utilization of the facilities fully, the type of data that are provided in the governmental publications are obviously very scanty. Two of such studies considered the question of effective utilization of the facilities given to backward students since independence. It is said that non-utilization of the facilities by backward students has been one of the factors responsible for non- realization of the objective of equality in education.

It is also contended that non-utilization is very closely

linked with a low degree of awareness about these facilities and also strong resistance from the non-backward communities to the special facilities made available to-backward class students. Based upon a sample study of 522 students and 179 teachers from colleges in Pune, Deshpande concludes that there is much to be desired in the means used to disseminate information about facilities available among backward- class students and their parents. In view of inadequacy of allowances made for these students there is a need for additional facilities and compensatory courses to ensure better and more effective utilization of educational facilities. Another study in the same field attempted to examine the extent to which education and other facilities were available to backward-class students in Jalna district in Maharashtra. This study also concluded that the type of facilities available were far from satisfactory. Though such statistical studies with reference to a particular location cannot be taken as the basis for drawing generalizations, the conclusion of the study regarding inadequacy of facilities can hardly be doubted.

Financing of Education

With increasing enrolments and the expanding scope of educational activities, coupled with decreasing resource availability for the educational sector (in view of competing claims from other sectors) the problem of finance has become increasingly formidable in all sectors of education. The problems are experienced at three levels. First, at the level of the educational sector as a whole; secondly, at the level of sub-sectors of education and thirdly, at the level of the individual educational institution. These financial pressures- sectoral, sub-sectoral and institutional-would each have its own externalities on students and parents so far as the education of the household is concerned. It also has implications for the quality of education currently provided and the capability of the sector to undertake innovative programmes.

Financial pressures, coupled with declining educational standards and the weakening capability of the educational sector to train and educate students according to certain requirements, have also given rise to a new class of institutions which are termed 'parallel educational institutions'. These trends emerged more and more clearly over the past decade or so. The general cost escalations have aggravated the problem of finance for education. In our federal framework, irritants in intergovernmental relations have created-additional dimensions to the problem. Studies in this field are therefore expected to consider new themes and issues. During the 1970s, most studies of educational finances related to examining the problems of individual educational institutions (such as those dealing with university finances sponsored by the ICSSR and UGC) and to the analysis of the prospects of individual sources of finance. From the studies that appeared during the 1980s, there seems to be a slight shift in focus, though the traditional themes have not been altogether abandoned by researchers.

Of the studies, abstracts of which were received for being reported in this survey, three were case studies of university finances, two dealt with the problem of educational finance for primary and secondary education. Two considered the basic question of the linkages between educational finance and the problem of social justice. Five studies considered the effectiveness of scholarships as an instrument for educational equality. Two examined the possibility of getting external funding for education and also the possibility of adopting an innovative approach in budgeting that, through savings within the educational sector, could provide a dependable source of educational finance.

As stated earlier, the studies in finances for higher education during the 1970s were largely case studies. On the same pattern, three more studies of higher education finances have come to our notice. A study of higher education finances in the newly created state of Manipur since 1949 clearly shows that the problems of educational finance which have been observed since 1949 in other parts of the country are also observed in the case of Manipur. There is an unplanned growth of institutions, imbalances in the course of expansion, improper budgeting systems, non-availability of the physical resources necessary for institutions of higher education, etc. While the expenditure on higher education in Manipur increased 727 times between 1949-50 and 1979-80, the UGC's contribution to the development of colleges was only marginal-only about nine per cent of the total expenditure of the colleges from 1960-61 through to 1974-75.

Administrative costs accounted for the bulk of university expenditure. It is intriguing that the increase in expenditure on libraries was minimal. By and large, the picture of higher education finances in Manipur presents a good idea of the crisis that the higher education sector as a whole is facing in India. The case studies of M.S. University of Baroda in Gujarat and Kumaun University in U.P. present the same bleak picture of higher educational finances at the institutional level. As the Baroda University study shows, normally there exists no correspondence of cost with fees in all the faculties and institutions in the country. The fees reflecting the price of education as paid by the students and parents are almost static and hence there is no correspondence at all between cost escalation and the price paid. The library is again a victim of financial crisis, allocations declining in view of the inelasticity of all sources of the income for the university. The grant-in- aid system for different universities was found to be more or less unresponsive to the financial crisis that the universities are facing, The principles of adequacy, efficiency, equity and elasticity which ought to be the bases for ensuring the financial soundness of a university do not seem to have received any pointed attention from the grant-in-aid system.

As a result, a university may have a skewed

development, with more resources going to certain faculties and to certain activities at the cost of other faculties and activities. In the case of Kumaun University, for instance, per student expenditure in the commerce and law faculties was found to be disproportionately low as compared to that in the case of the science faculty. The Nainital campus received favourable treatment at the cost of the campus at Almora. A study of finances of universities in Madhya Pradesh developed a comparative analysis of income, expenditure and unit cost of different universities in the state. The study shows that there is one significant effect of the existence of the government grant. Though the grants are far from adequate and progressive enough for the development of different types of universities in the state, they have nevertheless reduced them into extended wings of the department of education of the government. The Uchha Shiksha Anudan Ayog established by the state in 1973 has not made any change in the system of control of the government on the university finances and administration.

Most of the universities in MP are in the red, with large deficits in their budgets. The state and UGC grants for these universities could not change the picture for the better. It is noteworthy that, in spite of the Uchha Shiksha Anudan Ayog, the state UGC, the salary structure, library development, development of student services, etc., are not comparable for different universities in the state. The study identifies the major causes for the financial problems of the universities in terms of huge financial deficits, availability of UGC grants only for development and not for maintenance, the state government's inability to share the financial burdens of the universities, inadequate attention paid to improving efficiency and economy in university expenditure, unnecessary interference of the state in university financial management, and non-availability of reserve funds of endowments in the universities.

Problems of finance have been identified as the main hurdle in realizing the goal of universal elementary education for children below 14 years of age as directed by the Constitution. A study by Misra (1984) draws attention to the different dimensions of the problem of finance for primary education in India after independence. The study brings out the fact that there is very little scope for flexibility in the methodology of primary education adopted for achieving the targets set because of rigidity in allotting financial resources and also because of the fact that as much as 93 to 97 per cent of total expenditure on primary education is on salary and allowances of teachers. Hardly 3 to 7 per cent of resources are available for any deviation from the usual practice.

Adequate resource availability and a policy commitment to educational development seem to be the basic preconditions for the development and progress of primary education. Kerala, Tamil Nadu, U.P. and Maharashtra were found to be the states with best progress of primary education; Jummu & Kashmir, Bihar and Orissa present an example of very slow progress. What is true of higher education and primary education also seems to be true of secondary education. In fact, secondary education appears to be the weakest link in the educational system of the country, for elitist pressures ensure availability of finances for higher education and the constitutional directive ensures or at least announces the preparedness of the country to provide adequate resources to the development of primary education. No such commitment or pressure seems to be working effectively in the case of secondary education. A study by R.S. Yadav (1985), examining the priority accorded to secondary education vis-à-vis other sectors in the Five Year Plans in the context of Haryana, brings out some interesting facts relating to secondary education in India.

Haryana being one of the economically advanced states does not appear to reflect development in the country as a whole so far as secondary education is concerned. Though the state has been spending a small percentage for its revenue budget for education as a whole, as compared to other sectors, the expenditure on secondary education in the state was found to have been increasing much faster than the state's net domestic product. It is interesting to note that the districts of the state which were spending more per capita on education in general were also spending more on secondary education.

The state government was found to be providing increasingly larger assistance for recurring expenditures, such as teachers' and staff salaries. However, educational infrastructure, like school buildings and libraries, did not receive adequate support from the state grant. It is intriguing that, though expenditure on buildings from the nonrecurring budget increased, that on libraries in the secondary schools has been declining. It was also found that financial resources were allocated largely to meet the need for quantitative expansion and very little attention was paid to qualitative improvement. In the case of non- recurring activities like developing the infrastructure, private endowment seems to have taken the initiative to finance it. However, the grant-in-aid system based on the deficit principle has a built-in disincentive for mobilization of resources from the private sector for meeting recurring needs.

Financing of Education and Equity-Efficiency Goals

The problems of educational finance are not restricted to the question of mobilization of adequate financial resources. As indicated earlier, they include the matter of the efficient utilization of resources, their proper allocation so as to improve the institutional efficiency, and also to realize the objective of equality. The best system of educational finance is the one which enables the educational structure to mobilize adequate resources, which has in-built flexibility with regard to availability of resources as and when required, which allows unconstrained autonomy in allocation of resources, mobilized (subject to these allocations not having unduly unfavourable effects from the point of view of equity), and where there is also, by and large, self-reliance and the minimum of interference from outside agencies. Self-reliance is steadily enhanced by raising internal efficiency in the use of resources and by reducing educational wastage and stagnation. A number of studies conducted recently have these themes as their focus.

A comparative study of educational financing in Haryana and Kerala and also in UP and Kerala provides interesting insights on educational financing and the equity and equality. The studies conclude that free education will have a limited impact on equity and that a more effective compensatory finance measure is necessary for a break-through in inequity and inequality. Examining the pattern of educational financing in Kerala (with a higher level of equality in educational opportunities) and that in UP (with extreme inequalities), the NIEPA study points out that central assistance has also a role to play in achieving greater equality and that central assistance in the case of UP is far from satisfactory.. The study also draws attention to the importance of regionalization of financial policies of states in matters of allotting grants and funds to districts.

This district-specific approach, as opposed to the present methods of considering the state as a planning unit, actually needs to be further disaggregated so that the financial needs of the educational sector at the village and *panchayat* levels are also appropriately viewed. Though the overall policies relating to educational finance may have their implications for equity, the effects will at best be indirect. It is from this point of view that a target-oriented approach to solving problems of resource poverty in the field of education becomes extremely crucial. The community-oriented and individual-oriented approach is evident in the case of several subsidization schemes in education at different levels. There have been various schemes of providing scholarships to various socio- economically backward communities. A number of studies have been undertaken to evaluate the performance of these scheme.

The study by Rao and Mittal evaluating the government of India's scheme of scholarships in approve residential secondary schools reaches a categoric conclusion about the low level of effectiveness of such schemes because of various socioeconomic and institutional reasons and also laxity in implementation. Mostly, these scholarship schemes are introduced at the secondary and the higher educational levels. This seems to be one of the factors of their low level of effectiveness. Most of the socio-economically backward students may well have dropped out even at the primary stage owing to a number of socio-economic and financial reasons. This has been pointed in some of the studies. A series of studies of post-matric scholarships for SC and ST students undertaken by NIEPA has reached similar conclusions regarding the causes for the failure of such schemes. The studies highlighted the inadequacy of the scholarship amount, delays in the payment of the scholarship, administrative hindrances in the effective implementation of the scheme, etc.

It was also noticed that different welfare departments which managed the post-matric scholarships are not properly coordinated, resulting in laxity in the implementation of the scheme. Despite some of these difficulties, the post-matric scholarship scheme has proved to be quite useful for encouraging enrolment of SC and ST children in higher education. The usefulness of the scheme would increase significantly with interdepartmental co- ordination, proper monitoring, and compilation of exhaustive data about the awardees and a follow-up study of the awardees throughout their educational and post-educational career. If the internal resources of the country are inadequate for meeting both the efficiency goals and equity goals of the educational sector, dependence on an external source of finance becomes inevitable. However, external financing would have its implications for the prioritization of different schemes within the educational sector and it may also significantly influence the entire process of educational policy making.

The Padmanabhan-Tilak study shows that external aid was more available for higher education than for lower levels of education. It is intriguing that external aid was available in the past only to the elite sectors even in higher education itself. Even though the resource demands from the primary and secondary education are in actual practice overwhelming, the external aid has been found to be available largely for development of higher education and also for infrastructure and not so much for the development of manpower. The study indicates that the question of external financing of education needs to be thoroughly examined with scheme-wise analysis so that further insights about the intentions and the effects of external financing can be properly understood.

Generally, when there is a general resource crunch in the economy, its incidence is felt most in the educational sector. However, there is an improvement in the resource availability, the reverse attitude of making larger allocations to the educational sector does not seem to be working, and this is largely because the gains from the educational sector are intangible. Even within the educational sector, the real gain, improvement in the educational standards of the people, which is intangible, gets relegated to the background in preference to the tangible aspects of construction of school buildings, procurement of equipment, etc. Regar-ding the utilization of prevailing intrastructural facilities in educational institutions, the present position does not seem to be satisfactory. Library resources, school buildings, laboratory facilities, etc. are not fully and properly utilized in most cases.

It is here that clear proof of whether or not the supply of facilities and the demand for facilities created are in equilibrium lies. Even in the context of the educationally advanced state of Kerala, library services were found to be not fully utilized in the case of higher educational institutions, the students' record of borrowing books from the library was not satisfactory, though it was much better in the case of teachers. The pattern of expenditure and the efficiency-level of the school system are believed to be very closely related. In the case of schools of the Bangalore district, however, the expenditure-efficiency relationship was not clearly brought out. It is generally believed that highly paid staff is likely to be more efficient than low-paid staff, indicating that higher salary would lead to better organisational and personnel efficiency. Surprisingly, this belief also was not substantiated in the case of the Bangalore schools.

The efficiency-level of the secondary schools was found to be determined more by the non-physical variables than the physical ones. For the purpose of higher resource efficiency, institutional coordination and networking should be suggested as one of the useful measures as Manvikar (1984) has indicated. This particular conclusion seems to be valid in the case of schools in other states also, because a significant number of schools (55 per cent of them) had below optimum infrastructural facilities and inadequate sports and games facilities (35 per cent of them). In such a context, institutional networking seems to be an unavoidable measure. Zero-base budgeting to bring about economy in the face of a severe resource crunch has all the potentialities for adversely affecting the educational sector to a significant extent. This does not imply that resources are properly utilized in the educational sector and that zero-base budgeting has no relevance at all for the educational sector. In the case of higher educational institutions in particular, the concept of zero-base budgeting can prove quite effective in releasing unused resources for the purpose of financing of the educational sector. Some of these questions have been examined by Panchamukhi.

To what extent is resource-inefficiency in the educational sector due to the responses of the decision makers on the supply side, and to what extent is it due to the responses of the decision-makers on the demand side? The educational institutions are the decision makers on the supply-side. They are, by and large, responsible for allocating resources to different activities and schemes of the educational sector. Most often, these decisions are taken by the suppliers of education in anticipation of their proper utilization by the aspirants for education. However, resource-inefficiency also arises largely on account of the non-corresponding responses of the aspirants for education. Such responses may lead to wastage and stagnation at different levels.

A number of studies with a focus on wastage and stagnation at different levels of education have focused their attention on some of the crucial causes for these inefficiency-oriented aspects. The studies by Das (1979), Sharma (1982), and Sundar (1984) have examined some aspects of wastage in educational institutions. The conclusions of these studies are extremely revealing. Teacher- training does not seem to make a significant contribution towards reduction of wastage and stagnation so far as primary education is concerned. Only in the case of multiple-teacher schools was the training of teachers found not to have an impact.

The wastage at primary level in Rajasthan was found to be higher for girls than for boys, higher for SC students than for others and higher for ST students than for others. Even though the students do not drop out, leading to wastage, there may still be improper utilization of their school resources if there is absenteeism. Student absenteeism was found to be more prevalent in government schools than in aided schools. By and large, regular attendance of the students was about one-third of registration, which obviously was not satisfactory. The various deterrents applied by the schools to control absenteeism were not found to be effective to a significant extent in the context of Delhi schools, as revealed in Sundar.

More about Internal and External Efficiency

The question of educational finance in particular and resources for the purpose of education in general, crucially depends upon how the existing physical and financial resources are utilized in the educational sector. The question of utilization of the resources in the sector in relation to its output is concerned with what is generally known as the internal efficiency of the educational sector. In this context, the concept of unit cost comes in very handy as a too] of analysis of internal efficiency. The question of internal efficiency has long been considered by researchers in the context of wastage and stagnation in education. While wastage refers to student dropout before the course is completed and stagnation to continuation of the students beyond the stipulated course period, the question of internal efficiency has the wider connotation of utilization of physical and financial resources within the educational sector.

The problems of wastage and stagnation thus highlight only one of the crucial dimensions of inefficiency in the system. A number of research studies have been conducted with a focus on such problems of internal efficiency of the educational sector at its different stages. Obviously, such studies on internal efficiency call for a micro approach. This is because a detailed factual profile of the resources used in each educational institution needs to be developed before any general statement about the internal efficiency of the entire educational sector can be made. Thus, the studies in this particular field have concentrated on region-specific and stage- specific approaches. The question of unit cost in the context of different methods of education-formal, informal and non formal-should also be interesting. Some studies in this field have considered this question also and these should ultimately help to develop insights about the cost- effectiveness of the educational sector.

Studies by Kumaran (1982) and Chalam (1981) examine the question of internal efficiency of higher education. Kumaran's study, for example, analyses the revenue and cost of education' in Annamalai University during 1947-48 to 1978-79. Based upon an analysis of the university budget and employing simple statistical tools of regression analysis, the study tries to relate unit cost with age, enrolments, salary of the teaching staff, in ratio of the non-teacher cost to total cost. Interestingly the study notices that the administrative cost and miscellaneous cost of university education have fallen during the above mentioned period while the academic cost has increased. The unit costs in crucial faculties of humanities, agriculture, sciences, particularly marine biology, were found to be very high as compared to the unit cost for faculties of education, linguistics and languages. This is in line with the conclusions of other studies conducted in the context of other universities.

The study by Chalam in the context of higher education in Andhra Pradesh, using data for the period 1955-76, concluded that the expenditure on scholarships, buildings, etc. accounts for 42 per cent of the variation in indirect expenditure. The study also considered the question of external efficiency of higher education in the context of Andhra Pradesh. It revealed that rates of return for higher education had declined during 1959-60 to 1975-76 while those for primary and secondary education were found to be increasing. This is once again in line with the conclusion reached in some of the other studies. Two studies were reported in relation to the internal efficiency of secondary school education in a recent period. The study by Manvikar (1983) tried to compare the expenditure pattern of different types of secondary schools in Bangalore district, both rural and urban, schools with a view to finding out the relationship of factors like strength, age of the school, teacher's age, qualification and experience, on the one hand, with the expenditure and school efficiency, on the other.

As could be expected, the secondary schools in urban areas were found to be more efficient than those in the rural areas. Though the author has tried to study the statistical relationship of the variables mentioned above, it should be noted that the expenditure variables explain only 21 to 29 per cent of variation in the total efficiency of the secondary schools. This seems to have a significant policy implication in the sense that, for the purpose of internal efficiency in secondary schools, though the amount spent on education may be necessary, it is not a sufficient condition for ensuring internal efficiency. Internal efficiency is related more closely with variables other than the expenditure variables. This obviously means that for better utilization of resources, the pre- condition is not, largely, the availability of resources or not necessarily a different pattern of expenditure. The crucial determinant seems to be better management and a higher level of commitment of the staff to the functional goals stipulated for them.

Another study on some aspects of internal efficiency having interesting policy implications is the one by Kumar (1968) done for the 'backward' state of Rajasthan. The study is based upon the data collected from 71 schools. It found that the cost per pupil was in direct proportion to the teacher-pupil ratio. Most of the schools which had high unit costs, and hence were uneconomical, were located in sparsely populated habitations, indicating that schools should be located in densely populated habitations if costs alone are considered. The feeder population which supplies clientele for secondary schools thus becomes a crucial determinant of the internal efficiency. When the country is aiming at spreading educational facilities from one end to the other, irrespective of habitations, where these facilities have to be provided, this conclusion is quite significant for developing an understanding of the quantum of resources required for the purpose.

It should also be mentioned that this study related to a distant past so far as the numbers are concerned. The basic conclusions of the study, however, seem to be still valid. Two more studies on unit cost of primary education were brought to our notice. Dutt's study considered the question of unit cost at the primary educational stage in Haryana. It was based on data drawn from only three primary schools within a radius

of 8 km. It is more in the nature of a case study rather than a study providing a basis for generalization. The study by Dandavate, on the other hand, collected data on as many as 201 primary schools in Greater Bombay during the period 1962-80. Its main objectives were to examine whether the unit cost (better still, expenditure per pupil) has any relation with the period of establishment of the school. The study concluded that the size of the school, teachers' salaries per pupil and maintenance expenditure acted as major determinants of primary-school cost. There were three studies on the analysis of cost of different methods of teaching and education.

It was found that economies of large-scale operate in the case of teaching aids as well (Singh). 'High cost' of AV media was no longer costly when its coverage was extended to all schools of the country and at all stages of school education. Similarly, conventional teaching aids like charts were no longer 'low cost' when extended to all schools. The study examined a number of factors responsible for this finding which has significant implications for educational television. Whether or not adoption of educational television as a teaching aid should be based upon the cost consideration is an important question. When the formal system is proving to be increasingly inadequate to provide facilities for growing numbers of aspirants for education at different stages, it becomes imperative to search for alternative structures within the educational system. Externalization of education is one such method adopted as an alternative to the present procedures and processes in the formal educational system. Correspondence education as an alternative strategy has been introduced in India largely at the higher educational levels. The two studies which were brought to our notice consider the costing, financing and other economic factors of correspondence education.

The study by Pandey attempts to examine the effectiveness of correspondence education in Indian universities, making use of data from seven universities, viz., Meerut, Delhi, Punjabi, Bombay, Sri Venkateshwara, and Madurai

Kamraj universities. Interestingly, correspondence education has proved to be highly self-supporting. On the whole, correspondence education was also found to be cost-effective, for the average cost per student in the case of correspondence education was found to be lower than that for regular courses. Interestingly, the academic performance of correspondence education was found to be better than that of private education. The attitudes of students and teachers towards correspondence education were found to be quite favourable. Interestingly, correspondence education was not favoured by women. Also, unemployed students were not favourable disposed towards this method of education. This, indeed, is a surprising conclusion. Female students, for socio-cultural reasons, have the problem of finding time to devote to education.

Similarly, unemployed students, who might be expected to prefer correspondence education do not favour it because they have to spend long hours in search of jobs. The conclusions of this study appear to be somewhat biased in favour of the correspondence education conducted by Meerut University. The question of the external efficiency of allocation of resources for education has received the attention of a large number of researchers since 1960s when a number of studies followed the publication of the contributions of T. W. Schultz. Two such studies were brought to our notice. By and large, a number of socioeconomic variables, other than education, were found to be the major explanatory factors so far as the earning advantages of an educated people are concerned. Rates of return for higher education in the context of Karnataka (Madi) and Orissa (Debi) were found to be fairly high with the rates being higher for professional education than for general education. Though one might like to improve upon the general methodology of calculating the rate of return on education, the general conclusions that these studies on external efficiency of higher education have reached seem to be replete with policy implications.

The general assumption that the researchers in this field make, that education is an important determinant of earning-capacity needs to be reconsidered in the context of the conclusions in such studies which have highlighted the role of a number of socioeconomic factors other than education explaining variations in earnings. There is the heroic question, viz.: to what extent can earnings be considered an index of the value of education? It would be useful if, as a guide to policy making in education, the heroic assumptions made in such research studies were reconsidered.

Planning and Management Questions

The consideration of education-economy-society interlinkages, and issues of internal efficiency and finance, suggests that proper planning and management of education, on the one hand, and the economy and society, on the other, may enable us to realize more fully the potential of education as an agent of social change. In what follows, we briefly consider the question of management and planning of education. The management and planning of the economy and the society are outside the scope of this review. Questions of planning and management can be viewed from micro and macro points of view. While micro perspectives about the functioning of individual educational institutions provide insights into various economic aspects of educational development, the planning of education in an integrated fashion, so as to be consistent with every aspect of socioeconomic development of the country, requires a macro perspective.

For obvious reasons, this aggregative or macro perspective should be developed on the basis of micro perspectives themselves. Educational planning, which is one of the crucial aspects of the economics of education, would thus derive its strength from the micro-economic and macro-economic methodologies. In this background, it becomes extremely useful to develop an analysis of the determinants of supply of and demand for education. What are the socioeconomic determinants of educational demand? Can these demands be properly taken account of in the overall socioeconomic planning of the country? What are the implications of this demand for the objectives if inter-gender, inter-regional and inter-community equity and equality? Thus educational demand is not a homogenous phenomenon. Its different connotations depend upon the type of education, the regions where it is required, the cost of meeting the demand, etc. Therefore, educational demand needs to be further analysed, taking into account all these aspects.

While the demand for education comes under the significant influence of past socioeconomic developments in the country, in the subsequent period, it may itself have its influences on the nature of socioeconomic development. From this point of view, the influence of educational demand on the dimensions of development also becomes crucial. Educational planning is not a mechanical exercise of putting screws in the holes and tightening them. This is because the human element is involved in the entire process of educational planning. Attitudes and aptitudes of aspirants for education, capacities and competencies of educated individuals, interests and involvement of educated employees, amount of satisfaction derived from the jobs which are manned by educated individuals, etc., are some of the basic variables which need to be considered in the exercise of educational planning. To what extent can policy variables like wages and salaries, restrictions and control, transfers and placements, influence the basic variables is another dimension which deserves attention of analysts and policy makers. In recent years, researchers in the field of education in general and economists of education in particular have been taking interest in some of these questions.

We have already reviewed above, under the heading, 'Interdependencies between Economy and Education, some of the studies which have a bearing on only some of these aspects. The general impression one gets from a review of research work in this field is that educational planning is not seriously attempted in India. Haphazardness in educational expansion, indifference to the question of course-content, inadequate resource availability, etc, illustrate this. For obvious reasons, it may also be difficult to undertake rigorous planning of education in India. Resource allocation exercises in relation to education (which are generally residuary in nature) cannot in themselves be considered as planning without an effective monitoring system coupled with a reward/punishment mechanism. Possibly, for the same reason, research studies in this field do not seem to have made an impact. Even with regard to institutional planning and management, the research efforts are only few in numbers, though this area provides much scope for innovative approaches.

Management of the institutions in particular, and the educational sector in general, have increasingly become a specialized job, with the application of modern techniques of management to the various decision making situations. Management techniques in the educational sector have some unique features which are not shared by economic organizations such as companies and the firms. In the case of the educational sector, the problem is largely one of human resource management in the face of limited physical capital resources. Education is highly human-capital-intensive activity. Though ideas about management techniques developed in the context of educational institutions abroad cannot be imported into, it is still useful to examine the applicability of some of these ideas to Third World countries where serious attempts at restructuring educational systems are being made. A comparative analysis of university administration in India and the USA or other developed countries could bring out possibilities of using some of these innovations in India.

A micro approach to the administration of educational institutions at different levels should provide further insights into the crucial variables in educational management. Majumdar (1979) feels that some of the oldest universities in India have developed internal contradictions and hence their future is not very bright. This was the particularly painful conclusion drawn in the context of Calcutta University. A study in the context of a regional university also does not have very encouraging observations to make about university administration. In most of these universities there is no participatory management. This has resulted in low levels of efficiency. While this is the situation in the universities, the situation of the apex body charged with university development in India, the UGC is no less discouraging. A study of the organization and management of the UGC brings out some of the difficulties in the case of its functioning. The absence of a networking of the various apex institutions at higher education level such as the UGC, ICSSR, ICHR, ICPR, NIEPA, CSIR, and CAPART, is largely responsible for duplication of effort and also internal contradictions in the educational sector.

Studies on organizational aspects of schools are extremely important because, while at the higher educational levels there are serious attempts to employ some professional management approaches, there seems to be an attitude of indifference so far as the management of schools is concerned. The role of the head of the school, the organizational climate in the school, management behaviour, etc. should be some of the crucial variables for determining the effectiveness of the school as an institution. On the whole, the issues in planning and management of education do not seem to have found much favour with researchers in the field of economies of education.

Education on Women's roles in the society

The expectations held by a society define the roles of its members. While many factors influence the parts individuals play in their cultures and communities, education has always been the crucial element in the establishment of social roles. Education was the catalyst which changed women's roles in society from what they were in the late 1800s to what they are now. In the latter years of the nineteenth century, women's roles in American society underwent gradual but definite growth, spurred on by a rapidly changing society. As the nation recovered from its Civil War and slavery faded away, a massive transformation of industrialization took place, and revolutionary scientific ideas, such as those presented in Charles Darwin's Origin of Species, and by Sigmund Freud, caused people to question and to rethink fundamental aspects of their lives, religion, and beliefs. Social reforms in the fields of health, labor, and education developed as the publication of books and periodicals revealed to the public the problems therein. At the turn of the century, women's roles were severely limited by society's concepts of male supremacy and female inferiority. Women were perceived as weak, a notion upheld by the "prevalence of invalidism among nineteenth century women".

Fashions of the times didn't help either. Voluminous, billowing skirts hampered movement, and corsets caused dizzy spells and fainting. A woman's priority in young adulthood was to find a husband, and after doing so, raise a family and run a well-kept household. Women were not expected to harbor aspirations other than "... the acquisition of a husband, a family, and a home...." (Cowen, Ruth Schwartz) The male-dominated social order dictated that women be meek and obedient "domestic creatures," for the most part confined to housewifery and raising of children, deferential to men, and financially dependent on the husband. These very definite ideas about a woman's part in the overall scheme of things were responsible for the restricted part women played in their world. "... [A]n exclusively nineteenth century phenomenon among women... developed as a result of the concept of the 'woman's sphere,' whereby the woman's role in life was strictly limited to home and family. 'Sorority' as a social phenomenon seems to have passed away in the twentieth century as women's opportunities and roles expanded".

As slaves were forbidden to learn to read, women were likewise kept in their place through lack of substantial and purposeful formal instruction. In the late 1800s, women began to go to college to pursue "learning for its own sake, detached from professional motives". (Solomon, Barbara) Higher education was not intended as job preparation. Women were expected to marry and not pursue a career, thus having no practical use for their educations aside from what they learned in home economics courses. In the south, token education, 'finishing school,' was commonly regarded as proper for young women as "femininity [was] more valuable than scholarship". Women's uncertain place in the development of liberal arts curriculum was yet another factor contributing to lesser scholarship. Female students were not always taken seriously, and were frequently discriminated against, requested to withdraw from certain courses so that more men might enroll. Female faculties at Colleges were small and social constraints abounded, particularly in the Southern region of the country where the "cult of womanhood" was almost religiously upheld.

Smoking, drinking, and dancing were prohibited, and chaperones were present at most functions. There was also the "unmarried academic woman" phenomenon where women were either married or educated; Sweet Briar's first four presidents are an example. In light of the sexism present at institutions of higher learning, schools for women were started. They served different purposes, some merely finishing schools. Other colleges, like Sweet Briar, were founded on "the highest college standards" with demanding entrance requirements. The schools' aim of serving as a foundation from which women could move into professional work enabled them to leave college with "power and joy, and with courage to meet life's great adventure". (McVea) Women were urged to think about their role in the world, a world greater than just the confines of home. "The greatest advancements for women in the closing decades of the nineteenth century were in education".

Oberlin College began admitting women in 1837, becoming the first coeducational college, and Mt. Holyoke became the first women's college that same year. Bryn Mawr, Smith, Vassar, and Wellesley were all founded between 1861 and 1885. Many schools were founded with a purpose of "physical, moral, religious training, education and sound learning... [as befitted] useful members of society". Higher education for women became normal in the late 19th and early 20th centuries but often a college educated woman would retire to the home with a family and not pursue a career, especially in the South, where education was a social grace and not a practical necessity for Southern women. Many women, however, responded to their education by being eager to pursue a career. They were fascinated by the world opened up to them through education, new concepts such as Darwinism, and "intellectual experimenting". (Solomon)

Education did not guarantee pursuit of an occupation. Society's expectation that women care for home and family left little room for personal growth and professional development. Women who sought jobs or professional work were still rare. "...[W]omen who worked outside their homes did so only under duress or because they were 'odd'...". (Cowen) As things became more urbanized, the need for workers grew and thus the presence of women was required. But women were working in factories, as teachers, or in other womanly jobs only. "[A] woman's usefulness was not equated with professionalism". (Solomon) Women studied courses useful in their personal life such as home economics. There was neither focus on practical courses that would lead them to jobs nor any definite purpose of developing 'critical minds.'

Mary Boykin Chesnut was an educated woman but

despite this, she, like so many other women of the 1800s, was relegated to the home. Although she had had a thorough education which included extensive traveling and study of languages, literature, and history, her duties consisted solely of entertaining friends and her husband's colleagues. Childless and needing a challenge, she stood out as an exception to the rule, a woman who transcended the expectations of her society. She played an active though unofficial role in the day's political scene, and pursued personal interests by translating foreign works, teaching slaves to read, and writing. Foremost among her literary works is her Civil War journal, valued for her opinions and insights as well as historical value. But once women began receiving higher education, there was no going back. Education changed women's role in society dramatically. Occupations were limited but women began to seep into the male-dominated world.

After experiencing higher learning, aspirations changed and gradually society's expectations had to change as well. Education bred confidence and empowerment. With empowerment came the realization that women should not be considered lesser citizens than men and therefore should have the same rights enjoyed by men. Educated women were more apt to challenge men's role as the dominant figure and the flawed rationale for the denial of suffrage. Before this time, women were uneducated. How then were they capable of being voting citizens? Why should they be property owners? Without education nothing was expected of women. A narrowness of education resulted in narrowness of experience, outlook, and life. Once they began to go to college they began to challenge society's expectations as well as broaden their personal experiences.

Women became activists pushing for rights and eventually were successful. The gain of suffrage set the precedent for other future gains. "While acquisition of the vote for women may have signaled the end of the women's movement for millions of Americans, it represented a long-awaited opportunity to pursue previously slighted goals for a myriad of women activists". (Patterson) When women learned about social ills and had use of the vote, they fought for reform in factories and treatment of the insane, and worked against prostitution. Callie Khouri's 1994 Sweet Briar College commencement speech is significant not only in the messages it contains but in the circumstance of its delivery. Presented to young women about to begin a new adventure in life, many of them expecting to attend graduate school and embark upon professional careers, Khouri's speech represents a great deal of change from Mary Chesnut's time period and the mindset of late nineteenth century society. The importance of self-sufficiency and self-esteem is emphasized. She urges women to have aspirations and encourages late marriage, a radical idea by 19th century standards.

In Mary Chesnut's era, no one was delivering commencement speeches about self-sufficiency to women; indeed, young women had just begun to attend college as a regular matter of course. What would Mary Chesnut have said to a graduating class of young women? Women of the previous century had no one to urge personal independence and goals. Khouri's advice to young women is different from advice Chesnut might have given a young woman of her era; Khouri urges self-sufficiency, whereas to Chesnut that was a somewhat foreign concept. Sexism was not yet identified as a social wrong. For women of the late nineteenth century, higher education was an accepted innovation but not a necessity for daily living and for the future. Today, women study subjects of personal interest, pursuing degrees that match their talents, interests, and aspirations. Formal education beyond a four-year college is likewise common as women go on to earn their Master's degree and PhD.

The goals of education today are very different from the purpose of women's education of yesteryear. Going to college was an accepted part of life for both generations, but with different rationales and post-graduate aspirations. In a rapidly changing and growing world, higher education is not a nicety but a necessity to survive. Self-sufficiency is critical. As the number of educated women grows and as the level of education increases, the expectations become greater but at the same time more liberating.

Frequently, nineteenth century expectations of women were restrictive and while today's standards may call for a more difficult "juggling act" of roles of wife, mother, and career person, the female experience is much broader overall. The family is an interest not the interest. Women today still face discrimination in the form of income disparity, the "glass ceiling," and the notion of female professionalism as being unwomanly, but education is now a means of self-sufficiency and an opportunity to be seized with purpose. "When going to college became an accepted part of her life, a woman was empowered with [her] education and the self-confidence it engendered". (Patterson) The major catalyst of the women's movements was education, changing the role of women in society from a passive one to an active, vital force.

7

The Connection between Philosophy and Education

Three Conceptions of Philosophy

We should never be ashamed to approve truth or acquire it, no matter what its source might be, even if it might have come from foreign peoples and alien nations far removed from us. To him who seeks the truth, no other object is higher in value. As a matter of daily practice, educators formulate goals, discuss values, and set priorities. Anyone who gets involved in dealing with goals, values and priorities soon realizes that in a modern society such as ours there are many competing choices. Some are incompatible with others. Hard decisions have to be made. Here, for example, are some everyday dilemmas that educators confront: How do we treat a specific student's needs, yet deal fairly with a class of students as a whole? When, if ever, should we bend the rules? Should a teacher ever emphasize good behaviour over subject skills?

It is in trying to resolve such questions that the discussion becomes philosophical, even though it may not be recognized as such. And it is philosophy that can help us make better choices among goals, values and priorities. But what exactly is this "philosophy?" And how does it help? In daily use the term, "philosophy," is not clear-cut. TV programs offer us the personal philosophies of various religious or political leaders. Other people talk about their philosophy in choosing a kindergarten or a college. Some people believe a difference in philosophy distinguishes between Roman Catholic and public schooling practices. Still others talk about Progressive or Back-to-Basics philosophy.

We see then, that the word "philosophy" is vague, yet, asking someone for her philosophy on something is different from asking her how she feels about it. "How do you feel about divorce?" we ask. "I don't like the idea," comes the reply; "but my philosophy on divorce is that you have to consider whether it might not be better to give up rather than stay in a bad relationship." What, then, is philosophy? To shortcut discussion we can borrow distinctions made by philosopher John Passmore and separate out three common conceptions of philosophy: philosophy as wisdoms; philosophy as ideology; and philosophy as critical inquiry. These distinctions help us sort out different traditions within what is called philosophy by the man-on-the-street (although only critical philosophy is understood to be philosophy in Passmore's own academic tradition).

Although three conceptions of philosophy can be distinguished, there are many common elements shared by them. A person may derive an ideology from wisdom, and then subject it to critical philosophy. A truth discovered through critical philosophy may come to be uncritically venerated, as, for example, was the insight in America that education should center on the child. The three conceptions of philosophy, in practice, are found in a mix in the day-to-day practice of the schools. Almost every major philosopher in the critical tradition — famed philosophers like Socrates, Aristotle, Aquinas, Locke, Kant and others— have had much to say in the way of wisdoms about education and much in the way of ideology to say about how we should go about schooling.

Our primary interest in this essay is in philosophy as critical inquiry. Wisdoms and ideologies are usually inculcated into us in a way which gives us little opportunity for reflection and criticism: we are taught them as absolute truths as children. But critical philosophy, as we will see, is characterized by an attitude of critical reflection and a practice of analysis that inculcators of wisdoms and ideologies avoid. However, wisdoms, ideologies and critical inquiry are intimately and importantly related, especially in educational practice. Let's examine more closely the difference between these three ideas of philosophy and how each relates to educational practice.

Philosophy as Wisdoms

Philosophy, however one conceives it, is expected to be more than a passing feeling or a knee-jerk opinion. It's supposed to be a thoughtful response to a question or situation. The response may not be very extensively thought out, but it's got some element of reflection in it. Philosophy as wisdom incorporates, at the very least, this notion of reflection, of thoughtful response. This conception of philosophy as wisdoms includes two related ideas: personal reflections on broad questions, and prophetic wisdoms. Such philosophy is generally seen as arising out of personal experience or as having sacred origins. For these reasons we tend not to challenge them with a critical question such as, "How do you know that?"

For example, you have probably read or have heard people say things like

a. You can't expect too much from life without being disappointed sometimes; or
b. Live and let live, that's what I say;
c. Don't smile until Christmas (common advice to new teachers).

Such statements are thought to be philosophical. They are general, they are often offered as reasons for acting, and they have a certain air of thoughtfulness about them. We generally concede people the right to these sorts of reflective opinions and do not press them for further justification. Then there are the statements or writings of prophetic individuals many of us have been taught to consider both wise and worthy of veneration:

a. Do not covet the favors by which Allah has exalted some of you above others. (Koran, Women 4:30)
b. Thou shalt not bear false witness against thy neighbor. (Exodus, 20:16)
c. Train up a child in the way he should go: and when he is old, he will not depart from it. (Proverbs, 22:6)

Such wisdoms form the core of religious movements and are treated as sacred scripture. It is important to notice that when people offer philosophy in the form of sacred writings they do not welcome challenge. Indeed, a questioning or sceptical attitude is often thought to be rude or even blasphemous. Similarly, in education we frequently encounter some statements so deeply embedded in schooling culture that they are treated as religious fundamentals. For example:

a Every person should be educated to his or her fullest potential.
b. Always treat a child so as to bolster his or her self-esteem.
c. Practice makes perfect.

Philosophy as Ideology

Philosophy can also be thought of as ideology. An ideology is, by comparison with wisdoms, a more highly organized body of opinion. It usually serves programs of action and organizational needs. Philosophy as ideology is what we normally find in schools. For licensing purposes, state departments of education require schools, public and private, to have available a document that states the school's "philosophy" of education. Significantly, such school philosophies can be acquired pre-packaged. Educational accrediting agencies publish books of them that school planners and directors can use to choose among different philosophies of education like so many items on a menu. Here is an example of such an educational ideology:

The social development of elementary school student's proceeds as the child becomes aware of the various authority structures that operate throughout the school, the community, the region, and the nation. We believe the school must help the child establish a perspective on the responsibilities and opportunities inherent in the multitude of authority systems in a democratic social order. The point of ideology is to provide extensive suggestion as to how to structure and control an organization. This may be subject to debate. Although the example above mentions a" democratic social order," given its emphasis on authority, one could imagine that with this ideology, a school run like a miniature police-state could be rationalized.

In developing an ideology, the wisdoms of individuals, prophetic or otherwise, is called on to justify policies and day-to-day procedures. But did Moses, Jesus or Mohammed ever talk or write about hall passes, or detentions? No. What philosophy as ideology requires is an imagination that stretches the original intents and statements into broader or novel applications. Sometimes this imagination goes far beyond any reasonable interpretation. Indeed, deeply pious people may complain that the ideology of a church organization violates the essential spirit of the prophetic teachings, as when they complain that teachers in their schools fail exercise forgiveness as often as they should. A key point here is that organizational demands often substantially change the spirit of the original philosophy. Deep moral concerns may be lost in service of expediency.

Philosophy as Critical Inquiry

The American Philosophical Association, which represents professional academic philosophers in the critical tradition, characterizes the activities of philosophy this way:

Properly pursued, philosophy enhances analytical,

critical and interpretive capacities that are applicable to any subject-matter, and in any human context. It cultivates the capacities and appetite for self-expression and reflection, for exchange and debate of ideas, for life-long learning, and for dealing with problems for which there are no easy answers.

The distinguishing characteristic of philosophy as critical inquiry is its focus on careful questioning and systematic appraisal, with no special respect given to the sources of the opinions examined. It doesn't matter who said or wrote what. Nor does it matter what effect critical inquiry might have on an organization. The point of the activity is not to honor individuals or to bolster organizations, but to try to get to the truth.

Most importantly, in philosophy as critical inquiry, any statement purporting to be truth is challengeable. But what are the rules for making such a challenge more than just an expression of dislike? What rules there are have been developed through millennia in a literature tracing back to Plato and earlier. We will look more closely at these rules for challenge and investigation later.

Assumptions of the Tradition of Critical Inquiry

Early on in critical philosophy, Greek philosophers distinguished between what they saw as "received opinion" and "truth." This distinction mirrors the difference between what we are calling wisdoms — and their derived ideologies — on the one hand, and critical inquiry on the other. Received opinion might be true, but it was the task — those ancient philosophers believed — not of traditional or religious authorities but of critical analysis to determine if it was so. There is a potential here for significant conflict. It is important that a central story in the history of philosophy is that of Socrates. He was condemned to death by the Athenian Court for "impiety" and "corrupting youth" by teaching them critical inquiry.

To emphasize an important point, however, critical

inquiry is not confined to the irreligious. The tools of critical inquiry have long been recognized as useful by religiously committed philosophers in their struggle with the wisdoms of competing religious groups. There are recognized critical philosophers in many major religions. Islamic, Jewish and Christian philosophers have practiced in the tradition of critical inquiry. Philosophy as critical inquiry treats knowledge as tentative. For practical purposes we might accept something as true, yet later change our mind if the evidence warrants. Notice how different this is from the conceptions of philosophy as wisdoms or ideologies. Wisdoms and ideologies present what they offer as absolutes. Those who offer us such absolutes insist at some point that inquiry must stop, questioning is no longer allowed.

Critical inquiry, by contrast, will always - in theory, at least- allow questioning to proceed. For critical inquiry it is not acceptable to say, "This is so because I (or my prophet) say it is." Something different is required. These are reasonableness and evidence. What this specifically means, we will see later. To reiterate, just because something is commonly believed to be true, is not considered in critical philosophy to be an adequate reason for accepting it. Since it is method, not personal authority that establishes truth, critical philosophy does not encourage us to become followers, or true believers. Rather, each person is required to think for him or herself, following certain procedures which do not prejudice the outcome. Educators are well-served by learning these procedures, especially in a pluralistic society like ours where so many wisdoms and ideologies compete.

We live in a society where wisdoms and ideologies compete. Educators must be able to fairly select among them in a way which they understand to enhance their practice. Such a selection among competing wisdoms should be as reasonable and as unbiased as possible. Critical philosophy has at its disposal a wide variety of tools for analyzing and appraising educational debates. Educational disputes in our society tend to be particularly ideological. Practitioners need tools which are neutral to these disputes in order to deal with day-to-day problems in schools. Here, for example, is a list of the kinds of questions educators confront on a day-to-day basis, and, in effect, decide upon, whether thoughtfully or not:

1. Should a talkative student be silenced for the sake of the class?
2. Should student infractions of the rules ever be overlooked?
3. Should grading be based purely on achievement or should effort be factored in?

   These first three questions bring up the issue as to how the needs of individuals should be balanced against the needs of managing a group. Philosophy as ideology provides answers here; but there are competing ideologies. Philosophy as critical inquiry enables a reasoned choice. There are many other questions of similar importance that raise other philosophical issues. Consider these, for example:
4. Should students be taught to tolerate those things their parents believe are immoral?

   This question comes up, for example, when sexual preference or practice is a curriculum issue.
5. Should a teacher always follow administrative policy?

This may be an issue of how to handle a conflict between personal morality and school rules. The many wisdoms and ideologies of our pluralistic society offer competing, even contradictory answers to such questions. For question 5, for example, one ideology might state that a teacher's primary duty is to the school and the policies that govern it; therefore, the teacher should always follow policy. Another ideology might hold that the needs of the child come first in any educational organisation; therefore, there will be occasions when policies have to be ignored. Who is to say which of these two ideologies is better and why? Critical inquiry gives us the tools to answer this question.

Towards a Pragmatic Liberal Education

"Pragmatism is pouring over and through the academic dikes that long kept it outside the liberal arts...a broad consensus is therefore emerging around a view of liberal education that may be termed 'pragmatic'!"

The proposition that pragmatism is now becoming the legitimating theory of American liberal education suggests that close attention to where the educational enterprise is headed is not only warranted but might be, in fact, a transformative act. To this end, Rollins College president Rita Bornstein and Robert Orrill, executive director of Academic Affairs for the College Board, decided to convene a conference of college presidents, faculty and administrators to discuss the future of American liberal education.

An invitational colloquy, "Towards a Pragmatic Liberal Education: the Curriculum of the 21st Century" will include papers presented by experts in a number of fields and several moderated sessions. In addition, there will be small "teams" from approximately 35 colleges and universities. In the majority of cases, these "teams" will include the institution's president. Finally, a number of educators and organizational leaders have been invited because they have a particular interest in the evolution of liberal education. Charles Eliot, (president of Harvard during the late nineteenth century), made a break with the classical tradition, and John Dewey took this break as a given in his own thinking about the further reform of American liberal education.

Furthermore, it is this same break that Robert Hutchins sought to reverse and undo in a debate with Dewey that reverberated in the educational community throughout the first half of the 20th century. In addition to these considerations, Eliot wrote that the meaning of liberal education has sometimes in its history "quietly undergone many serious modifications" and that, at other times, conditions have changed so forcefully that its meaning had "to be fundamentally and openly changed." The heart of the matter for those attending the Rollins colloquy in February 1997 is perhaps whether it is one of these latter moments that we are entering at the close of the 20th century.

Pragmatism

Bruce Kimball identified six points of pragmatism in The Condition of American Liberal Education. They are:

1. that belief and meaning, even truth itself, are fallible and revisable;
2. that an experimental method of inquiry obtains in all science and reflective thought;
3. that belief, meaning, and truth depend on the context and the inter-subjective judgment of the community in which they are formed;
4. that experience is the dynamic interaction of organism and environment, resulting in a close interrelationship between thought and action;
5. that the purpose of resolving doubts or solving problems is intrinsic to all thought and inquiry; and
6. that all inquiry and thought are evaluative, and judgments about fact are no different from judgments about value.

"We believe that pragmatism, a uniquely American philosophy, has much to offer as Americans question the value of a liberal education and expect us to prepare students not only for personal development but for leadership in the community and the workplace," said Rita Bornstein. "The disuniting pressures of ethnocentrism, fundamentalism, and incivility are straining our ability to sustain a viable democratic nation. New workplaces and careers are requiring new skills, knowledge, and experiences. The pragmatist nexus between theory and practice, academic and applied learning, fact and value can help us reconceived liberal education for the twenty-first century," she explained.

Socialization and education in post-modern times

Education seems doomed to be a field plagued with paradoxes and contradictions. On the one hand, the conviction that education is important and school resources must be improved is, fortunately, on the rise. On the other hand, bewilderment and discontent grow before the undeniable failure of teaching institutions on too many occasions. It has become increasingly evident that there are more and more things that should be taught, but also that ever more students are unable to learn them or even comprehend the interest that their studies hold. While general, compulsory education should be the great equalizer of the social opportunities for young people, it instead reinforces inequalities; acting as a discriminatory filter.

One of the most significant problems-that of integration-finds in the school its most sensitive arenas. The general crisis occurring in education at the present is set within the framework of a greater crisis of values. This current crisis of values is characterized by the creation of a type of human being that-as Ortega would say-no longer knows what to hold to, but rather than anguishing over his dilemma or becoming distressed, accepts it as a natural fact. The question is not a rhetorical one, we are living at a time when two visions of the world overlap. One is that of the positive, optimistic neo-liberal economists for whom everything is going extraordinarily well. The existing problems are merely minor difficulties that will not take long to overcome. On the other hand, some authors and political observers (Alain Minc, Bordieu, Touraine) caution that we have never lived in such an uncertain world, a world which is on the verge of collapse, a collapse that would be absolute in such an interrelated world as ours.

As a social institution, the school is a place where groups of individuals from wide-ranging and different social circles come together. The dominant social culture as well as the economic and political context to which the school belongs, impregnates the human exchanges that occur within it. Thus, the contradictions that we find in the different demands of that social culture characterize the human exchanges within the school, as well. In other words, when discussing schools, we cannot place blame only on the teachers for the problems that arise. On Tuesday February 8 of this year, an article appeared in the ABC newspaper which presented an alarming statistic: 40% of British teachers and approximately the same percentage of French and German teachers (statistics were not provided for the Spanish) thought that the school was no longer a safe place. In the U.S. the statistics are even more alarming.

While the "national educational objectives" undertaken by the White House in 1991 foresaw that by the year 2000 "all American schools would be free of drugs and violence", their goals are nowhere near to being reached. The situation in Spain is not yet as serious as in other countries, but we will soon be on the same road if we do not take appropriate measures. The diagnosis, as we will see, is common to almost all countries with similar educational levels. It is clear that the presence of violence in schools in not an uncommon phenomenon nor is it restricted solely to them. Violent incidents and aggressive behaviour are manifested so assiduously in the media that it would not be farfetched to predict the disappearance of media or games that in a hypothetical-fictional case scenario decided to eliminate content of a violent nature.

They would simply disappear because their audience would feel deprived-in the emotional sense of the word-of the enchantment and anxiety that violence provides. Regardless of any ideological motives or intentions to mediate public opinion, the media describes violent behaviour as a semiotic necessity to safeguard the existence of its own discourse, and as such, the existence of its own economy. One might allege that the media does no more than register that which already exists in society. But that is not the problem-violence has always existed and even more than now. The problem lies in its intensity and the frequency of the message that violence, far from being perceived as an extraordinary event, has become normalized. Violence has come to form part of our everyday lives as something habitual and routine.

To begin with, we must understand that, overall, schools do not engender violence but suffer from it and in the worst of cases, they allow it to happen. Doubtless, it is the place chosen by violent adolescents to let out their pent-up rage by intimidating younger students (a result of the introduction of the "ESO"-compulsory secondary education). However we should not ignore the fact that what was originally a lack of discipline and which later turned into violence in the schools are mere symptoms of serious and complex social ills whose etiology includes family disorders, media pressure, parental disorientation, the desire for immediate satisfaction, and loss of authority. Yet while it is important to study the symptoms, it is even more important to study their causes.

It should not be surprising that in general the disappearance of authority and the weakened objectives and ideals of modern schools give rise to this diagnosis. But that is not enough. Over the last two decades an exceptional phenomenon has been occurring. On the one hand, the state is being challenged by an increase in illegal activity and on the other hand, the welfare state is being questioned as a result of the appearance of members who are excluded from the system. While the two processes are very different, they have a significant influence upon the school and bear witness to the failings of the structures of order. Here, order is understood in the classic sense of the word as submission to rule and law. But it is also understood as a social order that has culminated the social democratic dream of a population-from the poorest to the richest- which is wholly protected by the Welfare State. This time we cannot blame communism as the cause of all evil; we must also blame the shortcomings of a model that required an annual growth rate of 3% or 4% to run smoothly.

Those excluded from the system constitute, in their own way, a large "gray area." They are living proof of a world over which the State has increasingly less control. Some authors have called this phenomenon "the new middle ages" It is a phenomenon where anomie, marginality, and invisibility are present and is exemplified by the 100,000 young people that drop out of school to disappear into the bowels of the system. One only needs to take a walk around the outskirts of any city, not only the big cities, to realize that the presence of the State, police or otherwise, simply does not exist here. Why is this phenomenon exclusive to the schools and so present in them? Why is it so dramatically evident?

The answer can be found in the fact that the school is the only normative place that these representatives of the gray area are unable to sidestep. Their lives may be a series of dysfunctional contexts: family, social circles, etc...and suddenly school appears on the scene; a school which is parallel to the other circles in which they move and they do not know how to react; neither they nor the teachers. To resolve this problem is practically impossible. The instruments employed by the teachers and the education administration run head on into anomie (a breakdown of social norms) and aggressiveness; as does the symbology to which they are accustomed. The tools we do possess are inefficient and to use force would not change their system. In spite of this, we cannot allow our will to crack, even when it is difficult for us to contemplate these issues and not be able to resolve them. But deep down we know we are right and will continue to be so.

To this first "gray area" of social outcasts, we must add a second one; made up of marginal micro-communities that live entwined around the heart of society but which do not identify with the system. How many thousands of young people believe themselves to be independent and unaccountable to the rules! In contrast to the youth of '68 who were politicized and hence revolutionaries, these do not even bother to reject the system. We should not forget, however, that hate constitutes a social bond.

These young people ignore the system, despise it and get around it. Self-sufficient, thanks to the society as benefactor- be it in the form of parents or State, these young people reinvent a primitive model which has been closely studied by anthropologists. It is a model in which power is held by those who ensure survival and where violence is the most natural way for its members to relate to one another, with the exception of those who sign the "pact." Who can exercise the least authority over these youths, their parents? They are out of touch. For a long time now they have been disarmed and powerless social workers? Trained to remedy the world's misery, they freeze up before phenomena such as these which are resistant to generosity and altruism.

The causes for this phenomenon are varied:

a. The influence of the American model of culture which worships money while ignoring the moral and religious counterweight inherent to Protestant and Catholic Europe.
b. Individualism that has led people to give preference to their interests perinde ac cadaver.
c. The collapse of the great institutions: State, Church, Political Parties, Syndicates.
d. The disappearance of class struggles and social conflicts that have given way to mimetism between professional circles and the desire to imitate (the appearance of emblematic figures that are dishonest and cunning).

It seems as if the realm of the real world and the realm of the legal world were divided in their jurisdictions, and that the latter is increasingly on the defensive. The less transparent a society and the more oligarchy prevails over democracy, more incrusted becomes the gray, illegal society in the structures of power. The State should accept a reality it does not quite want to admit: its incapacity to control whole sectors of society. How strange in a century which sought to know all, dominate all and submit all to reason!

The only way to ease inequality

The school and the entire educational system, in spite of its meritocratic nature and its function as a reproducer of social hierarchies, is probably the most egalitarian of all social subsystems. As a social institution in which different groups of individuals come into contact with one another, the school exercises a powerful socializing influence. Inevitably, the dominant social culture within the political and economic framework of the school impregnates the human exchanges that occur within it.

The contradictions that we find today in our lives are replicated in the schools. Both teachers and students have assumed contradictory values in the three spheres of social life.

a. A demand for attention, care, affection, and generosity in the family.
b. A tendency to competitiveness, egoism, individualism, gives importance above all to money and productivity in the workplace, the economy and the labour market.
c. The conviction that everyone is equal at least in theory and by right of law, political participation, a commitment to the common good, and the collective responsibilities of democratic societies.

These contradictions take on meaningful nuances in our times. The family is no longer a unifying force, nor is it the homogenous and inalterable sphere of thirty years ago. The economy calls for new forms of behaviour, new attitudes and new skills. Politics has become mere marketing with scant citizen participation. Absolute cultural and historical relativism; the ethical pragmatic that "everything goes"; superficial tolerance understood as a lack of commitment and orientation; ferocious competitiveness; egocentric individualism coupled with social conformity; the importance of appearances, fashion, of having over being; the exaltation of all things ephemeral and changing; and the obsession to consume should all be regarded as a logical consequence of the way in which economic relations are conceived.

Relations which condition the lives of human beings are regulated exclusively by market laws. Of course all these aspects of contemporary post-modern culture are present in everyday exchanges in and out of the school and they unquestionably lead to the acquisition of specific conducts, values, attitudes and ideas. In short, the success of our schools is short-lived. Three keys functions are concentrated in the school that cannot be found in other social realms.

a. The social function of the school, which transmits the basics of public education to all strata of society, is indispensable in order to guarantee the training of human resources required by the job market for it to run smoothly. The higher the educational level, greater is the possibility to adapt to the ever-changing demands of the economic world today. Thus, we are able to affirm that the school carries out a social function characterized by the perfection of spontaneous processes of socialization; with its virtues and contradictions.
b. The political function of the school as a free and compulsory public service for all citizens up to a certain age -16 years in Spain-aims to compensate for the deficiencies in these spontaneous processes of socialization. This is true of the generalized shortcomings of these same processes with respect to different fields of study, as well as to the profound inequalities they cause in the social and cultural origins of different groups of people. In this way, public education tries to alleviate the effects that the inevitable inequalities of the market economy have produced in different social groups. It is here where the school has been left on its own as a place which is capable of containing and resolving the problems that open, democratic societies do not know

how to resolve. However, the school is neither capable, nor knows how to, nor is equipped with the instruments to force a change in the often negative and opposing tendencies of its younger members.

c. Also of importance, is the school's educational function. When the school teaches purely academic material of little consequence to real life, it is learnt merely for the sake of passing exams and quickly forgotten. The stimulus is lacking to apply what is learned in a conscientious and reflexive manner to everyday life and the school's duties are not of an educational but a socializing nature. The educational function requires intellectual autonomy and independence and is characterized by a critical analysis of those same processes and socializing influences. To break the artificial barriers between school and society and to convert the educational center in an open and flexible place where participation is expected, discrepancies tolerated and initiatives are encouraged is to complete its educational function.

Schools have been burdened with a task that not even society would take on. Politicians have refused by decree to treat the problems of socialization and social inequality in schools. It is as if the school was a conveyor belt: the problematic, dysfunctional student enters in one end and comes out the other in a state of perfect integration and self-awareness. We have already mentioned that when disorder advances in the heart of democratic societies, the problem is eschewed by making it invisible; in this case by placing it in the school. The idea in itself is not bad: inequality in the processes of socialization-a key problem in formal democratic societies which are ruled by the law of the free market-becomes invisible when the school is entrusted with the task of eliminating it. It is naive to think that schools will be able to overcome such economic and cultural inequalities. But they can and should provide the opportunity to compensate in part for the effects of such alarming discrimination in the individual development of the most marginal groups.

Schools should be equipped with appropriate tools which would allow them to successfully integrate those students that are difficult or distanced from public education with other students that have assumed academic or educational models. The more academic we are with this type of non-integrated student, the greater the distance and the drop-out rate will be for those who do not find support or encouragement in their family or peers. To say it another way: there should be transitional classrooms (some do already exist de facto) that facilitate the move towards intellectual cultural. This takes on even more importance since it is only in the school where intellectual culture can be experienced and enjoyed.

In new and different ways schools in post-industrial societies seem to achieve this complex and contradictory set of functions: socialization, transmission of education, preparation of human resources or compensation for the effects of social and economic inequalities. But it will only be educational when it is able to make reflection, the construction of autonomous thought and individual conduct possible.

It is evident that post-modern thought has demonstrated the enormous shortcomings that the modern age overlooked: the nature of corporeality, the moment, the world of emotions and feelings, the limitations of the logos, the importance of the present, the importance of micro politics, the non-universal nature of norms, the positive evaluation of aesthetics and expressiveness, the importance of tolerant and respectful attitudes, the demystification of the principles and role of science and technology, the rejection of militancy and the deification of reason.

We are entering a world where we will no longer find solid, unifying principles.

a. Nor religious principles, for obvious reasons.
b. Nor ideological principles: the notion of progress as ultimate ratio will be short-lived. It is evident that progress has not disappeared, and less so the belief in

progress itself, but it is only one conviction among many that is offered in the market of ideologies.

c. Nor cultural principles. The American model manipulates the symbols as if it were the dominant model, yet entire areas of the world, such as Asia, resists its model.

d. Nor economic principles: financial and industrial realities must coexist with historical events and strategic dynamics that keep them from determining the concerns of our societies.

If we can no longer hope for absolute certainties from the sciences, nor the arts, nor culture or philosophy with respect to knowledge or values which dictate human exchanges and the management of public affairs; if situational certainties are reached through a common search, experimentation and evaluation of democratically encouraged and controlled projects; if public life is to embrace individual liberties, guarantee equal opportunities and protect different manifestations and minority proposals, they should all be the consensual result of a democratic, informed and reflexive participation of the members of a social community. The emergence and strengthening of the subject should become the main priority of education.

The State should recognize that nowadays the school does not only resolve problems related to education, but also socio-political ones and should, therefore, modify its approach towards the most well-prepared of all institutions. But at the same it is one of the most overlooked institutions in the social and political realm. For those that work in education and who are confronted with an increasing number of problems, it is a profession lacking in incentives. If the State does not take on this challenge, schools will be divided into two types of institutions: elitist institutions that will resolve educational issues and other "integrating" institutions that will resolve or at least try to resolve social and political issues. They will however, ignore academic and educational questions, sentencing all those boys and girls to dysfuncionality; boys and girls who are determined to work hard, become part of the system and take on educational challenges.

Socialization in "progressive" education

Wayne Dunn's article on "progressive education" in the school systems discusses the origin and obsession of school educators with socialization as the primary goal of grade school education. Dunn writes, "the socialization mongers are busily sacrificing kids' minds for the sake of society." I cannot agree more with this. After spending a good deal of time reading through the arguments over home schooling in an Internet Infidels forum - and finding great pleasure in the articulate postings of Lisa Pea (Elisabeth Higgins) - I find myself more and more turned off with people citing socialization as the key benefit to conventional public schooling.

Dunn provides some background information on progressive education to help readers understand why and how educators have become obsessed with using this idea as the central focus of grade school education. The shortage of factual content in public schools is no accident. It's a consequence of a doctrine of education teachers themselves learn in the universities, called "socialization." The socialization approach, known by the innocuous title "Progressive education," has dominated the educational establishment ever since philosopher John Dewey ushered it in early last century. According to Dewey, the purpose of school is to encourage "the child's own social activities."

"The mere absorbing of facts and truths," Dewey maintained, "is so exclusively individual an affair that it...tends toward selfishness. There is no obvious social motive for...mere learning, there is no clear social gain in success thereat." Imagine if Galileo had spurned the "mere" truths of astronomy in order to bow to his era's social standard, Church dogma. I'm glad to finally know where this "socialization" idea as it refers to education comes from because it gets thrown around liberally by people who argue that home scholars will fail to benefit from the great socialization lessons learned in school. It's difficult to avoid the "What about socialization" question when you talk to someone about home schooling. But, being people who favour ideas that are viewed as fringe, such as home schooling and even attachment parenting, we're used to these types of questions.

The people who ask them, on the other hand, have read very little about what they question and, it appears, have thought just as little about the issues as well. Martha Ransom provides an interesting response to people who ask the question, "What about socialization?" Oh, I think the word you are looking for is socializing. Socialization is actually defined as the process by which the norms and standards of our society are passed from one generation to the next. I've never really thought that a complete strangers six-year old child would be a good source of information on the correct standards of behaviour in our family and in society as a whole. Harsh! Not what I would choose to say. In general, I think, people refer to socialization as the process of learning to engage in social activities. Socializing is quite precise, but people refer to socialization as if it were meant to convey some different meaning. In the final analysis, I take the meaning of socialization to be teaching children for 12 or so years to conform rather than to be individuals.

Groups of people who riff on the socialization and education aspect of Dewey summon the "S word" in arguments about home schooling, calling it the key benefit of school and one of the main reasons why home schooling is a bad idea. Socialization is the most important aspect of education? Wow. I agree with those people who thought that learning would be the most important aspect of education. To pronounce the importance of only one aspect of childhood development, very often misses the fact that the imparting of knowledge to students is as important if not more important than learning to be socially adept. Why is it so difficult to try to take a holistic view of education and not deem one approach to learning as right and another wrong?

In the Internet Infidels thread, a few people have actually claimed to prefer to be socially adept and stupid than to be smart and socially inept. Wow! I find that sad. I personally don't see why one can't become both, especially as someone who lives in a busy and culturally diverse city that offers social opportunities every time we walk out our apartment door. But besides the fact that I refuse to generalize here about what works best for whom, I know that what some kids learn from school socializing is how to be treated like a social outcast, how to deal with cliques (avoiding them or trying to join them), and how to suppress individuality to become more accepted. Some kids learn how to overpower others and use power to be cruel. Some kids experience this. Other kids escape unscathed and are able to survive the social life of school.

The thing that I find particularly irksome is that when people talk to you about school and you mention your interest in home schooling, without knowing your child and his needs, they are very often quick to try and persuade you away from it because of this socialization issue. It's truly amazing, the amount of unsolicited advice you begin to get when you become a parent. Such generalizations with ignorance to individual needs don't interest me, but a well-rounded education on my part of what our options are does. With every piece of literature or email discussion that I read that informs my growing capability to parent, I become more and more equipped to debate in public the ideas we are forming and the decisions we are trying to make to support our child without conforming to conventional practice.

Education as Socialization and as Individualization

When people on the political right talk about education, they immediately start talking about truth. Typically, they enumerate what they take to be familiar and self-evident truths and regret that these are no longer being inculcated in the young. When people on the political left talk about education, they talk first about freedom. The left typically views the old familiar truths cherished by the right as a crust of convention that needs to be broken through, vestiges of old- fashioned modes of thought from which the new generation should be freed.

When this opposition between truth and freedom becomes explicit, both sides wax philosophical and produce theories about the nature of truth and freedom. The right usually offers a theory according to which, if you have truth, freedom will follow automatically. Human beings, says this theory, have within them a truth-tracking faculty called 'reason', an instrument capable of uncovering the intrinsic nature of things. Once such obstacles as the passions or sin are overcome, the natural light of reason will guide us to the truth. Deep within our souls there is a spark that the right sort of education can fan into flame. Once the soul is afire with love of truth, freedom will follow - for freedom consists in realizing one's true self, that is, in the actualization of one's capacity to be rational. So, the right concludes, only the truth can make us free.

This Platonic picture of education as the awakening of the true self can easily be adapted to the needs of the left. The left dismisses Platonic ascetism and exalts Socratic social criticism. It identifies the obstacles to freedom that education must overcome not with the passions or with sin but with convention and prejudice. What the right calls 'overcoming the passions', the left calls 'stifling healthy animal instincts'. What the right thinks of as the triumph of reason, the left describes as the triumph of acculturation - acculturation engineered by the powers that be. What the right describes as civilizing the young, the left describes as alienating them from their true selves. In the tradition of Rousseau, Marx, Nietzsche and Foucault, the left pictures society as depriving the young of their freedom and of their essential humanity so that they may function as frictionless cogs in a vast, inhuman socioeconomic machine. So, for the left, the proper function of education is to make the young realize that they should not consent to this alienating process of socialization.

On the leftist's inverted version of Plato, if you take care of freedom - especially political and economic freedom - truth will take care of itself For truth is what will be believed once the alienating and repressive forces of society are removed. On the original, rightist and the inverted, leftist account of the matter, there is a natural connection between truth and freedom. Both argue for this connection on the basis of distinctions between nature and convention and between what is essentially human and what is inhuman. Both accept the identification of truth and-freedom with the essentially human. The difference between them is simply over the question: Is the present socioeconomic set-up in accordance, more or less, with nature? Is it, on the whole, a realization of human potentialities, or rather a way of frustrating those potentialities? Will acculturation to the norms of our society produce freedom or alienation?

On abstract philosophical topics, therefore, the right and the left are largely in agreement. The interesting differences between right and left about education are concretely political. Conservatives think that the present set-up is, if not exactly good, at least better than any alternative suggested by the radical left. They think that at least some of the traditional slogans of our society, some pieces of its conventional wisdom, are the deliverances of 'reason'. That is why they think education should concentrate on resurrecting and re-establishing what they call 'fundamental truths which are now neglected or despised'. Radicals, in contrast, share Frank Lentricchia's view that the society in which we live is 'mainly unreasonable'. So they regard the conservative's 'fundamental truths' as what Foucault calls 'the discourse of power'. They think that continuing to inculcate the conventional wisdom amounts to betraying the students.

In the liberal democracies of recent times, the tension between these two attitudes has been resolved by a fairly simple, fairly satisfactory, compromise. The right has pretty much kept control of primary and secondary education and the left has gradually got control of non-vocational higher education. In America, our system of local school boards means that pre-college teachers cannot, in the classroom, move very far from the local consensus. By contrast, the success of the American Association of University Professors (AAUP) in enforcing academic freedom means that many college teachers set their own agendas so education up to the age of 18 or 19 is mostly a matter of socialization - of getting the students to take over the moral and, political common sense of the society as it is. It is obviously not only that, since sympathetic high school teachers often assist curious or troubled students by showing them where to find alternatives to this common sense.

But these exceptions cannot be made the rule. For any society has a right to expect that, whatever else happens in the course of adolescence, the schools will inculcate most of what is generally believed. Around the age of 18 or 19, however, American students whose parents are affluent enough to send them to reasonably good colleges find themselves in the hands of teachers well to the left of the teachers they met in high school. These teachers do their best to nudge each successive college generation a little more to the left, to make them a little more conscious of the cruelty built into our institutions, of the need for reform, of the need to be sceptical about the current consensus. Obviously this is not all that happens in college, since a lot of college is, explicitly or implicitly, vocational training. But our hope that colleges will be more than vocational schools is largely a hope that they will encourage such Socratic scepticism.

We hope that the students can be distracted from their struggle to get into a high-paying profession, and that the professors will not simply try to reproduce themselves by preparing the students to enter graduate study in their own disciplines. This means that most of the skirmishing about education between left and right occurs on the borders between secondary and higher education. Even ardent radicals, for all their talk of 'education for freedom', secretly hope that the elementary schools will teach the kids to wait their turn in line, not to shoot up in the johns, to obey the cop on the comer, and to spell, punctuate, multiply and divide. They do not really want the high schools to produce, every year, a graduating class of amateur Zarathustras. Conversely, only the most resentful and blinkered conservatives want to ensure that colleges hire only teachers who will endorse the status quo. Things get difficult when one tries to figure out where socialization should stop and criticism start.

This difficulty is aggravated by the fact that both conservatives and radicals have trouble realizing that education is not a continuous process from age five to age 22. Both tend to ignore the fact that the word 'education' covers two entirely distinct, and equally necessary, processes - socialization and individuation. They both fall into the trap of thinking that a single set of ideas will work for both high school and college education. That is why both have had trouble noticing the differences between Allan Bloom's The Closing of the American Mind and E. D. Hirsch's Cultural Literacy. The cultural left in America sees Bloom and Hirsch as examples of a single assault on freedom, twin symptoms of a fatuous Reaganite complacency. Conservatives, on the other hand, overlook the difference between Bloom's Straussian doubts about democracy and Hirsch's Deweyan hopes for a better educated democratic electorate: They think of both books as urging us to educate for truth, and to worry less about freedom.

Let me now put some of my own cards on the table. I think that Hirsch is largely right about the high schools and Bloom largely wrong about the colleges. I think that- the conservatives are wrong in thinking that we have either a truth-tracking faculty called 'reason' or a true self that education brings to consciousness. I think that the radicals are right in saying that if you take care of political, economic, cultural and academic freedom, then truth will take care of itself. But I think the radicals are wrong in believing that there is a true self that will emerge once the repressive influence of society is removed. There is no such thing as human nature, in the deep sense in which Plato and Strauss use this term. Nor is there such a thing as alienation from one's essential humanity due to societal repression, in the deep sense made familiar by Rousseau and the Marxists. There is only the shaping of an animal into a human being by a process of socialization, followed (with luck) by the self-individualization and self-creation of that human being through his or her own later revolt against that very process.

Hirsch is dead right in saying that we Americans no longer give our children a secondary education that enables them to function as citizens of a democracy. Bloom is dead wrong in thinking that the point of higher education is to help students grasp the 'natural' superiority of those who lead 'the theoretical life'. The point of non-vocational higher education is, instead, to themselves - that they can rework the self-image foisted on them by their past, the self-image that makes them competent citizens, into a new self-image, and one that they themselves have helped to create. I take myself, in holding these opinions, to be a fairly faithful follower of John Dewey. Dewey's great contribution to the theory of education was to help us get rid of the idea that education is a matter of either inducing or educing truth. Primary and secondary education will always be a matter of familiarizing the young with what their elders take to be true, whether it is true or not.

It is not, and never will be, the function of lower-level education to challenge the prevailing consensus about what is true. Socialization has to come before individuation, and education for freedom cannot begin before some constraints have been imposed. But, for quite different reasons, non-vocational higher education is also not a matter of inculcating or educing truth. It is, instead, a matter of inciting doubt and stimulating imagination, thereby challenging the prevailing consensus. If pre-college education produces literate citizens and college education produces self-creating individuals, then questions about whether students are being taught the truth can safely be neglected.

Dewey put a new twist on the idea that if you take care of freedom, truth will take care of itself. For both the original Platonism of the right and the inverted Platonism of the left, that claim means that if you free the true self from various constraints it will automatically see truth. Dewey showed us how to drop the notion of 'the true self, and how to drop the distinction between nature and convention. He taught us to call 'true' whatever belief results from a free and open encounter of opinions, without asking whether this result agrees with something beyond that encounter. For Dewey, the' sort of freedom that guarantees truth is not freedom from the passions or sin.

Nor is it freedom from tradition or from what Foucault called 'power'. It is simply sociopolitical freedom, the sort of freedom found in bourgeois democracies. Instead of justifying democratic freedoms by reference to an account of human nature and the nature of reason, Dewey takes the desire to preserve and expand such freedoms as a starting point - something we need not look behind. Instead of saying that free and open encounters track truth by permitting a mythical faculty called 'reason' to function unfettered, he says simply that we have no better criterion of truth than that it is what results from such encounters.

This account of truth - the account that has recently been revived by Jürgen Habermas - amounts to putting aside the notion that truth is correspondence to reality. More generally, it puts aside the idea that inquiry aims at accurately representing what lies outside the human mind (whether this be conceived as the will of God, or the layout of Plato's realm of ideas, or the arrangement of atoms in the void). It thereby gets rid of the idea that sociopolitical institutions need to be 'based' on some such outside foundation. For Dewey, as for Habermas, what takes the place of the urge to represent reality accurately is the urge to come to free agreement with our fellow human beings - to be full participating members of a free community of inquiry. Dewey offered neither the conservative's philosophical justification of democracy by reference to eternal values nor the radical's justification by reference to decreasing alienation. He did not try to justify democracy at all.

He saw democracy not as founded upon the nature of man or reason or reality but as a promising experiment engaged in by a particular herd of a particular species of animal - our species and our herd. He asks us to put our faith in ourselves - in the utopian hope characteristic of a democratic community - rather than asking for reassurance or backup from outside. This notion of a species of animals gradually taking control of its own evolution by changing its environmental conditions leads Dewey to say, in good Darwinian language, that 'growth itself is the moral end' and that to 'Protect, sustain and direct growth is the chief ideal of education'. Dewey's conservative critics denounced him for fuzziness for not giving us a criterion of growth. But Dewey rightly saw that any such criterion would cut the future down to the size of the present. Asking for such a criterion is like asking a dinosaur to specify what would make for a good mammal or asking a fourth-century Athenian to propose forms of life for the citizens of a twentieth-century industrial democracy.

Instead of criteria, Deweyans offer inspiring narratives and fuzzy utopias. Dewey had stories to tell about our progress from Plato to Bacon to the Mills, from religion to rationalism to experimentalism, from tyranny to feudalism to democracy. In their later stages, his stories merged with

Emerson's and Whitman's descriptions of the democratic vistas - with their vision of America as the place where human beings will become unimaginably wonderful, different and free. For Dewey, Emerson's talent for criterion less hope was the essence of his value to his country. In 1903 Dewey wrote: '[T]he coming century may well make evident what is just now dawning, that Emerson is not only a philosopher, but that he is the Philosopher of Democracy.' Dewey's point was that Emerson did not offer truth, but simply hope. Hope - the ability to believe that the future will be unspecifiably different from, and unspecifiably freer than, the past - is the condition of growth. That sort of hope was all that Dewey himself offered us, and by offering it he became our century's Philosopher of Democracy.

Let me now turn to the topic of how a Deweyan conceives of the relation between pre-college and college education, between the need for socialization and the need to remove the barriers that socialization inevitably imposes. There is a standard caricature of Dewey's views that says Dewey thought that kids should learn to multiply or to obey the cop on the comer only if they have democratically chosen that lesson for the day, or only if this particular learning experience happens to meet their currently felt needs. This sort of nondirective nonsense was not what Dewey had in mind. It is true, as Hirsch says, that Dewey 'too hastily rejected "the piling up of information"'. But I doubt that it ever occurred to Dewey that a day would come when students could graduate from an American high school not knowing who came first, Plato or Shakespeare, Napoleon or Lincoln, Frederick Douglass or Martin Luther King, Jr. Dewey too hastily assumed that nothing would ever stop the schools from piling on the information and that the only problem was to get them to do other things as well

Dewey was wrong about this. But he could not have foreseen the educationist establishment with which Hirsch is currently battling. He could not have foreseen that the

United States would decide to pay its pre-college teachers a fifth of what it pays its doctors. Nor did he foresee that an increasingly greedy and heartless American middle class would let the quality of education a child receives become proportional to the assessed value of the parents' real estate. Finally, he did not foresee that most children would spend 30 hours a week watching televised fantasies, nor that the cynicism of those who produce these fantasies would carry over into our children's vocabularies of moral deliberation.

But Dewey's failures of prescience do not count against his account of truth and freedom. Nor should they prevent us from accepting his notion of the socialization American children should receive. For Dewey, this socialization consisted in acquiring an image of themselves as heirs to a tradition of increasing liberty and rising hope. Updating Dewey a bit, we can think of him as wanting the children to come to think of themselves as proud and loyal citizens of a country that, slowly and painfully, threw off a foreign yoke, freed its slaves, enfranchised its women, restrained its robber barons and licensed its trade unions, liberalized its religious practices, broadened its religious and moral tolerance, and built colleges in which 50 per cent of its population could enroll - a country that numbered Jefferson, Thoreau, Susan B. Anthony, Eugene Debs, Woodrow Wilson, Walter Reuther, Franklin Delano Roosevelt, Rosa Parks and James Baldwin among its citizens. Dewey wanted the inculcation of this narrative of freedom and hopes to be the core of the socializing process.

As Hirsch quite rightly says, that narrative will not be intelligible unless a lot of information gets piled up in the children's heads. Radical critics of Hirsch's books have assumed that he wants education to be a matter of memorizing lists rather than reading interesting books, but this does not follow from what Hirsch says. All that follows is that the students be examined on their familiarity with the people, things and events mentioned in those books.

Hirsch's radical critics would sound more plausible if they offered some concrete suggestions about how to get such a narrative inculcated without setting examinations tailored to fists like Hirsch's or if they had some suggestions about how 18-year-olds who find Newsweek over their heads are to choose between political candidates.

Let us suppose, for a moment, that Hirsch's dreams came true. Suppose we succeed not only in inculcating such a narrative of national hope in most of our students but in setting it in the larger context of a narrative of world history and literature, all this against the background of the world picture offered by the natural scientists. Suppose, that is, that after pouring money into pre-college education, firing the curriculum experts, abolishing the licensing requirements, building brand new, magnificently equipped schools in the inner cities, and instituting Hirsch-like school-leaving examinations, it proves possible to make most American 19-year-olds as culturally literate as Dewey and Hirsch have dreamed they might be. What, in such a utopia, would be the educational function of American colleges? What would policymakers in higher education worry about?

I think all that they would then need to worry about would be finding teachers who were not exclusively concerned with preparing people to be graduate students in their various specialties and then making sure that these teachers get a chance to give whatever courses they feel like giving. They would still need to worry about making sure that higher education was not purely vocational - not simply a matter of fulfilling prerequisites for professional schools or reproducing current disciplinary matrices. They would not, however, have to worry about the integrity of the curriculum or about the challenge of connecting learning - any more than administrators in French and German universities worry about such things. That sort of worry would be left to secondary school administrators. If Hirsch's dreams ever come true, then the colleges will be free to get on with their proper business. That business is to offer a blend of specialized vocational training and provocation to self-creation.

The socially most important provocations will be offered by teachers who make vivid and concrete the failure of the country of which we remain loyal citizens to live up to its own ideals - the failure of America to be what it knows it ought to become. This is the traditional function of the reformist liberal left, as opposed to the revolutionary radical left. In recent decades, it has been the main function of American college teachers in the humanities and social sciences. Carrying out this function, however, cannot be made a matter of explicit institutional policy. For, if it is being done right, it is too complicated, controversial and tendentious to be the subject of agreement in a faculty meeting. Nor is it the sort of thing that can be easily explained to the governmental authorities or the trustees who supply the cash. It is a matter that has to be left up to individual college teachers to do or not do as they think fit, as their sense of responsibility to their students and their society inspires them. To say that, whatever their other faults, American colleges and universities remain bastions of academic freedom is to say that the typical administrator would not dream of trying to interfere with a teacher's attempt to carry out such responsibilities.

In short, if the high schools were doing the job that lots of money and determination might make them able to do, the colleges would not have to worry about Great Books, or general education, or overcoming fragmentation. The faculty could just teach whatever seemed good to them to teach, and the administrators could get along nicely without much knowledge of what was being taught. They could rest content with making sure that teachers who want to teach a course that has never been taught before, or assign materials that have never been assigned before, or otherwise break out of the disciplinary matrix that some academic department has been perpetuating are free to do so - as well as trying to ensure that teachers who might want to do such things get appointed to the faculty.

But, in the real world, the 19-year-olds arrive at the doors of the colleges not knowing a lot of the words on Hirsch's list. They still have to be taught a lot of memorizable conventional wisdom of the sort that gets dinned into the heads of their co-evals in other countries. So the colleges have to serve as finishing schools, and the administrators sometimes have to dragoon the faculty into helping with this task. As things unfortunately - and with luck only temporarily - are, the colleges have to finish the job of socialization. Worse yet, they have to do this when the students are already too old and too restless to put up with such a process. It would be well for the colleges to remind us that 19 is an age when young people should have finished absorbing the best that has been thought and said and should have started becoming suspicious of it. It would also be well for them to remind us that the remedial work that society currently forces college faculties to undertake - the kind of work that Great Books curricula are typically invented in order to carry out - is just an extra chore, analogous to the custodial functions forced upon the high school teachers.

Such courses may, of course, be immensely valuable to students - as they were to Allan Bloom and me when we took them at the University of Chicago 40 years ago. Nevertheless, carrying out such remedial tasks is not the social function of colleges and universities. We Deweyans think that the social function of American colleges is to help the students see that the national narrative around which their socialization has centred is an open-ended one. It is to tempt the students to make themselves into people who can stand to their own pasts as Emerson and Anthony, Debs and Baldwin, stood to their pasts. This is done by helping the students realize that, despite the progress that the present has made over the past, the good has once again become the enemy of the better. With a bit of help, the students will start noticing everything that is paltry and mean and unfree in their surroundings. With luck, the best of them will succeed in altering the conventional wisdom, so that the next generation is socialized in a somewhat different way than they themselves were socialized.

To hope that this way will only be somewhat different is to hope that the society will remain reformist and democratic, rather than being convulsed by revolution. To hope that it will nevertheless be perceptibly different is to remind oneself that growth is indeed the only end that democratic higher education can serve and also to remind oneself that the direction of growth is unpredictable. This is why we Deweyans think that, although Hirsch is right in asking, 'What should they know when they come out of high school?' and 'What remedial work remains, things being as they are, for the colleges to do?', the question, 'What should they learn in college?' had better go unasked. Such questions suggest that college faculties are instrumentalities that can be ordered to a purpose. The temptation to suggest this comes over administrators, occasionally, as does the feeling that higher education is too important to be left to the professors.

From an administrative point of view, the professors often seem self-indulgent and self-obsessed. They look like loose cannons, people whose habit of setting their own agendas needs to be curbed. But administrators sometimes forget that college students badly need to find themselves in a place in which people are not ordered to a purpose, in which loose cannons are free to roll about. The only Point in having real live professors around instead of just computer terminals, videotapes and mimeo lecture notes is that students need to have freedom enacted before their eyes by actual human beings. That is why tenure and academic freedom are more than just trade union demands. Teachers setting their own agendas - putting their individual, lovingly prepared specialties on display in the curricular cafeteria, without regard to any larger end, much less any institutional plan - is what non- vocational higher education is all about.

Such enactments of freedom are the principal occasions of the erotic relationships between teacher and student that Socrates and Allan Bloom celebrate and that Plato unfortunately tried to capture in a theory of human nature and of the liberal arts curriculum. But love is notoriously untheorizable. Such erotic relationships are occasions of growth, and their occurrence and their development are as unpredictable as growth itself. Yet nothing important happens in non vocational higher education without them. Most of these relationships are with the dead teachers who wrote the books the students are assigned, but some will be with the live teachers who are giving the lectures. In either case, the sparks that leap back and forth between teacher and student, connecting them in a relationship that has little to do with socialization but much to do with self-creation, are the principal means by which the institutions of a liberal society get changed. Unless some such relationships are formed, the students will never realize what democratic institutions are good for: namely, making possible the invention of new forms of human freedom, taking liberties never taken before.

I shall end by returning to the conservative-radical contrast with which I began. I have been trying to separate both the conservative's insistence on community and the radical's insistence on individuality from philosophical theories about human nature and about the foundations of democratic society. Platonism and Nietzsche's inversion of Platonism seem to me equally unfruitful in thinking about education. As an alternative, I have offered Dewey's exaltation of democracy for its own sake and of growth for its own sake - exaltation as fruitful as it is fizzy. This fuzziness annoys the conservatives because it does not provide enough sense of direction and enough constraints. The same fuzziness annoys the radicals because it provides neither enough fuel for resentment nor enough hope for sudden, revolutionary change. But the fuzziness that Dewey shared with Emerson is emblematic of what Wallace Stevens and Harold Bloom call 'the American Sublime'. That Sublime still lifts up the hearts of some fraction of each generation of college students.

Socialisation

Human infants are born without any culture. They must be transformed by their parents, teachers, and others into cultural and socially adept animals. The general process of acquiring culture is referred to as socialization. During socialization, we learn the language of the culture we are born into as well as the roles we are to play in life. For instance, girls learn how to be daughters, sisters, friends, wives, and mothers. In addition, they learn about the occupational roles that their society has in store for them. We also learn and usually adopt our culture's norms through the socialization process. Norms are the conceptions of appropriate and expected behaviour that are held by most members of the society. While socialization refers to the general process of acquiring culture, anthropologists use the term enculturation for the process of being socialized to a particular culture. You were enculturated to your specific culture by your parents and the other people who raised you.

Socialization is important in the process of personality formation. While much of human personality is the result of our genes, the socialization process can mold it in particular directions by encouraging specific beliefs and attitudes as well as selectively providing experiences and these very likely accounts for the difference between the common personality types in one society in comparison to another. For instance, the Semai tribesmen of the central Malay Peninsula of Malaysia typically are gentle people who do not like violent, aggressive individuals. In fact, they avoid them whenever possible. In contrast, the Yanomamö Indians on the border area between Venezuela and Brazil usually train their boys to be tough and aggressive. The ideal Yanomamö man does not shrink from violence and strong emotions. In fact, he seeks them out. Likewise, Shiite Muslim men of Iran are expected at times to publicly express their religious faith through the emotionally powerful act of self-inflicted pain.

Successful socialization can result in uniformity within a society. If all children receive the same socialization, it is likely that they will share the same beliefs and expectations. This fact has been a strong motivation for national governments around the world to standardize education and make it compulsory for all children. Deciding what things will be taught and how they are taught is a powerful political tool for controlling people. Those who internalize the norms of society are less likely to break the law or to want radical social changes. In all societies, however, there are individuals who do not conform to culturally defined standards of normalcy because they were "abnormally" socialized, which is to say that they have not internalized the norms of society. These people are usually labeled by their society as deviant or even mentally ill.

Large-scale societies, such as the United States, are usually composed of many ethnic groups. As a consequence, early socialization in different families often varies in techniques, goals, and expectations. Since these complex societies are not culturally homogenous, they do not have unanimous agreement about what should be the shared norms. Not surprisingly, this national ambiguity usually results in more tolerance of social deviancy—it is more acceptable to be different in appearance, personality, and actions in such large-scale societies.

Socialization is a learning process that begins shortly after birth. Early childhood is the period of the most intense and the most crucial socialization. It is then that we acquire language and learn the fundamentals of our culture. It is also when much of our personality takes shape. However, we continue to be socialized throughout our lives. As we age, we enter new statuses and need to learn the appropriate roles for them. We also have experiences that teach us lessons and potentially lead us to alter our expectations, beliefs, and personality. For instance, the experience of being raped is likely to cause a woman to be distrustful of others. Looking around the world, we see that different cultures use different techniques to socialize their children. There are two broad types of teaching methods—formal and informal. Formal education is what primarily happens in a classroom.

It usually is structured, controlled, and directed primarily by adult teachers who are professional "knowers." In contrast, informal education can occur anywhere. It involves imitation of what others do and say as well as experimentation and repetitive practice of basic skills. This is what happens when children role-play adult interactions in their games. Most of the crucial early socialization throughout the world is done informally under the supervision of women and girls. Initially, mothers and their female relatives are primarily responsible for socialization. Later, when children enter the lower school grades, they are usually under the control of women teachers. In North America and some other industrialized nations, baby-sitters are most often teenage girls who live in the neighborhood. In other societies, they are likely to be older sisters or grandmothers.

During the early 1950's, John and Beatrice Whitiing led an extensive field study of early socialization practices in six different societies. They were the Gusii of Kenya, the Rajputs of India, the village of Taira on the island of Okinawa in Japan, the Tarong of the Philippines, the Mixteca Indians of central Mexico, and a New England community that was given the pseudonym Orchardtown. All of these societies shared in common the fact that they were relatively homogeneous culturally. Two general conclusions emerged from this study. First, socialization practices varied markedly from society to society. Second, the socialization practices were generally similar among people of the same society. This is not surprising since people from the same culture and community are likely to share core values and perceptions. In addition, we generally socialize our children in much the same way that our parents socialized us. The Whitings and their fellow researchers found that different methods were used to control children in these six societies.

For instance, the Gusii primarily used fear and physical punishment. In contrast, the people of Taira used parental praise and the threat of withholding praise. The Tarong mainly relied on teasing and scaring. This cross-cultural study of socialization is provocative. Perhaps, you are now asking yourself what methods you would use to control the behaviour of your children. Would you spank them or threaten to do so? Would you only use praise? Would you belittle or tease them for not behaving? Would you try to make your children independent and self-reliant or would you discourage it in favor of continuing dependence? At some time in our lives, most of us will be involved in raising children. Will you do it in the same way that you were raised? Very likely you will because you were socialized that way. Abusive parents were, in most cases, abused by their parents.

Likewise, gentle, indulgent parents were raised that way themselves. Is there a right or wrong way to socialize children? To a certain extent the answer depends on the frame of reference. What is right in one culture may be wrong in another. Even seemingly insignificant actions of parents can have major impacts on the socialization of their children. For instance, what would you do if your baby cried continuously but was not ill, hungry, or in need of a diaper change? Would you hold your baby, rock back and forth, walk around, or sing gently until the crying stopped, even if it took hours. The answer that you give very likely depends on your culture. The traditional Navaho Indian response usually was to remove the baby from social contact until the crying stopped.

After making sure that the baby was not ill or in physical distress, he or she would be taken outside of the small single room house and left in a safe place until the crying stopped. Then the baby would be brought indoors again to join the family. Perhaps as a result, Navaho babies raised in this way are usually very quiet. They learn early that making noise causes them to be removed from social contact. In most North American families today, we would hold our baby in this situation until the crying stopped. The lesson that we inadvertently may be giving is that crying results in social contact. Is this wrong? Not necessarily, but it is a different socialization technique.

The socialization process

Socialization refers to the development of the individual from infancy upwards; it is intertwined with the educational system, whether through formal education in schools, through non-formal programmes, or through informal education such as family upbringing. It is intrinsically based upon the right to education and hence the maximization of the potential of the individual in the process of development. Two basic questions are of interest to this study. First, to what extent does technology contribute to the socialization process in general, particularly in the educational system? Second, to what extent does technology help to promote human rights education in particular?

Technology and the Educational System

The present formal educational system in Thailand is based upon six years' compulsory education, which is being extended to nine years. At the primary level, the enrolment rate is over 90 per cent, but the numbers of those reaching secondary school and tertiary institutions are less impressive. There is a high unemployment rate among axstudents in certain quarters (particularly among law students). According to the statistics of the Ministry of Technology, the past decade some 247,000 students of science and technology have been produced by the formal educational system. Yet currently there is a great shortage of technically proficient personnel. The institutions producing engineers and technicians complain that they are unable to meet the demands of industry in view of Thailand's rapid industrialization.

The demand and supply pattern is illustrated in tables 6-8. Beyond the industrial spectrum, the impact of education and technically proficient students on the country's development process is less clear. While computerization has arrived at universities and vocational training institutions in urban areas, it has yet to arrive at the classroom in rural areas. There are also some misgivings among educators that technology will make students lazy. The advent of calculators, for example, has meant that many students are unable to do simple calculations without resorting to these calculators. On the other hand, simple educational technology such as overhead projectors and videos is still insufficiently used in the classroom, even if it is available. The classroom methodology tends to perpetuate the old style of lecturing and learning by rote, with the teacher in a magisterial position.

At another level, one is tempted to ask the following questions, for which there are no ready answers. Has the formal educational system really helped to upgrade agricultural techniques and to improve the condition of rural people? Has it prevented the brain drain of rural students to urban areas in search of jobs in industry? From the standpoint of non-formal and informal education, the impact of technology is felt among the ordinary population in both positive and negative ways. A number of courses offered by the Ministry of Education and the Ministry of Agriculture to those who are out of school provide for technological training, e. g. basic mechanics.

Television and radio programmes also provide key information which may help the ordinary population; the radio is a particularly effective means of communicating with outlying areas, and its educational programmes often offer tips to farmers concerning technology and farming needs. Yet the impact of technological knowledge has its negative side. As already noted, the excessive dependency of farmers on pesticides and fertilizers has vast personal and ecological repercussions of a detrimental kind. The message for the future seems to be to stress the importance of the type of technological knowledge that will enable people to choose between different forms of technology so as to minimize negative consequences.

Technology and Human Rights Education

The field of human rights education poses a great challenge to educationists in Thailand today precisely because it has been neglected for so long. While substantive courses on human rights are found at the tertiary level, the other levels of education only have fleeting references to it. At the secondary level, there are no substantive courses on human rights, but there may be reference to human rights in the elective course on law which students may choose to do. The human rights message may also be conveyed through other courses relating to social sciences. At the primary level, the situation is similar; there is no substantive course on human rights, but there may be reference thereto in the courses on life experiences and general knowledge.

However, one may generalize that, up to the tertiary level, formal schooling tends to inculcate a sense of duties rather than rights.[88] Children are taught about the duty to pay tax, the duty to register births and deaths, and the duty of conscription, without necessarily being offered a broader vision of human rights and current problems pertaining to them in Thai society. A key example is the paucity of references to children's and women's rights from childhood upwards. Which classroom raises the issues of child labour and child prostitution, which are widespread in Thai society?

Of course, there are exceptions to the rule, and well-read teachers will no doubt refer to such issues. However, unless these issues of human rights are inserted directly into the curriculum, particularly at the primary and secondary levels, the obligation to disseminate human rights will be missing. What is the impact of technology on such education? Again the message of the uninventive classroom pervades many educational institutions. The formal lecture still persists in pedagogy, coupled with the dominant role of the teacher and lack of participation on the part of students. The stifling of critical analysis and of active interchange of views is commonplace. Likewise, when there are non-formal training programmes, there is still a lack of imagination on how to diversify educational materials and methodology.

In this respect, one may claim that the appropriate use of technology for human rights education can help to instil a deeper consciousness of human rights issues. For instance, one need hardly observe that a lecture about child prostitution is likely to be bland unless it is accompanied by a slide show or video of the problem of prostitution. The affective, the cognitive, and the psychomotor can all be influenced by proper educational technology. Some of the recent experiments in Thailand in this regard include non-formal courses for villagers, children out of school, and youth about the law and their basic rights. An example is the programme initiated by various law faculties and the Department of Public Prosecutions offering courses to village leaders. There are usually accompanied by an initial needs assessment of the target groups themselves, i.e. what are their problems and how should the course respond to their needs?

The programmes vary in length and content, but there has been a gradual recognition of the need to diversify the teaching technology. Thus the use of transparencies, videos, games, cartoons, and plays has become more common in the training process. On another front, the rise of concern for women's and children's rights has led to courses with more imaginative use of educational materials. The materials produced include games on the rights of child labourers, cartoons on the rights of child labourers and the dangers of child prostitution, consumer protection, and the hazards of drug abuse. It is also felt that one must reach out not only to the potential exploited person but also the potential exploiter.

For example, the Law Communicators Group has produced, with the Child Labour Home in Bangkok, a little diary for children warning them of the dangers of child labour, the risks of signing contracts without reading the contents, and the addresses of institutions providing help if in need. Complementary to this, as a catalyst to stimulate the concern of the potential abuser, the group is also producing a calendar to educate employers about labour law and warn them against violations. In this sense, technology can exert a preventive impact on potential human rights violations.

One of the latest experiments is to train rural youth in law and basic rights. The Child Welfare Association, in cooperation with law teachers and students, is undertaking the training of youth from all over the country. The materials prepared are in response to a feasibility study to assess the target groups' needs. The educational materials produced in keeping with these needs include games, videos, posters, cartoons, and simple handouts concerning such issues as land law, criminal procedure, environmental concerns, and contractual obligations. These are tested with some of the target groups to see whether they respond to the latter's needs before they are widely disseminated.

Equally important in the educational process is the evaluation of the impact of the information conveyed. Traditionally, the technique for doing this was based upon general examinations. However, these often failed to take into account the long-term implications of education, particularly the aspects of social consciousness and community involvement. Long-term impact assessment is now being tried in Thailand by monitoring the trainees over a long period to observe the consequences of what they have learnt and how they perform in community life.

Working for social mobility

Who is responsible for widening participation in higher education? Too often answers to this question - being debated at fringe meetings at the three main political conferences this autumn - shift responsibility between universities and schools, parents and communities. This game of pass-the-parcel doesn't help anyone, but it's easy to see why it happens. Realistically, what are higher education institutions (HEIs) or schools expected to achieve? Educational inequalities correlate closely with just about every other sort of inequality from income and employment to housing and health. Indeed, schools and HEIs are both part of the solution and part of the problem. Many failing schools serve areas of deprivation, whereas research-intensive institutions take four-fifths of their students from better-off backgrounds. Both reflect and reproduce inequality.

The real question is not who should be responsible for widening participation to HE - schools, colleges, higher education establishments and government all have a role to play - but what we should be doing about it. We should get away from sentimental appeals to middle-class conscience on the one hand, and unrealistic expectations matched by scare-mongering about social engineering on the other. Better to focus on what can practically be done. For Hefce (the Higher Education Funding Council for England), the question is: what contribution can higher education make?

Growth in poorest communities

This is the first of a series over the coming weeks looking at action being taken by the sector to help widen participation. Interventions include working with schools; supporting learners (mentoring, summer schools and student ambassadors); fair admissions; opening up new kinds of opportunity and ensuring learners' success. So is there any evidence that we are making progress? It is often argued that the middle classes were the ones to benefit most from HE expansion, so much so that social mobility has declined. But this misreads social trends in the last quarter of the 20th century. The growth of inequality during the 1980s may have cramped the life chances of a generation, but if social mobility has stalled now it is because the growth in managerial and professional jobs has slowed, not because more of the middle classes have degrees.

Remarkably, data on HE participation shows a rapid growth among young people who grew up in the 80s in the poorest communities. Since 1998, participation from the most deprived areas has increased by 33% (4.5 percentage points), compared to 4% (1.8 percentage points) from the least deprived areas. The difference in the rate of growth is dramatic. The chances of young people going into HE from the most deprived 20% of areas was increasing around eight times faster than the least deprived 20% of areas.

Data on the social class gap tells a similar story. Participation among the top three social groups actually fell between 2002 and 2006, while participation among the lowest increased. This has narrowed the social class gap by over six percentage points. Progress has not been uniform, nor would we expect it to be. In the early 1980s, before the big expansion of HE, the top three social groups entered HE at 4.7 times the rate of the lower socio-economic groups. In the 1990s, the absolute gap in percentage points between social groups widened. Now it is narrowing absolutely and proportionately and there is no doubt about the long-term trend.

Social mobility

At the end of the century that advantage was reduced to 2.6 times. And when the data is examined more closely, it is participation among people from routine and manual occupational backgrounds where growth is strongest. Higher education has always been an important factor in the social mobility of individuals from communities without the economic resources and social connections of their wealthier neighbours, and it still is. Progress in addressing social inequality is slow, with no short fixes, but clearly crucial for reasons of social justice and economic competitiveness.

The rate of progress could be better but there are no short-term fixes. Social inequality is the result of a dynamic set of relationships; gaps closed in one direction repeatedly open up in another. The sector's commitment to widening participation, led by Hefce, weighs in on the side of greater equality and opportunity. It mitigates disadvantage and provides the encouragement, insight and support that releases potential. Higher education cannot resolve social inequality on its own. If institutions are to build on the progress already achieved, incorporating a commitment to widening participation into the way they understand their mission and purpose is key.

Education and Social Change

The role of education as an agent or instrument of social change and social development is widely recognized today. Social change may take place – when humans need change when the existing social system or network of social institutions fails to meet the existing human needs and when new materials suggest better ways of meeting human needs. According to Maclver social change takes place as a response to many types of changes that take place in the social and nonsocial environment. Education can initiate social changes by bringing about a change in outlook and attitude of man. It can bring about a change in the pattern of social relationships and thereby it may cause social changes.

Earlier educational institutions and teachers used to show a specific way of life to the students and education was more a means of social control than an instrument of social change. Modern educational institutions do not place much emphasis upon transmitting a way of life to the students. The traditional education was meant for an unchanging static society not marked by any change. But today education aims at imparting knowledge. Education was associated with religion.

It has become secular today. It is an independent institution now. Education has been chiefly instrumental in preparing the way for the development of science and technology. Education has brought about phenomenal changes in every aspect of men's life. Francis J.Brown remarks that education is a process which brings about changes in the behaviour of society. It is a process which enables every individual to effectively participate in the activities of society and to make positive contribution to the progress of society.

Social Inequality and Exclusion

In every society some people have a greater share of valued resources-money, property, education, health and power than others. These social resources can be divided into three forms of capital-economic capital in the form of material assets and income; cultural capital such as educational qualifications and status; and social capital in the form of networks of contacts and social associations. Often these three forms of capital overlap and one can be converted into the other. For example a person from a well-off family can afford expensive higher education and so can acquire cultural or educational capital. Patterns of unequal access to social resources are commonly called social inequality. Social inequality reflects innate differences between individuals for example their varying abilities and efforts. Someone may be endowed with exceptional intelligence or talent or may have worked very hard to achieve their wealth and status. However by and large social inequality is not the outcome of innate or natural differences between people but is produced by the society in which they live.

8

Education on Consumer Behaviour with Social Change

Education is closely related to social change, because inventions and discoveries take place due to education. Consequently, change comes in society also. The changed society again gives direction to education according to its new form. The education and social change have a sort of action and inter-action. It is the duty (function) of society to bring progressiveness in society and make the attitude of its members liberal and wide. But liberal outlook does not mean that one should adopt a thing without properly knowing and understanding it. Instead, it means that he should not hesitate or discriminate in accepting a correct fact or product. It is very necessary to encourage inventions, discoveries, researches, and tests etc. for bringing progress in society through education.

Some check on this progress is also necessary so that undesirable elements do not increase in society as a result of changes due to progress and new gains. Thus the nature of education also continues to change and at the same time this changed form becomes pragmatic and the aim becomes, preservation of old society and establishing of new values in society. For e.g., as the people get aware the importance of the computer, the organization as well as people purchasing the computers for fast and accurate processing to save the time and money. Thus big and specific institutions of society whether they are religious or political, scientific or vocational, sales or marketing – take the help of education for progress and to establish the new market. In the absence of education, man cannot take advantage of progress due to inventions, discoveries and researches nor can he develop his personality.

However much he may do hard work and however, much he may develop his culture and society by using his imagination, but the fact is that he cannot get pleasure and satisfaction with this progress without proper education and guidance, because he is not able to utilize it. Education has to be given right direction for pleasure and satisfaction by utilizing progress and development. Its aims are to be determined and the representatives of the society have to come for performing this task. They determine the aims of education in order that a person may be successful in establishing good social relations by developing his personality to the maximum extent. In determining the educational aims, the capacity, age and social environment of man have to be kept in mind.

For such new customers who are in the first stage of education or gaining the product knowledge, the aims are different from those for customers receiving higher education or already used or using the product. Cultural and physical objects have developed due to education. But there are many abstract things, which are very important and effective. The most glaring example is that of language. Language is the strongest of all material things and its social and cultural importance is supreme. A living creature or ignorance of the new inventions cannot make progress in the absence of education. The extensive influence of education is proved by other facts also.

The relation of invention and discoveries of knowledge is influenced by education because changes come due to inventions and discoveries which affect man and society.

In this field, education has two distinct functions. First, to preserve material and non-material objects of its culture or preserve its old culture and second, to encourage new inventions and discoveries in order that new facts may be found out and new truths may be brought to light which may strengthen progress still further and can increase the market size. Thus education performs these two important function. It develops social institutions in order that there may be progress in social life. At the same time it helps in the development of personality of the individual in order that he may render help in the progress and development of society and through social institutions. I have noted that social change is a continuous process.

It is natural and necessary. The form of change is determined by people or by those persons of the society who realize its importance. In a democratic system the people exert their influence on these changes through their elected representatives. The function of education is to give a desirable direction to social changes, which come automatically without any aim. I have noted above that cultural changes have their impact on society and changes automatically come in society. The study of these automatic changes is necessary for providing them a right direction. The aim of education is not to allow people to become indifferent to these changes. In fact, the apathy of the people should be removed in a planned manner. The co-operation of the people may be obtained in this effort. As has been said above, education has some responsibilities in this connection and these responsibilities are of two kinds.

Firstly, to create such consciousness in the public that they give desired direction to the automatic changes. Secondly, to produce such individuals who can recognize the movement of the people and can understand which changes are in the interest of society and how they can be brought about. A system and well-organized education system has the capacity for creating that consciousness in the customer which may enable them to understand the need for desirable changes. In the absence of such educational system, the customer cannot evaluate good or bad system connected with administration, vocation, recreation, health, market potential, product knowledge etc. So it requires planned efforts for the full co-operation of the people. This work is only possible through a systematic and well-organized education.

The customer generally feel hesitant in discarding old traditions and customs and hesitate to accept a new system, however, better it may be. The customer in the beginning resists every change. So it is the function of education that it prepares customer for accepting a change, explains to them the need of change and gives them knowledge of those mean which fulfill the need. So it should be the aim of education to provide so much ability and capacity to customer that they make the automatic changes useful for the society. It is the function of education to preserve old culture and transmit it to the next generation.

It is undisputed that a customer cannot move forward without any foundation or previous knowledge of product and the past is that foundation on which future is constructed i.e. brand name of the organization or previous product, but care has to be taken that useless and untimely knowledge from the past knowledge is removed. It is injurious to accept everything old blindly and it has had its adverse effect, too. So it is necessary in the interest of the society that old traditions and customs are impartially analyzed in view of the present circumstances and lifeless knowledge is weeded out. In this analysis and sorting, history can render necessary help and we should take the best advantage to crate the new market of the new invented product with the help of education and social change.

Adult Education for Social Change

Popular education is a form of adult education that

encourages learners to examine their lives critically and take action to change social conditions. It is "popular" in the sense of being "of the people." Popular education emerged in Latin America in the 1960s-1970s; Paulo Freire is its best known exponent. However, its roots may be found in the French Revolution, in workers' education of the 1920s-1930s, and in such movements as the Highlander Folk School in Tennessee. The goal of popular education is to develop "people's capacity for social change through a collective problem-solving approach emphasizing participation, reflection, and critical analysis of social problems". Key characteristics of popular education are as follows: everyone teaches and learns, so leadership is shared; starting with learners' experiences and concerns; high participation; creation of new knowledge; critical reflection; connecting the local to the global; and collective action for change. This digest describes popular education methods, addresses challenges, and offers some insights for adult educators.

The Popular Education Process

Because it is strongly community based, popular education takes a wide variety of forms. However, the process usually follows a pattern or cycle described as action/reflection/action or practice/theory/practice. Beginning with people's experience, the community initiates problem identification; then they reflect on and analyze the problem, broadening it from local to global in order to develop theory; next, participants plan and carry out action for change. Adult educators can facilitate the process by serving as democratic collaborators who ensure that learning takes place and leadership and self-direction develop in the group. Facilitators keep the group on track and encourage participation, but they should also try to foster a longer-term perspective on the problems addressed, helping the group place the issues in social, historical, and political context.

One important aspect of popular education is the way it often draws on popular culture, using drama, song, dance, poetry, puppetry, mime, art, storytelling, and other forms. Proulx (1993) distinguishes "popular culture" from cultural institutions often perceived as elitist and from instruments of mass culture such as the media, identifying popular cultural forms as those in which "working class adults recognize their life and their values". The use of these forms can enhance communication among audiences with an oral tradition, demonstrate respect for community cultural values and enhance group spirit, demystify the information conveyed and make it accessible and relevant, and encourage participation and learning by appealing to different modalities.

Arnold and Burke (1983) recommend the use of a variety of techniques for popular education, based on the assumption that learning is most effective if participation is active, different learning styles are addressed, content is relevant to learners' lives, learners are treated as equals, and the learning process is enjoyable. Examples include theater—participants act out a situation from real life experience using words, movement, gestures, and props; drawing—which appeals to those with a strong visual learning style and helps crystallize or symbolize ideas; and sculpturing—people physically position themselves in ways that depict their understanding of an issue or theme.

Challenges to Popular Education

Popular education is often seen as different from, threatening to, or marginalized by dominant institutions. Popular educators thus face a number of challenges illustrated in the examples that follow: the demands or constraints of funding sources; perceptions of the role of facilitators; disconnection between program goals and participant objectives; failure to address gender issues (ibid.); and the perception that popular education is too radical or revolutionary. Describing how university-based adult educators can play a role in facilitating community learning, Zacharakis-Jutz et al. (1991) give examples of successful and unsuccessful popular education efforts at the Lindeman Center at Northern Illinois University.

Instead of acting as experts, educators demonstrated their view of the community as co-researchers and co-learners by assisting public housing residents in developing their own capacity for leadership and their own knowledge about tenant management. On the other hand, an attempt to develop an intergenerational home repair cooperative in an impoverished neighborhood failed because facilitators neglected community-based needs assessment and strategy development and because a city agency that provided funding imposed "top-down" decision making and insisted on selecting participants.

Facilitators of Casa en Casa, a project in an Hispanic health clinic, sought to train community volunteers to be health promoters in their neighborhoods. However, volunteers did not assume leadership roles or organize for collective action because they received no orientation to the purpose of training or the role of promoters. Training emphasized content knowledge but not the skills to use it for community action. Overly concerned with imposing their own agenda, project facilitators abdicated their responsibility to guide the learning process. As Merideth puts it, "starting where the people are does not mean staying there".

A popular education program in Paulo Freire's own city, Sao Paulo, Brazil, sought to develop citizenship for the radical transformation of political and social structures through literacy education. However, civic and political content was infrequently addressed and discussions were not always tied to learners' understanding of how the subjects affected their lives. "There was a substantial disjunction between efforts to make them discuss political issues in class and the type of political discourse they engaged in daily life".

Although most of the facilitators and participants were women, the program did not explicitly address gender issues. Although the overall objective was increasing citizen participation, this goal was not strongly connected to the objectives of participants, many of whom were primarily interested in social interaction or satisfaction of personal needs. Ultimately, the program encountered—and was terminated by—a major obstacle of popular education: opposition of political groups threatened by an agenda of social change.

Insights for Adult Educators

How can adult educators address these challenges to popular education? Stromquist (1997) recommends that community needs and goals should form the basis for a popular education agenda and those facilitators should be trained in critical dialogue that blends political content with instructional practices and connects the issues with participants' immediate reality. Beder (1993) maintains that "power is a critical resource ...because change cannot be accomplished without power". However, power must be owned by the group, but exercised by individuals on behalf of it. Facilitators should neither impose an agenda nor abdicate responsibility.

They should recognize that merely incorporating participatory learning techniques and democratic structures does not necessarily enable people to challenge their internalized beliefs and develop critical abilities, and they should have a clear vision of social change and how their work fits into the broader picture. Zacharakis-Jutz et al. (1991) conclude that the role of university-based educators is not to precipitate action but to support actions the community takes on its own behalf. They suggest finding ways in which university resources can work for the community. Merideth (1994) notes how popular education programs may be constrained by the mandates and regulations of funding sources.

Heaney (1992) reinforces the pitfalls associated with public funding, suggesting that popular educators keep the proportion of public funds in the overall budget low, form an umbrella organization to channel funds, or "promote and support indigenous resources within the community, helping local groups to build strong organizations under local control". Stromquist (1997) emphasizes that empowerment and emancipation are not generic: they have different meanings and implications for men and women. Gender relations must be part of the analysis of power relations and social conditions that takes place in popular education.

Walters and Manicom (1996) recommend strategies that take women's standpoint, drawing on women's experiences in a way that illustrates that "woman" is not a homogeneous category; explore the intersection of gender, race, class, and culture; and enable women to find space, time, and a place for learning. Popular education is not limited to addressing the needs of identifiable cultural groups or the poor and the powerless.

It has wider application as a method of developing critical understanding, building self-confidence and analytical skills, and linking them with social action in a variety of contexts and socioeconomic levels. Education that has as its goal social transformation faces formidable challenges, as shown by some the programs described here. However, education for social transformation is an ongoing effort. Although a particular program may appear to have failed in its immediate goals, it may represent one step in the slow, complex, and cumulative process of social change.

The Concept of Social Process

A scientific vocabulary for sociology can be produced in two ways: by inventing new terms, by re-defining common-sense words. The second method is most widely used with resulting confusion to both sociologists and the public. But common conceptual orientation is a necessary preliminary to research in a natural science. Social process is used with many shades of meaning and is often treated as if it were a natural science concept. This view is denied by the paper. When used singularly, it merely denotes the existence of societal activities that are continuously changing. Many other terms, such as social interaction, social change, social dynamics, social organization, etc., convey much the same meaning.

Social process is too ambiguous, too indefinite, too inclusive, to be useful as a natural science concept. Historically, it has served to indicate the dynamic as opposed to the static nature of societal phenomena as well as to emphasize the non-normative nature of them. But these usages are philosophic and methodological, not natural scientific. There are fundamental differences between the concepts of natural science, philosophy, and methodology. Social process belongs in the last two categories.

Used plurally, "the social processes" concept is indefinite because the processes are too numerous, and each is specific. The emphasis should be upon the kinds of activities involved, not upon the fact that they occur. To add "process of" to integration, assimilation, conflict, etc., does not add anything to the meaning and so is tautological. The conceptual content is not in "process of" but in the governed noun. Methodologically, "the social processes" is a convenient term to designate a number of social processes without enumerating them, but such a usage is no more a natural science concept than is a-b. Hence, to treat process or processes as if it were a natural science concept is very confusing. A sociological concept must generalize specific, observable, repetitive, societal phenomena.

A. H. Lloyd used to say poets and philosophers have one thing in common, to wit, their licentious use of language. In this respect, sociologists are partly poets or philosophers, or both, for we certainly take liberties, if not license, with language. In our attempt to create a natural science vocabulary for sociology, that is, a system of concepts having identical meanings for all, at least for all sociologists, two courses are open. One, we can invent terms, usually constructed from Latin or Greek, or both, to describe typical forms of social behaviour. This is the narrow way of neologism, often used by the physical and biological sciences. It is logically and scientifically the best method, but it has the disadvantage that the public, and even scientists in other fields, do not understand the terms until they have been popularized.

This usually corrupts their original logical purity. Socius, telesis, mores, and consensus are sociological examples. Two, we can attempt to put the new wine of scientific precision into the old verbal bottles of common sense. This has the twofold disadvantage that the public never understands the terms, and sociologists themselves seldom exhibit a high degree of agreement. This is the broad way of slowly evolving consensus to which we seem committed. Culture, human nature, isolation, competition, attitude, wish, etc., are examples. It invites endless word-wars and terminological disputes.

However, if sociologists can agree upon the meanings of concepts as a means to, or as a result of, significant research, we shall eventually gain as much popular understanding for our technical terms as now exists for such concepts as heredity, ignition, radio activity, blood count, contagion, and so on. But such a desirable consummation cannot be achieved unless and until we can define our concepts with sufficient clarity and precision to make them useful tools for significant research. The conception of science without concepts, that is, without hypothetical generalizations, is nonsense. It is equally nonsensical to suppose that we can derive significant concepts by mere word-spinning. We must test them in the hot fires of actual research if they are ever to attain scientific validity, as Ogburn has said. But there must be some tentative conceptual agreement as a preliminary to comparable research.

Without repetition of research on the same problem, there can be no valid scientific concepts. Without clearly defined concepts there can be no identical problems and hence no comparable research. This criticism and clarification of concepts in the light of accumulating research findings is one of the functions of the theorist. Of course he may suggest hypotheses synthesize and interpret facts and findings, but he must also criticize concepts, logic, and methods, disagreeable task though it be. It is my purpose to examine a term that has become widely used in recent years. It appears in all kinds of connotations and combinations, singular and plural, definite and indefinite, governed by all kinds of nouns, modified by all kinds of adjectives, and finally have attained the apparent conceptual dignity of titling our program. I shall try to avoid mere word-juggling by analyzing the meanings involved rather than by criticizing the words by which these meanings are conveyed.

Yet it is very important that language should be used with nicety and precision in verbalizing scientific concepts. "Process" and seventeen derivatives are listed by Eubank in his sociological vocabulary. Almost every recent writer devotes some space to these terms. "Process" occurs almost as frequently as "social," and is usually as indefinite and ambiguous. Social is used with several different shades of meaning. It may refer to instinctive adjustments that result in corporate action, as in "social" animals and insects; to human behaviour regarded as good, in contrast to asocial; to similar responses to a given stimulus, as in crowd action; to adjustive behaviour based upon interaction of mechanisms acquired through communication, and so on.

It has become a commonplace with sociologists that the social sciences deal with a fourth order of natural phenomena, superimposed upon the inorganic, organic, mental triad, or derived from it, either by emergent or non-salutatory evolution. If this be true, it is evident that "social," for sociologists, should refer to societal, cultural, super organic, or sociological phenomena, the fourth of the usages mentioned above. In discussing the concept of social process we shall use this sociological definition of the social. Mead has defined "social" in a somewhat different way' which I think depends for its validity upon the fact that human beings are capable of acquiring sufficiently similar action patterns to permit reciprocal behaviour. Etymologically, "process" merely means "the fact of going on or being carried on: progress, course."

Murray mentions thirteen main substantive usages. Some sociologists adhere to the etymological implication of progressive action or advance, but the more common usage emphasizes the dynamic, changing characteristics of social phenomena without any commitment on the normative nature of the activities or occurrences. There is also the implication that the goings-on are regular, continuous, and repetitive. Stripped of verbiage, then, the social, or societal, process means social or societal interaction; the kind of activities, movements, or occurrences that go on between culture-making animals in their corporate capacities. As a concept, it merely means that natural phenomena of the fourth order, like those of the other three orders, are characterized by change; that it is a universal trait of socii and groups of socii in contact to interact, to influence each other reciprocally.

As a scientific concept, this tells us precisely nothing. It does not differentiate types of social interaction, or add to, or extend, or clarify the common-sense observation that human beings can and do react to each other. It is as barren as the universally valid (or invalid) concept that all things exist. Hayes says, "The social process is composed of all the activities that go on in association", Park and Burgess, "Social process is the name for all the changes which can be regarded as changes in the life of the group."

These, and many similar statements, show conclusively that "the social process" can never tell us anything about societal interaction, except that it exists. Hence, "the social process" can lay no claim to being a natural science concept since it does not and cannot, by its very nature, aid us in observing and classifying similar societal phenomena so that uniformities not obvious to common sense may be ascertained. It is true that Cooley's idea of social process as relatively unconscious, unplanned organic growth does add something to the common-sense idea of social interaction (vid., note 6, supra), but it is significant that even the penetrating insight of a Cooley could not say anything very illuminating about "the social process" in general. His real contribution is his discussion of certain typical forms of societal behaviour. This is equally true of all who attempt to discuss societal phenomena in a way that goes deeper than the superficial observations of common sense. Case well says,

To appreciate the larger units of life requires the synthesizing work of art, religion, and philosophy, all of which aim to grasp the meaning of the whole. To understand the smaller units we have recourse to the analyzing, abstracting methods of science, which splits the world of phenomena into separable, countable, measurable, and ever minute parts, and takes no thought for the whole.

The social process concept was a protest against both static, descriptive sociology and the normative implications of progress and social evolution. This was decidedly necessary thirty years ago, and is still, especially with reference to normative implications. But in both these senses, it is a philosophic and methodological, not a natural science, concept. Regularity and continuity of change is a necessary philosophic assumption for natural science. The non-normative nature of these changes is both a philosophic and methodological concept. The concept of social process has done yeoman service in both respects. One of the commonest errors in scientific thinking is the reification of philosophical and methodological concepts with the futile and confusing consequence of treating them, or trying to, as if they were conceptualizations of sense experience.

They are scientific concepts, of course, if we mean by science any systematized body of knowledge, but they are not natural science concepts if natural science means a system of conceptual knowledge derived from observable, natural phenomena by means of methodological devices. In this broadest sense of the term, there are three kinds of science: 1. Natural. 2. Philosophic. 3. Methodological. The first consists of physical, biological, and societal sciences; the second, of synthetic and normative; the third, of logical and mathematical. "The social process" concept belongs in philosophy and methodology. As a philosophic concept it is useful to indicate the relatively regular on-going-ness of societal phenomena; as a methodological concept it is useful to indicate the non-normative nature of societal phenomena; as a natural science concept it is useless and meaningless.

Instead of the social process concept, one might equally well use such terms as social interaction, socialization, organic social growth, social evolution, social organization, social dynamics, social change, or, if normative-minded, social progress. These terms are so inclusive and indefinite that all social data are implicit in them. All social activities could be discussed equally well under each term. All have the common element of suggesting change, but none of them denote any specific societal data that can be observed. Hence, they are philosophic rather than scientific concepts. All are equally useless and equally meaningless for natural science until they are broken up into definitive concepts by which we may observe, classify, symbolize, and generalize actual societal phenomena.

And this is precisely what all the writers do. When "the social process" becomes "the social processes," something is gained, but something is also lost, namely, the illusion that social process is a natural science concept. I have shown that it is too inclusive, too ambiguous, too indefinite, to have any value or validity for natural science. It is pseudo-science, a pretentious verbalism that adds little or nothing to common-sense observation. It is an elaborate conceptualization of the very obvious. All that is contended here is that it is useless for a natural science whose concepts must denote actual, sense-observable objects and occurrences. Its philosophic and methodological value is granted.

When "the" social process is pluralized, we get such phrases as processes of selection, industrialization, history, assimilation, social change, valuation, projection, imitation, communication, and so on, indefinitely. It is evident at once that the conceptual content of these multitudinous phrases is the type of interaction, or behaviour, or activity, and not the fact that the activity occurs or proceeds. Competition, conflict, accommodation, assimilation, etc., are activities, are kinds of observable and possibly measurable behaviour that can be defined, identified, classified, and possibly generalized. Hence, they may be, or may become, scientific concepts. It is mere tautology to add "process of." In all the literature I have read dealing with "processes of" this and that, "process of" could be deleted without causing confusion or obscuring any shade of meaning.

It is clear that one could not deal so cavalierly with a legitimate natural science concept. So we must render a verdict of pseudo-science alike for the singular and plural form of social process. It should be mentioned here that Professor Hayes makes a very nice distinction between social processes, or specific activities, and social relations, or the modes by which social activities are causally influenced. He would call competition, conflict, and accommodation, etc., relations, and dispense altogether with assimilation. While I agree that social processes must designate specific kinds of activities, I think the weakness of his position lies in the fact that the above concepts may refer to specific and observable societal behaviour. He tacitly admits this when he says, "Communication is used either as a name for a relationship which may be unintended, or for an activity intended to establish that relationship. Most of the words for social relationships unfortunately have this double signification. "

Hayes made a real contribution by insisting that

activities are the essence of the scientific data of sociology and that descriptive concepts must be based upon observation of these. The processes are activities, and the conceptualization must deal with the relatively stable uniformities exhibited by these activities. Whether his contention that the relation-concept of condition-consequent is "the most important of all realities for scientific explanation" and is "the pons asinorum of social theory" is sound, I do not know, but I have my doubts. I am not sure that anything is necessary for scientific explanation beyond the determination of unexceptional, repetitive uniformities under defined conditions. Any so-called explanation beyond this strikes me as unnecessary verbal meringue upon the pie of scientific procedure.

It is obvious that the kinds of societal activities that can be designated are almost innumerable. The number of valid scientific concepts would equal the number of such activities exhibiting enough repetitive uniformity to permit prediction of sufficient accuracy to be useful in making societal adjustments. Doubtless such uniformities are appearing and disappearing all the time. Whether there are concepts of sufficient generality to be universal and of sufficient definiteness to be scientifically valid, I do not know, nor is it the purpose of this chapter to inquire. My guess is that whenever any concept is defined rigidly enough to describe societal variables accurately enough to permit valid prediction, such prediction will be found applicable only to limited areas over limited periods of time. I do not know whether there are one (Tarde), or two (Binder), or three (Case), or four (Park and Burgess), or eleven (Hayes), or eleven hundred "fundamental" social processes. I would be inclined to guess the latter figure if by "fundamental" one means types of societal behaviour possessing sufficient stability to permit valid prediction.

One should not conclude that the writer thinks "process" and "processes" are words too licentious and

Bibliography

Ayyar, Vaidyanatha R.V., (1997), 'Educational Planning and Administration in India: Retrospect and Prospect', *Journal of Educational Planning and Administration,* Vol. XII, No.2, April 1997, pp.167-214.

Ayyar, Vaidyanatha R.V.,(1997), 'Basic Education and Human Rights', *Journal of Educational Planning and Administration,* Vol. XI, No. 1, January 1997, pp.67-87.

Basu, A.N., (1947), *Education in Modern India,* Orient Book Co., Calcutta.

Bhola, H.S., *Campaigning for Literacy,* UNESCO, 1984.

Dayal, Bhagwan (1955), *The Development of Modern Indian Education,* Orient Longman, Bombay.

Department of School Education, Government of Madhya Pradesh, Bhopal, *Annual Administrative Report* (1996-97).

Department of School Education, Government of Madhya Pradesh, Bhopal, *Annual Administrative Report* (1997-98).

Department of School Education, Government of Madhya Pradesh, Bhopal, *Annual Administrative Report* (1998-99).

Directorate of Public Instruction Madhya Pradesh, Bhopal, *Basic Educational Statistics* (1997).

Education and National Development Report of Education Commission, July 1996.

Education Policy in India 1968, Ministry of Education, Culture and Social Welfare, GOI, New Delhi, Aug. 1968.

Education for All - The Indian Scene, Department of Education, Ministry of Human Resource Development, GOI, Dec., 1993.

Gore, M.S., (1995), *Indian Education: Structure and Process*, Rawat Publication, Jaipur.

Govinda, R., (1997), *Decentralisation of Education Management: Experiences from South Asia*, International Institute for Educational Planning, Paris.

Haq, Ehsanul., (1997), *Education, Polity and Society*, Shipra Publications, Delhi.

Jolly, K.G., (1992), *Literacy for All by 2001: Strategies at District Level*, D.K. Publishers, New Delhi.

Limaye, P.M., (1945), *Education in India Today*, Deccan Education Society, Poona.

Mahajan Baldev and Others, (1994), *Education Administration in Madhya Pradesh (NIEPA)*, Vikas Publishing House, New Delhi.

Mehta, P.L. and Poonga, Rakhi (1997), *Free and Compulsory Education*, Deep and Deep Publications, New Delhi.

Naik, J.P., (1975), *Elementary Education in India: A Promise to Keep*, Allied Publishers, Bombay.

Naik, J.P., (1966), *Elementary Education in India - The 'Unfinished Business'*, Asia Publishing House, New Delhi.

National Policy on Education 1986, Ministry of Human Resource Development, GOI, New Delhi.

Premi, M.K., (1972), *Educational Planning in India*, Sterling Publishers, New Delhi.

Ramachandra, Vimala,(1996),*Women and Girls' Education in South Asia*. India Country Paper, (mimeo), 1996.

Rao, D. Pulla (1998), *Economics of Primary Education*, Rawat Publications, Jaipur.

Rao, Digumarti Bhaskara (1997), *Success story of a Primary Education Project,* APH Publishing Corporation, New Delhi.

Sen, Amartya and Dreze, Jean, (1995), 'Basic Education as a Political Issue', *Journal of Educational Planning and Administration,* Vol- IX, No. 1, January 1995, pp. 1-26.

Sharma Amita & Gopal Krishnan R., (1999), *A New Strategy for the Total Literacy Campaign* (Document 5, Rajiv Gandhi Mission, June 1999).

Sharma Amita & Gopal Krishnan R., (1996), *Bringing the People Back In: From Lok Sampark Abhiyan to Education Guarantee Scheme* (Document 3, Rajiv Gandhi Mission, October 1996).

Sharma Amita & Gopal Krishnan R., (1999), *Universal Primary Education and Total Literacy in Madhya Pradesh: A Proposal for Institutional Reform* (Document 4, Rajiv Gandhi Mission, March 1999).

Sharma Amita & Gopal Krishnan R., (1999), *Bringing the People Back In: From Lok Sampark to Education Guarantee Scheme,* (Document 5, Rajiv Gandhi Mission, March 1999).

Sharma Amita & Gopal Krishnan R., (1996), *Wanted, A New EGS: An Education Gaurantee Scheme* (Document 1, Rajiv Gandhi Mission, August 1996).

Sharma, S.N., (1995), *Elementary Education: Experience and Expectations,* Kanishka Publishers, New Delhi.

Singh, U.K., and Sudarshan, K.N., (1996), *Primary Education,* Discovery Publishing House, New Delhi.

Sinha, Amarjeet (1998), *Primary Schooling in India,* Vikas Publishing House, New Delhi.

Tilak, J.B.G., (1992), *Educational Planning at Grassroots,* Ashish Publishing House, New Delhi.

J.B.G., (1995), 'Elementary Education in India in the 1990s, Problems and Perspectives', *Journal of Educational*

Planning and Administration, Vol. 4, No.2, April, 1995, pp. 387-407.

Venkatesh, B. and Athreya, Sheela Rani Chunkath, (1996), *Literacy and Empowerment*, Sage Publishing.

Weiner, Myron, (1996), 'Child Labour in India: Putting Compulsory Primary Education on the Political Agenda', *Economic and Political Weekly*, Nov. 9-16.

Zellener, A. A. (1951), *Education in India*, Bookman Associates, New York.